FRANK & FEARLESS

Nicholas Cowdery AO QC was the Director of Public Prosecutions for New South Wales (known as the DPP) from 1994 to 2011. Previously he had been a barrister since 1971, working in Papua New Guinea and at the Sydney Bar. Since 2011 he has focused on helping developing countries improve the rule of law and protect human rights, especially through professional prosecution systems, and giving advice on how to maintain the rule of law and improve criminal justice in Australia. One example of this is his work with a number of organisations dedicated to reducing Indigenous over-representation in the criminal justice system. Nick is a University of New South Wales visiting professorial fellow and adjunct professor at the University of Sydney.

Rachael Jane Chin practised as a lawyer before becoming a non-fiction writer. Her first book, *Nice Girl: The story of Keli Lane and her missing baby Tegan*, was published in 2011. From 2002 to 2004 she was employed as a journalist by the *Australian Financial Review*. Her website is <www.rachaeljanechin.com>

NICHOLAS COWDERY

WITH RACHAEL JANE CHIN

FRANK & FEARLESS

NEWSOUTH

A NewSouth book

Published by
NewSouth Publishing
University of New South Wales Press Ltd
University of New South Wales
Sydney NSW 2052
AUSTRALIA
newsouthpublishing.com

First published 2019

10 9 8 7 6 5 4 3 2 1

A catalogue record for this book is available from the National Library of Australia

ISBN 9781742236377 (paperback)
9781742244617 (ebook)
9781742249100 (ePDF)

Design Josephine Pajor-Markus
Cover design Peter Long
Cover image 25 August 2009: Sydney, NSW. Director of Public Prosecutions, Nicholas Cowdery QC, at his office in Sydney during an interview with *The Daily Telegraph*. Photograph by Cameron Richardson. *Newspix*
Printer Griffin Press

This book is printed on paper using fibre supplied from plantation or sustainably managed forests.

CONTENTS

INTRODUCTION

For 16 and a half years, from 1994 to 2011, I was the Director of Public Prosecutions (DPP) for New South Wales. The DPP is the chief prosecutor, and a gatekeeper for the criminal justice system. He or she decides if, when and how a police investigation into a serious criminal offence is to be tried in a court of law.

The role of DPP is extremely stressful. In addition to managing an office of hundreds of professionals, it involves being immersed in the very worst and saddest of human behaviour, making sometimes extraordinarily difficult and often unpopular decisions, dealing with a lot of attention from the media, and dealing with pressure from public figures, particularly politicians, that is not usually helpful or necessarily fair.

When I walked through the office door each day, I knew that almost every decision I made would make somebody unhappy. If I decided to prosecute someone, he or she would be unhappy. If I decided not to prosecute, a victim or a police officer or both would be unhappy. If I decided to appeal against an inadequate sentence, the prisoner would be unhappy; if I declined to appeal, the law-and-order brigade would erupt. Almost any decision I made could make the media, a politician, or both, unhappy for a multitude of reasons, or for no good reason at all. Members of the community would express their unhappiness with what I did, individually or in groups. Excessive demands upon staff were always a cause for angst.

This all went with the job, however, and any concerns about such effects had to be suppressed. The DPP's office will always be an unusual working environment and not attractive to many – but those who work there render great service to the community. I had chosen to work with them and I thoroughly enjoyed it (for the most part).

In my previous career as a barrister practising largely in crime, I was familiar with the work of the crown prosecutors and the role of the DPP, but I was unprepared for both the managerial role and the level of active outside attention the position attracted. When I was appointed DPP by NSW Premier John Fahey in 1994, I expected the role to be an interesting and stimulating challenge and the high point of my career. I was willing to take on the responsibilities of the office and, if I could, work improvements in the criminal law and its processes. I didn't realise how controversial that modest aim could become. I knew that my predecessor had carried out reforms, but in a style that did not attract public attention. I quickly formed the view that I should do it differently, explaining to the community as I went the reasons why changes should be made for its benefit. I was – temporarily – blind to the politics of that course.

During my tenure, the Office of the Director of Public Prosecutions (ODPP) had a staff of around 300, rising to over 600. That included the senior crown prosecutor, deputy senior crown prosecutors, crown prosecutors, lawyers and administrative staff located in ten offices around the state. I worked closely with many of the prosecutors, some of whom featured prominently in the media because of the cases they conducted.

In the course of an average year, the ODPP had up to 18000 cases before the courts and in preparation by the end of my tenure. I was not involved in all of them, but the more serious cases – either because of their nature (e.g. involving a death or serious abuse), public profile, legal complexity or contentiousness – would all come to me for final decisions at various stages of prosecution. It was always satisfying to have a conviction in a case where I thought that should be the just outcome, according to the law – though as this book shows, some cases and convictions did pose larger questions of whether the law needs reform to better serve the interests of justice.

This book shows what the rule of law looks like in the

prosecutor's office, and describes some of the most significant cases that came across my desk. A properly functioning criminal justice system involves the DPP and having to deal with situations where there are usually no winners and no limits to the awfulness.

Why would anyone in their right mind put themselves through such pain? Former Justice of the High Court Michael Kirby AC CMG once summed up why the criminal justice process appeals to legal professionals:

> No other branch of the law is so important. It is where our commitment to fair trial and the rule of law are tested every day, in courts throughout the nation. It is where fear of wrongdoers intersects with respect for basic human rights.

Ever since humans began to live together, we have needed rules for our conduct. Rules allow us to live together harmoniously and to have ways of resolving disputes. Those rules are often enacted in our laws. Inevitably criminal laws intersect with other systems of rules based on morals, ethics, religion and philosophy. Criminal laws apply to all of us – they cannot be evaded or applied selectively – but those other systems, and even the criminal laws, sometimes require choices to be made in their application.

People sometimes accused me of being insensitive, cold-hearted or unrealistic in the decisions I made as DPP. But what they failed to take into account was that the DPP is really a split personality.

One half is the normal human side. The other half is the professional, disciplined side. I had to develop a way of putting aside the normal human reaction to what was before me, to filter out any purely personal beliefs and all of those emotional and other professionally irrelevant aspects. This ability gets better the more practice you have. Of course, once a decision is made you can then allow yourself a normal human reaction to the situation, sometimes in discussion with others. Examples of such dilemmas are prosecutions for low-level drug offences and for assisting terminally ill people to die; but any allegation – for example, of sadistic child abuse – may throw together normal human responses and professional, legal standards to be applied.

In our system the vast bulk of minor crimes are prosecuted by police prosecutors in the Local Court. The ODPP prosecutes some of those offences (e.g. all child sexual assaults, high profile matters, offences by police) and all the more serious crimes, known as indictable offences. When homicide in any of its forms (or any other serious indictable crime, such as armed robbery or serious sexual assault) has occurred and someone is a suspect, it is the DPP who has to decide if there is a reasonable prospect of conviction by a court and whether or not a prosecution will proceed. Under a system of formal delegations, in other defined circumstances decisions may be taken at a lower level in the office hierarchy.

No matter how passionately the police, the family and friends of a victim or anyone else may feel, only evidence capable of being admissible in criminal proceedings according to the law and the Prosecution Guidelines can be considered. It is not enough to have suspicion or to say the admissible evidence shows the suspect probably did it or might have done it (as will appear later). The question is whether there is a reasonable prospect that the admissible evidence would convince a reasonable jury, who have been properly instructed as to the law, that there is no reasonable doubt that the suspect is guilty. That is a high bar and consequently the hurdles that have to be cleared before a prosecution can even begin are high.

So take a seat in the DPP's chair and brace yourself for a stormy passage. The shocks and blows come from all angles and often without warning. It is not pretty, but it is all part of the application of the rule of law in our modern society.

And I am greatly privileged to have been a DPP.

Chapter 1

ENOUGH IS ENOUGH: THE MURDER OF MICHAEL MARSLEW

In a civil society, everyone accused of a crime, including (and especially) those accused of the most horrific crimes, must have a fair trial.

The desire for revenge, to inflict violence or death on those who have hurt or killed a loved one, arises in even the most law-abiding people. Because serious crime is so devastating, the process of holding trials and deciding punishments has to be in the hands of disinterested strangers. 'Justice' cannot be in the hands of a vigilante mob or the outraged family of a victim. The most involved the family and friends of a victim can be in a trial is as a witness or, in some cases, as a secondary victim. A more common role is as an observer of the trial.

The reasons for excluding those who have strong emotions from deciding what happens in the criminal justice system are well established; but how do the families of victims feel about that?

I dealt with Michael Marslew's case soon after I had been appointed DPP in 1994. It was my baptism by fire in the area of victims' rights. Michael's father Ken made it clear he was not going to leave me alone unless I lived up to his expectations. I hadn't had to deal with this sort of situation previously. It was the beginning of my policy of consulting with victims and families of victims when circumstances made it appropriate to do so. This ultimately became part of the Prosecution Guidelines. Part of that consultation was explaining why some charges would be proceeding and others would not.

The facts of Michael Marslew's case are as follows. On 3 March 1994, about seven months before I was appointed DPP, two little boys, Joshua and Paul, were playing on the banks of a river, searching among the mangroves for lost tennis balls. Joshua's family was nearby.

Paul saw what he first thought was the oar of a boat resting on the smelly mud. However, as the boys got closer, they saw it was something else. Paul picked it up. It looked heavy and dangerous. The two 11 year olds decided to carry the thing back to show Joshua's father.

As the two boys came into view, Joshua's father realised they were carrying a shotgun. He yelled at them to put it down and ran off to get the car. While Joshua's father was searching for his keys, Joshua's older brother picked up the grime-covered shotgun to show his mother. A spent cartridge fell out.

Joshua's father ordered his older son to put the shotgun and the spent cartridge in the car. Having made things as safe as he could, he then told Joshua and Paul to get in and drove to the nearest police station. Joshua's father then carried the shotgun and the spent cartridge into the police station, accompanied by the two little boys.

Officers at the station realised the boys had probably found what the Homicide Squad had been searching for in the same river the day before. Detectives and officers from the police ballistics team arrived to examine the firearm. It was a Bentley 12-gauge pump-action shotgun, and dirty from being immersed in river water. It was also loaded. Detective Beresford made the shotgun safe by ejecting five live cartridges. He and the other detectives believed this was almost certainly the weapon used in a failed armed robbery a few days earlier that had resulted in the death of 18-year-old Michael Marslew.

Michael was a university student who had a part-time job as a delivery boy at a Pizza Hut in Jannali, a suburb in Sydney's south. On the evening of Sunday, 27 February 1994, at around 11.30 p.m., Michael and three other employees were preparing to shut the shop, having locked the front door so no more customers could come in.

Caroline was an 18-year-old part-time kitchenhand. She and Michael were mopping the floor. Fellow kitchenhand Lisa was at the cash register checking the pizza order dockets against the register's total. The duty manager, Mikel, was organising the night's takings. Piles of counted cash were sitting on the table used for cutting up pizzas, ready to be placed into the safe, which was open.

One of the last chores was to put the rubbish into the skip in the car park at the rear of the shop. Having finished mopping the floor, Michael told Caroline that he would take the rubbish out. As she walked to the front of the shop, she heard him open the heavy back door.

Caroline then heard something odd and turned to see what it was. She saw Michael standing in the doorway. Near him was a tall, skinny man wearing a mask.

'Get down!' shouted the masked man. Caroline yelled out to the duty manager, Mikel, and then dived to the floor near the counter. Before she hit the ground she heard a loud bang from near the back door. Lisa also heard the loud bang, but thought it was just Michael putting the rubbish out via the heavy back door. Caroline's yell to Mikel made her turn around. She saw Caroline diving to the ground and the masked man behind her. She crouched where she was. Mikel didn't hear the bang over the sound of the exhaust from the pizza ovens behind him, but he did hear Caroline yell his name, and turned around. By this time the masked man had taken a couple of steps towards the counter where Lisa was crouched on the other side of the open door of the safe. Mikel saw the masked man and dropped to the floor.

All three Pizza Hut employees were on the ground, but the masked man, who was panicking, didn't know what to do next. 'Get down!' he shouted again. Then, as quickly as he came, he disappeared.

Nobody moved for a few seconds. Then Mikel got up and ran to a phone on the counter to call the police. He also activated the alarm button in the safe. Unsure of where the masked man was, Mikel then crawled towards the back of the shop. He saw Michael lying on his back, his feet towards the open back door. A large pool of blood was forming under him. Mikel had no choice but to step over Michael so he could close the back door. After satisfying himself that the masked man was no longer in the shop, Mikel also called out to Lisa to phone emergency services. He then bent down to see if Michael was breathing. He wasn't. Caroline crawled to where Lisa was crouched near the counter with the phones, and stayed with her as she called emergency services. Mikel called out to Lisa to ask for an ambulance. Having made the call, Lisa and Caroline made their way to where Michael lay. Lisa felt his neck for a pulse and told the others she could feel one. Mikel got a foil blanket out of the first aid box and covered Michael, who was still not breathing and very pale. Within minutes the ambulance and police arrived, but Michael had died.

A police sweep of the area recovered a black balaclava on a nearby street. A black bag and a small torch were found near Michael's body. Michael Marslew had been killed during a failed robbery. The cause of death was a gunshot wound to the back of the neck. Police now faced the task of telling the young man's family.

A couple of days after Michael's death, his father Ken appealed to the public for help to find whoever killed his son. Michael's mother was too distraught to speak. Within a fortnight, the state government offered a $50 000 reward for information about the crime. Three months later that amount was increased to $250 000. This was on top of the $10 000 reward offered by Pizza Hut.

The serial number on the shotgun found by the two little boys on the banks of the river revealed that it was stolen. Information from a police informant and further police inquiries led detectives to a man named Andrew in Queensland. In mid-June, nearly four months after Michael's death, New South Wales detectives spoke to Andrew. Faced with evidence about the stolen shotgun, Andrew made admissions about his role in Michael's death. He also mentioned a man named Vincent, who he said was part of the failed armed robbery and to whom he had sold the stolen shotgun. When questioned by police, Vincent made admissions about his role in the killing. He also told police about the involvement of a man named Karl, Andrew's brother. Karl in turn admitted to being involved in the crime. All three men mentioned a fourth man. Andrew and Karl knew him as 'Doug' but did not know his last name. Vincent didn't know the fourth man's name at all.

The events that led to Michael's death emerged. On the morning of Sunday, 27 February 1994, 20-year-old Vincent woke up and went to the pub. There he met his new friends Andrew and Karl, brothers who were both in their early twenties. The young men drank and played pool. Later that morning they all decided to go back to Vincent's place and began to discuss an idea that Karl would later claim was Vincent's. They could all do with some extra money, especially to buy furniture. Vincent, who worked at a restaurant, was earning $350 a week. Karl and Andrew were unemployed. They had just moved out of home and into a flat not far from where Vincent lived. The young men agreed a robbery would solve their money problems.

Vincent told the others he knew of a place they could rob. It was a Pizza Hut in a quiet suburb where no one knew them. Vincent knew that all Pizza Huts closed around midnight and that one of the final jobs the staff had to do before closing was to throw all the rubbish out. When one of the staff at the Pizza Hut he had in mind opened the back door to do that, they would be able to force their way in and steal that night's takings.

Sometime during the afternoon, Vincent and Andrew went to an army disposal store and bought four balaclavas and a torch. Afterwards, Karl and Andrew went back to their flat. Karl called Doug to tell him something he might be interested in was being planned, and to make sure he brought his car. At around 7.00 p.m., Doug arrived at Karl and Andrew's place. Karl told Doug that a robbery was being planned. Doug wanted to be involved. All three then went back to Vincent's to talk about the plan, drink and wait. Doug never introduced himself to Vincent, preferring to remain a nameless stranger while in his home.

Karl, Vincent and Andrew would all make different claims about who produced the shotgun that night and who loaded it, but at about 10.30 p.m. the four men were driving in Doug's car towards the Pizza Hut. All of them, with the possible exception of Doug, knew there was a loaded shotgun in the car.

They parked the car in a backstreet not far from the back door of the Pizza Hut.

Karl tied a shirt around Andrew's head, while Vincent put on the only balaclava they had brought with them and took hold of the loaded shotgun. Vincent and Andrew then walked to a spot behind a parked car near the rear of the Pizza Hut and waited for someone to open the back door. Karl found a spot to observe everything from a distance. The moment the back door began to open, Andrew charged forward with Vincent close behind.

Vincent was holding the loaded shotgun so it was pointing forward. When later interviewed by police, Vincent would admit he had never handled a shotgun before that night. The closest he had been to any sort of firearm was when he was a little boy and his grandfather had shown him his guns, taking care to point out where the safety catches were. But here was Vincent that night in 1994, after a day of drinking, pointing a loaded shotgun at a door, not knowing who or what was behind it.

In front of Vincent, but hidden from those inside the Pizza Hut by the partially opened door, was Andrew. Having charged into the door, Andrew had collided with Michael, who was on his way out. Andrew and the 183-centimetre, well-built Michael found themselves jammed in the doorway. They jostled to get free of each other. Vincent, who was following Andrew, didn't know this was going on. Unable to see into the shop, Vincent took the loaded shotgun into one hand, and with the gun still pointing up but across his body, he used his other hand to further open the door. By this time Andrew had pushed past Michael and was yelling at the other staff to get down. With the loaded shotgun pointing into the Pizza Hut, Vincent made it into the doorway where Michael was standing. Shocked by the unexpected sight of the pizza delivery boy, Vincent shot him.

Hearing the shot, a panicked Andrew looked back and saw the boy he had just jostled lying on the ground. Andrew dropped the torch and the bag he had brought to put the money in and ran back outside. The failed robbery was over in a matter of seconds.

Andrew and Vincent ran back to the car. Karl and Doug were already inside. 'Vincent shot someone,' said Andrew and they drove away with the car lights off, all screaming at each other, with the exception of Vincent, who was silent with shock. Coming across a river, Karl instructed Doug to stop and one of them threw the loaded shotgun in. A couple of days later, Andrew fled to Queensland.

The relief Michael's family felt once police arrested his killers was replaced with fury and outrage. Michael had been murdered by dangerous fools. His parents had to find some way of coping, for their own sakes and for the sake of their other son. They got in touch with a support group for relatives of victims of homicide. Some of these people had become victims themselves, unable to find any joy or purpose in life. Michael's father Ken was determined not to be a victim. While waiting for the trials of his son's killers to begin, he began an organisation called Enough is Enough. Its goal was to reduce the amount of violence in society, and its members would be those who had lost family members to violence, just as his family had lost Michael.

Right from its inception, the media gave Enough is Enough a lot of attention. Ken was often quoted in the papers and interviewed on radio and television. But no matter how much energy he put into making something positive come out of Michael's death, anger always threatened to overwhelm him. The stupidity of those who killed Michael didn't help. Vincent told police he was having second thoughts about the armed robbery during the car trip but he went along with it because he didn't know how to unload the shotgun. Before his trial, Karl changed his testimony in an attempt to claim he didn't know the shotgun was loaded. Andrew threatened to call their mother as a witness to give evidence about how dishonest Karl was. When police tracked down Doug, a young unemployed man of no fixed address, it emerged he got involved so he could have some money for drugs.

On 11 October 1994, during one of the committal hearings, it all became too much for Ken. The police video of Andrew describing how he ran past Michael's body as he rushed back out the door was played in court while Andrew was crying in the dock. Ken stood up from his seat in the public gallery and walked towards him.

'Fuck you!' Ken yelled, standing directly in front of the dock. Court officers quickly restrained him, and he was ordered to leave the courtroom. Outside, he punched a wall.

Ken was not only angry at the men who killed his son, he was also angry at the legal system. He refused to describe the process as the 'criminal justice system' – he insisted on calling it the 'criminal legal system'. He hated the way Michael was referred to simply as 'the deceased'. He hated the attention given to the rights of the accused, which left those who loved Michael as mere spectators. He was angry that when he said something from the public gallery during one of the pre-trial hearings, the magistrate told him that this was between the defence and prosecution, not him.

In December 1994, two months after Karl, Vincent and Andrew were ordered to face trial, Ken told the NSW Parliament of his plans to make Enough is Enough a nationwide organisation. Aware of all of the media attention he was generating, politicians were all ears.

During his trial in June 1995, Vincent decided to change his plea to guilty. He was sentenced to 18 years with a non-parole period of 13 years for the murder of Michael Marslew.

'What was Michael's life worth?' asked a furious Ken in front of the TV cameras outside the courtroom. He was also open about his belief in the death penalty. Weeks after Vincent's sentence was handed down, the *Daily Telegraph* published more about Ken's outrage over Vincent's sentence under the headline 'Five-Star Jail No Punishment'.

In early October 1995, Premier Bob Carr announced that families of murder victims would now be able to make submissions to the Parole Board against the early release of prisoners. The premier said he had been convinced of the need for this change after speaking with Ken and other families of murder victims.

In November 1995, despite all his efforts to portray Vincent as the ringleader and himself as only being involved in a feeble effort to make sure Vincent didn't kill anyone, Karl pleaded guilty to murder by way of common purpose. The sentencing judge took the view that Karl was the ringleader who got the others to do his dirty work, describing Karl as a 'calculated and practised liar' before sentencing him to 18 years with a non-parole period of 11 years. Weeks before Karl pleaded guilty to Michael's murder, the *Daily Telegraph* praised Ken and Enough is Enough for 'giving voice to the victims'.

In February 1995, on the weekend following Doug's committal to face trial for manslaughter, Ken and others involved in Enough is Enough had featured in a group photo that was published as part of a two-page spread in a Sunday paper. The accompanying article made the point that this was a club no one wanted to join. The day the group photograph was taken, one of its members, a parent unable to deal with their grief any longer over the murder of their child, committed suicide.

Ken was furious that any of the accused would face anything less than a murder charge. I met with him to explain why Doug was facing manslaughter and Andrew was facing both murder and manslaughter charges, but it all sounded technical and uncaring to him. After the meeting, Ken went home and put two large olives in a jar, vowing to himself that one day he would replace them with my testicles.

The wheels of justice kept turning. In July 1996, having been found by a jury to be not guilty of murder but guilty of manslaughter, Andrew was sentenced to a non-parole period of six years and eight months. The media kept swinging its spotlight onto Ken.

In 1996, two years after Michael's murder, Ken's campaigning led to a new law that officially gave a voice to victims and their loved ones. No longer confined to just giving evidence as witnesses or remaining silent as courtroom observers, the family of someone who had been murdered or otherwise unlawfully killed could have their say once a conviction had been reached and before the sentence was decided. In cases of other very serious crimes, such as violent assaults and sexual assaults, the victims themselves could make such statements. Of course, the final decision about a sentence would be in the hands of the justice system, but devastated relatives and victims would at least know their point of view had been heard in their victim impact statements.

Just over a year later, the premier gave $200 000 to another new program Ken had advocated that involved offenders serving jail sentences facing the families of their victims.

These were significant achievements, and when approached by journalists, Ken continued to be an excellent media performer. Many in the media took to asking Ken for his opinion about any issue of criminal law that happened to be news, even if it had nothing to do with Michael's case, victim impact statements or offenders coming face to face with the families of victims.

Facing an election in 1999, Premier Carr announced a new policy that would force judges to impose minimum sentences set by the government. Enough is Enough and other victims of crime groups supported this minimum sentencing policy.

Even though Ken described it to the media as 'judicial education', lawyers knew minimum sentencing was really about politicians stopping judges from doing an important part of their job, namely using discretion to decide the appropriate sentence in each case in order to do justice to the community and to the offender. Lawyers also knew the new policy was pretending to the public that sentencing issues were simpler than they really were. The NSW Bar Association and I publicly criticised the premier's new sentencing policy as being created only for 'naked political ends'. To put it bluntly, the new policy didn't help the justice system at all. It was just intended to attract votes in the upcoming election campaign.

The media paid scant regard to my or the Bar Association's protests. With the sympathy the public naturally felt for Ken, the popularity of his criticisms of the legal system would hold the interest of media and politicians for years.

Chapter 2

WHICH BROTHER? THE GILHAM FAMILY STABBING DEATHS

In late July 2000, I had to decide whether a young man named Jeffrey Gilham should be prosecuted for the killings that occurred in his family home at Woronora, south of Sydney, during the small hours of 28 August 1993. A huge cloud of suspicion hung over Jeffrey's head, but his account of that night threw doubt over who the killer was. This was a contentious and unnerving case that underlined how a prosecution can only go ahead if there is sufficient evidence to create a reasonable prospect of conviction.

Just before 4 a.m. that night in 1993, a neighbour was reading in bed when she heard the sound of screaming, frantic voices. It sounded like it was coming from the house just down the hillside, where the Gilham family (Jeffrey, his parents and his brother) lived, and went on for five or so minutes. A neighbourhood dog started barking. The neighbour got out of bed to look out of her window, but she couldn't see anything. Then it was silent, except for the barking dog.

The dog belonged to Mr and Mrs B. They hadn't heard any frantic voices, but their dog woke them up. About half an hour later, at around 4.30 a.m., a now wide-awake Mr B was walking around the outside of his home trying to see what had upset his dog so much when he saw smoke rising from under the roof tiles of the Gilham family home. Then he saw something flickering inside one of the windows. He rushed inside and told his wife to call the fire brigade.

While Mrs B made the call, another set of neighbours, Mr and Mrs W, heard a knock on their front door. Mr W had only just fallen asleep, having been woken earlier by the sound of loud, heated arguing somewhere in the neighbourhood. He got out of bed, opened the door and found 23-year-old Jeffrey Gilham wearing only a pair of boxer shorts. Jeffrey was in a highly agitated state and mumbling about needing to call triple zero because his house was on fire. Mr W ushered Jeffrey inside, where his wife joined them.

'They're all dead. He killed them, set up [sic] them on fire,' Jeffrey said, jumbling his words. 'Mum and Dad are both dead. He's burnt them. I've killed him for what he did to them.'

It had been raining earlier that night, it was still misty, and it seemed that Jeffrey could be in shock, so Mrs W set about finding a jumper and a blanket for their young neighbour. Jeffrey's home was right next door and there was no fence separating the properties, which both backed onto the river. While trying to make sense of what Jeffrey was saying, Mr W noted to himself that as he hadn't heard the noisy latch of their front gate, Jeffrey must have come via the rear lawn.

Mr and Mrs W led Jeffrey to their landline phone, but Jeffrey, shaking and unable to stand still, was too distressed to dial emergency services himself. Mr W made the call for him. The emergency operator asked Mr W if Jeffrey had been drinking. He leant over to quietly smell Jeffrey's breath. There was no smell of alcohol, but Jeffrey smelt like smoke and kerosene, a smell Mr W remembered from when he first opened the door.

The emergency operator then asked to speak to Jeffrey.

'Easy. Calm down, calm down and just tell me mate,' said the operator.

'I walked in … through the door …' said Jeffrey.

'You've walked in from where? Out … being outside somewhere?'

'Mum called me … called me …'

'Right.'

'And … I came up … and … I see him there … with a knife,' said Jeffrey.

Mr and Mrs W heard Jeffrey tell the operator that his brother had killed his parents, that his parents were on fire and that he killed his brother after chasing him down the stairs. Mr and Mrs W also heard Jeffrey say he didn't know why he chased his brother. As they listened they noticed Jeffrey had become breathless while talking to the operator.

All they could do was to wait for the emergency services to arrive. Jeffrey sat on the leather settee and then stood up, obviously agitated. Mrs W handed him a burgundy coloured jumper. She and her husband noticed that Jeffrey was very cold and dry to the touch. They also noticed what looked like blood on his left lower leg that had been largely wiped or washed away. Still in just his boxer shorts, Jeffrey cuddled the jumper with his hands but didn't put it on. Instead, he lay down on the kitchen floor in the foetal position. Mrs W draped a blanket over his shoulders. Mr W thought he saw blood in the quick of some of Jeffrey's fingernails. Curled up on the floor, Jeffrey was quiet. At one point he stood up, grabbed a nearby fire extinguisher and told them he was going back to fight the fire, before Mrs W took it from him.

Less than 15 minutes after Mr and Mrs W's and Mr and Mrs B's emergency calls, fire fighters arrived. The upper level of Jeffrey's family's split-level house was ablaze. One fire fighter found Jeffrey standing alone near the garage at the rear of the property. 'Don't go in there. Someone's got a knife,' Jeffrey said to him. Soon after, three other firemen approached the blazing house. They found Jeffrey at the base of the stairs leading from the street, crying, disoriented and speaking incoherently. One of the officers thought Jeffrey's hair looked slightly wet. Another officer led Jeffrey to the street where Mr W was waiting. A fireman at the rear of the fire truck smelt petrol on Jeffrey, who was standing about a metre and a half away.

From their house, Mr and Mrs B saw Jeffrey and Mr W together on the street as the firemen set about controlling the fire. Mrs B saw Jeffrey with a blanket around his shoulders, waving his arms about, talking gibberish, then jumping and running in a strange, side to side gait along each side of the burning house. Mr B joined his neighbour on the street and the two men took turns holding Jeffrey, who was now shaking uncontrollably.

Meanwhile, the fire fighters tried to enter the house by opening the sliding glass doors from the living room onto the balcony. They succeeded in getting them open but it was too hot to enter. The rear bedroom window exploded. The officers went to the master bedroom window where flames were shooting through, turned on a fire hose and blanketed the bedroom with water. As the fire was now less intense, fire fighters wearing breathing apparatus were able to crawl in with a second fire hose and relieve two of the first three, who had been singed by the raging fire reacting to the cold water.

Through the flames and thick smoke they found the body of Jeffrey's mother, Helen Gilham. She was lying on her back in the hallway outside of the master bedroom, badly burnt. Then, after returning to the master bedroom, they found the equally badly burnt body of Jeffrey's father, Stephen Gilham, lying face down. There was an axe on the floor, the handle parallel to the bed.

Shortly afterwards, the fire fighters kicked in the rear door to the lower floor and found the body of Jeffrey's 25-year-old brother, Christopher Gilham, lying between the spiral staircase and his bedroom, near the pool table. The fire hadn't taken hold here and Christopher's body wasn't burnt. Rather, water from fighting the fire upstairs had run down stairs, wetting Christopher's hair and forming a few small puddles pink with blood. There wasn't much blood on the tiled floor near his body, nor was there much on the nearby walls, although there were small blood spatters on the nearby banister and railing. Christopher was wearing a dark grey dressing gown but no pants. There was no blood on Christopher's legs or feet. A knife was found next to him, partly under his lower left arm. It was clearly a crime scene, so the fire fighters did their best not to move anything while they got the blaze under control.

Just before 5.00 a.m., less than ten minutes after the fire fighters arrived, an ambulance arrived, followed within minutes by the police. Jeffrey was sitting on the footpath with Mr W nearby. Jeffrey was led into the ambulance, where an ambulance officer asked him what happened.

'My brother killed my parents. He had a knife and set fire to them,' Jeffrey said.

The ambulance officer asked him why his brother would do that.

'There had been a lot of arguments,' replied Jeffrey as a police officer joined them in the ambulance. Jeffrey then told the police officer that he stabbed his brother to death because his brother had killed his parents and set them on fire.

The police began to examine the crime scene and Jeffrey was taken into custody. Photographs and swabs were taken of the possible bloodstains on his left shin, inner right foot and right hand. Water had spread to the downstairs billiard room to such an extent that a tarpaulin was erected above Christopher's body to avoid contamination of the crime scene. Police found a length of garden hose that had been freshly cut from a hose in the garage where the cars were kept and a 25-litre jerry can with a very small amount of petrol in it in a brick alcove at the front of the house. Another section of hose was found under the family's small yacht and trailer. Jeffrey's boatshed bedroom at the rear of the property was found locked and the sheets of his bed pulled back quite neatly. In the lower level laundry police found a syringe filled with paracetamol, an empty packet of 24 paracetamol tablets, a knife and a glass mug containing paracetamol residue. No fingerprints were found.

Later that day police walked Jeffrey through the burnt remains of his home. He told them that he was asleep in his boatshed bedroom in the small hours of the morning when his mother called him over the intercom at about 4.30 a.m. He couldn't make out what she was saying, but she was screaming. He got out of bed, pulled on his boxer shorts, locked the boatshed door behind him as was his habit and made his way to the house. He didn't hear any commotion in the house as he rushed up the garden stairs to the upper level. He entered via the sliding glass doors and saw his brother setting his mother alight with a match. He says his brother then told him that he had killed both of their parents and set them on fire. Jeffrey said he then walked to where his mother lay, and saw through the master bedroom door that his father was already alight. He said he made no attempt to put out the fire, which was spreading quickly, because he did not think of it. He said he did not know whether his parents were alive or dead and did nothing to check whether they were alive, but saw that neither of them was moving. Then, seeing a knife on the floor near the piano, Jeffrey grabbed it, chased his brother down the spiral staircase and stabbed him repeatedly in the pool room.

'Why would you kill your brother?' asked police.

'I don't know, I was just there and I just …'

'Was he armed at the time?'

'I don't think so,' answered Jeffrey.

'Well, what do you mean, you don't think so? Was he armed or wasn't he armed?'

'I didn't see anything.'

'So you're saying that your life was not in fear [sic] at the time that you stabbed your brother?'

'No, no it wasn't.'

'So why did you stab your brother?'

'I just – just did. I saw everything there and I picked up the knife and chased him.'

Jeffrey told police he could not remember what he did with the knife after he stabbed his brother. After stabbing him, he went back upstairs, which was by that time full of smoke to the height of the top of the piano. He said he then left through the glass doors and went up to the street to his neighbours' house to raise the alarm.

Jeffrey also told police he didn't know why his brother would do such a thing, although he did think there had been tension between his brother and his father over the last few days, to the point that Christopher had pushed and shoved their father. Jeffrey said he knew nothing about the axe found near his parents' bed or the syringe filled with paracetamol and the other items found in the lower laundry.

Dr Christopher Lawrence, the government medical officer, attended the scene at 8.00 a.m., examined the bodies, took photographs and subsequently performed the post mortem examinations that revealed that Jeffrey's parents and his brother had been stabbed to death. Jeffrey's father had been stabbed 28 times, sustaining 16 wounds to the front of the chest, apparently in an attack without warning as he lay in bed. Jeffrey's mother and his brother, Christopher, had each been stabbed 17 times; 13 were to the back of Jeffrey's mother's chest and 14 were to the front of Christopher's chest. It seemed Jeffrey's mother had been attacked just after her husband, probably while she was trying to both reason with and get away from the attacker. Her body was found lying near the intercom that linked the house with the boatshed at the rear of the property that Jeffrey used as a bedroom. The intercom was on a table alongside the landline phone, which was near the front door.

The kitchen knife found near Christopher's body was quickly established as the weapon used in each killing. Despite this, there was no visible blood on the knife. There were also other things that seemed a bit odd. Christopher needed glasses to properly see further than an arm's length away. However, Christopher wasn't wearing his glasses. It seemed he hadn't been wearing them at the time of his parents' killing or his own death. Christopher's bedroom was on the bottom level of the house and there were signs that he had lain in his bed that night. The way he was dressed, a robe with no pants, and the fact he wasn't wearing his glasses, raised suspicions that maybe Christopher was the one roused from his sleep, not Jeffrey.

The knife used in all three killings was found in a very unusual position: it was blade up, resting on Christopher's left hip with Christopher's left lower arm across the handle. The 14 stab wounds to Christopher's chest in close proximity suggested they were made while Christopher lay on the floor. Given Christopher's arm across the handle, it was difficult to see how the knife could have landed where it was found if Jeffrey had simply dropped the knife. Also, a question arose over whether Jeffrey could have seen his father's body from where his mother's body lay. If Jeffrey stood near his mother's extended right hand, at most he could see only his father's left hand.

As he walked through the charred remains of his family home, Jeffrey told police about the jerry can at the front of the house and the length of garden hose that had been cut off. He said that earlier in the evening, he and his father had tried to siphon some petrol out of the car to use in their boat, but it was the wrong kind of petrol, adding that was why there was very little petrol in the jerry can found by police.

As police began to question neighbours and friends, one of the most extraordinary aspects of this case emerged. There was no known motive for either brother to murder their parents. Jeffrey's family were highly respected, free from mental instability or problems with drugs, alcohol, gambling or anti-social behaviour. Both Jeffrey and Christopher were university students, with Jeffrey approaching the end of his civil engineering degree and Christopher, who had completed a chemical engineering degree but been unable to find employment in that field, studying for a Bachelor of Education. There were differences in personality between the brothers. Jeffery was outgoing with many friends and sporting success, while Christopher was reserved, with few friends and career frustrations. But nothing could explain why either of them would murder their parents.

Nonetheless, one thing was clear: Jeffrey had killed Christopher, and police charged him with the murder of his brother the day following the night his family were stabbed to death.

Five days later, the clothes Jeffrey had been wearing earlier that night were found, burnt but with no bloodstains on them, under the lounge inside the house. This seemed a little odd to police, given Jeffrey said he was sleeping naked in the boathouse before pulling on his boxer shorts when woken by his mother on the intercom. Did it follow that Jeffrey was saying he undressed in the house, then walked through the winter evening dressed only in his boxer shorts to go to bed in the boatshed? More questions arose. Did Jeffrey wash himself before going to the neighbours' house? Were Jeffrey and Christopher left-handed or right-handed?

However, at this stage Jeffrey had retained a solicitor and was exercising his right to silence by refusing to answer any further questions. Police could only speculate as to which hand each brother would have held the knife in, what the clothes in the house meant, how the knife came to be found under Christopher's arm, why Jeffrey had so little blood on him when he turned up at Mr and Mrs W's home, and the significance of a document headed 'Evidence at the Scene of a Crime' found in a wastepaper basket that appeared to be part of Christopher's teaching materials.

Jeffrey's friends and his girlfriend revealed to police that Jeffrey had told them Christopher had been acting weirdly towards his father in the weeks before the murders. Jeffrey's grandmother also mentioned that Jeffrey's mother had said that Christopher's behaviour had been 'a bit off'. People who worked with Jeffrey's mother recalled her being very worried about one of her sons, but they couldn't be sure which one she was talking about. A few months before the murders, Jeffrey's mother told a friend that during a lunchtime party the two boys said they were planning to kill their parents and take their money. Jeffrey's mother took this as a joke. This friend thought nothing of it until she discussed it with another friend who was at a dinner at Jeffrey's home prior to Christmas 1992. During that dinner Christopher said, 'We'll kill you and get all your money.' Everyone laughed at the time.

A couple of years after the murders, Jeffrey's account of what happened that night in 1993 was still the only one that existed. To disprove that account and convict Jeffrey of killing his parents would mean convincing a jury that an intelligent and well-adjusted young man planned the murder of his parents for a number of weeks by spreading stories about his brother's aggression towards their father, then stabbed his parents to death while his brother slept in the house, set fire to his parents, stabbed his fit younger brother to death, sought help from his neighbours, and then admitted almost immediately to killing his brother because he was confident he would be treated leniently. Jeffrey's parents' murderer had to be either Jeffrey or Christopher, and even though Jeffrey had admitted to one act of extreme violence, the evidence as to which brother murdered their parents was unclear.

In 1995 Jeffrey asked for his murder charge to be reduced to manslaughter on the grounds that he had been provoked into killing Christopher.

The statement of agreed facts submitted to the sentencing court jointly by the Crown (meaning the state, the police and prosecutors) and Jeffrey's legal team stated:

> [Jeffrey] has given an account of events to Police which in their simplest form are a feasible account of what may have happened. The investigation to date has been unable to refute that scenario, despite a thorough scientific analysis and evaluation of the scene and available evidence.

While the Crown accepted Jeffrey's manslaughter plea, the ferocity of his attack on Christopher led the Crown to ask the sentencing judge to impose a custodial sentence. However, Jeffrey received a suspended three-year sentence and a five-year good behaviour bond. In June 1995, a month after his suspended sentence was handed down, a coroner found that Jeffrey's brother Christopher murdered both their parents.

It seemed that the events of the night Jeffrey's brother, mother and father died had been explained. Jeffrey's extended family accepted his claim that Christopher, the less successful, more socially awkward of the two brothers, was the one who murdered their parents. But the following year, a dispute over the parents' estate prompted some of the family to publicly accuse Jeffrey of being the one who murdered his parents.

Helen and Stephen Gilham's joint estate was worth around $900 000, including $46 000 held in trust for the paternal grandfather and a property valued at $180 000 in which the paternal grandmother held a life interest. Their wills left their estates to each other, then passing to their sons. Even if the terms of their wills had never been discussed with their sons, it would not be unusual for both Jeffrey and Christopher to have believed they would inherit.

There were different views as to Jeffrey's entitlement under his parents' respective wills, especially given that Christopher had died by Jeffrey's hand. Jeffrey attempted via his solicitor to persuade his elderly paternal grandparents to forgo their interests. Both grandparents refused and his grandmother initiated a court action to counter Jeffrey's claim. In 1996 Jeffrey's grandmother called one of his uncles, Tony, to complain that Jeffrey had been harassing her, demanding she hand over her share of the estate to him. Tony began to believe that it was Jeffrey who stabbed his brother Stephen and sister-in-law Helen so as to get his hands on their estate, an estate he wouldn't have to share with Christopher. Tony approached police with his new suspicion. He learnt that the police also suspected that Jeffrey may have murdered his entire family. However, given the manslaughter plea and the coroner's finding, without any new evidence there wasn't any prospect of Jeffrey being prosecuted.

Tony was determined to get what he considered justice. He began to constantly call the offices of the DPP and besieged his local member of parliament and verbally abused staff. He convinced the television current affairs program *60 Minutes* to take an interest in the case. Producers of the show approached a barrister and a forensic pathologist, who both expressed the view that the stab wounds showed that one person stabbed all three of the deceased. The forensic pathologist, Dr Godfrey Oettle, was happy to ask a television audience of over one million whether Jeffrey could have so little blood on him after stabbing his brother 17 times unless he had washed himself. The program, aired in November 1997, suggested the need for further investigation into whether one person had stabbed all three members of the Gilham family to death on that night in 1993.

Under renewed pressure from the police, who had collected the opinions of other forensic medical and fire experts since the *60 Minutes* program, I sought a further opinion from another forensic pathologist before deciding what, if anything, was to happen next. A 1998 DNA test of the swab from Jeffrey's right foot showed the blood could have been his or his mother's. (This was before DNA technology became as sophisticated and reliable as it is today.) The new expert opinions gathered by police and by my office raised plenty of suspicion, but my deputy and I agreed that there still wasn't a reasonable prospect of Jeffrey being convicted of the murders of his parents. However, I did request a re-opening of the coronial inquest into the house fire and the deaths of Helen and Stephen Gilham.

In 1999, six years after their deaths, a second coronial inquest was held. The experts approached by police and by the *60 Minutes* program – Dr Lawrence, Dr Oettle, Dr Cala and Professor Cordner – gave conflicting opinions on the stab wounds.

Dr Lawrence had performed the post mortems, and in accordance with usual practice had made no comment in his autopsy report on any similarities between the wounds.

For the purposes of the second inquest, Dr Lawrence prepared a generic anatomical drawing of the upper body on which he marked arrows indicating the general direction from which the stab wounds to the chest and back were delivered to Christopher and both of his parents. He also prepared a transparent overlay of the same pro forma anatomical drawing he used in the autopsy, on which he traced the wounds from the post mortem drawings for each of the deceased, so as to enable an easy comparison of the wounds.

At the inquest Dr Lawrence said, 'I honestly cannot recall a group of three sets of wounds that looked this much the same. And I've dealt with other triple homicides before.' However, he added, importantly, that this did not establish that one person was responsible for the three murders.

Having already appeared on national television, Dr Oettle had also made a number of his views known to police. One of these was that 'the pattern of stab wounds in all these three people was very similar being concentrated in the area involving the heart and lungs'.

Professor Cordner was not impressed with this observation. 'This is a true statement about stabbings in general. The vast bulk of homicidal stabbings involve the chest,' he said, and went on:

> The only similarity here is the number and the fact that they could all have been inflicted with the same knife. There is no specific peculiarity to tie the three together in my mind. Indeed, there are some differences … I do not think it is safe to conclude that the distribution and number of stabbed incised wounds in these three deaths are such as to indicate that the three deaths were by the one hand. I do not even think that it is a probable factor to be weighed in the balance – it is neutral in trying to conclude whether there was one or two murderers in this case.

Professor Cordner then said something that would ultimately see him excluded from giving evidence at Jeffrey's murder trial 15 years later: 'Conversely, one could say that as the wounds are consistent with being caused by the one knife, in this respect, the findings are consistent with Jeffrey's story.'

Dr Cala disagreed with Professor Cordner. 'The pattern of injury and indeed the causes of death in all three cases are extremely similar. The number of stabbings in two of the three victims are identical (17 times) … that these people should die in extraordinarily similar ways suggests to me the possibility that only one person was involved in the three deaths.'

Professor Cordner was also not impressed with Dr Oettle's view that Jeffrey must have washed himself and the knife.

> Assuming that Jeffrey was spattered with blood, why wash – and if he washed where and how did he do this? The inference is that he washed because he had some of his mother's and father's blood on him too. He had no need to wash (assuming he is acting rationally, which may be a significant assumption) if it was only his brother's blood because he is going to concede that he killed his brother. But why wash the knife too? Blood

> from all the victims would be on it however the murders happened. (Incidentally, I can see no report of a formal examination of the knife to confirm the absence of blood, although as far as one can see from the photographs, there is no obvious blood on it. In the absence of any blood, an additional question would need to be asked – was it indeed the weapon?)

Professor Cordner recommended submitting Christopher's dressing gown and Jeffrey's boxer shorts, if they were still available, to analysis for hydrocarbons and accelerants and reviewing the formal report of the examination of the knife. He also suggested that Jeffrey's clothes and shoes found upstairs be submitted for examination, particularly for hydrocarbons or blood.

However, Christopher's dressing gown, Jeffrey's boxer shorts, Jeffrey's other clothes and the knife, plus Christopher's fingernail scrapings, samples from the bedding, the jerry can, the petrol sample, the garden hose, clothing recovered from Stephen and Helen, carpet samples, the intercom which Jeffrey said his mother had used to frantically call him to the house, Christopher's computer and a set of keys, had all gone missing, probably having been destroyed after the 1995 manslaughter plea. Years later it would be revealed that the knife used to stab all three members of Jeffrey's family, while photographed and analysed for fingerprints, had never been formally examined for blood before it was destroyed or lost. Police also couldn't find Christopher's glasses or records of their discovery at the scene in Christopher's bathroom, which was close to his downstairs bedroom.

Dr Oettle and Dr Cala maintained that as the wounds on all three deceased were strikingly similar, it could be assumed that one person was responsible. Dr Lawrence and Professor Cordner did not think this conclusion could be made safely, with Professor Cordner going one step further to state the only real conclusion was that one knife was used for all three, just as Jeffrey said.

Recollections of jokes made by both brothers about killing their parents for money, and the fact they were made around the time of the highly publicised US trial of the Menendez brothers for the 1989 murder of their millionaire parents, were also aired at the second coronial inquest.

There was expert evidence on where the fire probably started. Jeffrey had told police that Christopher set fire to their mother and then the fire immediately spread to their father. From the testing of carpet samples around where the bodies were found, it was established that mineral turpentine was the accelerant used, not petrol as originally thought. No carpet sample from between the bodies had been taken and it was not possible to say if turpentine was spread between the bodies.

Suspicions that Jeffrey was lying were heightened as it emerged the bulk of the evidence collected by the fire officers and fire investigators suggested that, contrary to Jeffrey's account, the fire began in the main bedroom where his father's body was and spread to the lounge room. Jeffrey refused to answer questions on the basis that he might incriminate himself, which was his legal right (the so-called right to silence).

Unlike the first inquest, this coroner concluded there was evidence capable of satisfying a jury that Jeffrey was the one who murdered his parents. His uncle Tony was elated. However, was there really enough evidence to prosecute and convict Jeffrey? This was the question I faced in July 2000.

To begin with, what constitutes evidence in a coronial inquest may not make it in front of a jury. For example, the disbelief police expressed at parts of Jeffrey's version of events in filmed interviews with him would be inadmissible in criminal proceedings because it was strictly irrelevant and would unfairly prejudice a jury against

Jeffrey. The rules of evidence do not apply in an inquest, but they do in a criminal trial.

Dr Oettle's opinion was good television and made a big impression at the coronial inquest, but to my mind, most of it would not stand up in a courtroom. Dr Oettle's view that the wounds were strikingly similar was within his area of expertise, forensic pathology, but to then take a further step and express the view that this similarity meant one person was responsible for all three murders constituted not expert opinion but speculation that would not be permitted in criminal proceedings. To make such a leap would require expert consideration of other relevant facts, such as the brothers being of similar height, the same knife being used in all three stabbings and whether each brother was right-handed or left-handed. I thought the same problems existed for the opinion put forward by Dr Cala.

Dr Lawrence, who visited the crime scene just hours after the murders, also had the opinion that the wounds on all three deceased were strikingly similar, but unlike Dr Oettle and Dr Cala, he did not then claim this could prove one person stabbed all three. I thought his expert opinion was far more likely to carry weight in a murder trial and it was supported by the opinion of Professor Cordner, whose opinion that these similarities didn't prove which of the brothers murdered their parents also stood a good chance of being admissible. On balance, the expert evidence on the stab wounds that I thought likely to be admissible wasn't enough to disprove Jeffrey's claim that Christopher was the murderer and prove that Jeffrey was.

A lack of either parent's blood on Christopher would be an obvious piece of circumstantial evidence capable of weakening Jeffrey's claim that Christopher was the murderer. Forensic testing of Christopher's dressing gown carried out in 1993, before it was lost, revealed plenty of Christopher's blood, as was to be expected. But there were also stains of a blood type that both Christopher and his mother shared.

DNA testing would have provided a more definitive answer to whether his mother's blood was also on Christopher's dressing gown, but the laboratories used by police investigating this case in 1993 didn't perform DNA testing. The decision not to go to the time and expense of sending Christopher's dressing gown to a laboratory that performed DNA testing would prove to be a major stumbling block for a definitive answer as to who murdered his parents. Given the loss of this critical piece of evidence, there was no way of improving on the blood type testing. The possibility that his mother's blood could have been on Christopher would always remain. The remarkable lack of blood on Christopher's feet and legs, which would be expected to have blood on them if he stabbed his parents while not wearing shoes, might be explained by water from upstairs washing it away, given the amount of water that had pooled around Christopher's body was enough to make his hair wet.

As the *60 Minutes* program stressed, the unexpectedly small amount of blood on Jeffrey when he turned up at his neighbours' house could suggest that he had washed or cleaned himself. The need to wash would make sense if Jeffrey had the blood of his parents on his body, rather than just that of his brother whom he openly admitted he had stabbed to death. However, the lack of blood on Jeffrey could be explained by Christopher's dressing gown capturing most of his blood as the knife repeatedly penetrated his body, a point that Professor Cordner had raised. This possibility would also explain why only very small blood spatters were found on the wall near Christopher's body in areas that couldn't have been washed by water running down the stairs. Also, there was some blood found on Jeffrey's right foot, blood that also matched his mother's blood type. Even if subsequent DNA testing could determine that it was actually his mother's blood on his foot, its presence fitted with Jeffrey's claim that he walked near where his mother lay on the floor after she had been stabbed to death by Christopher.

The blood on his foot could also be used to argue that Jeffrey didn't wash at all because, if he did, that blood wouldn't have been there. The police didn't ask Jeffrey directly whether he had washed himself before he refused to answer any more questions. The shower recesses in the house hadn't been tested for the presence of blood. Even if blood from either of his parents had been found on Jeffrey, it wouldn't be conclusive evidence of guilt as his story involved a violent struggle with Christopher, who Jeffrey said had killed their parents.

The absence of any visible blood on the knife was similarly unexpected, as it was used to stab all three of the victims. Again, this might be explained by Christopher's dressing gown wiping the knife clean after each stab. More importantly, even if it could be established that Jeffrey had washed the knife, this wouldn't prove anything. The presence of his parents' blood on the knife could be explained by Jeffrey's claim that Christopher was the one who stabbed them. The knife was never scientifically tested for the presence of blood and no fingerprints were found before it was destroyed or lost after the 1995 manslaughter plea. However, this was not really so important because it would not prove Jeffrey's guilt if the blood of all three of the deceased or his fingerprints were all over the knife. That would be expected if he stabbed Christopher after his parents had been stabbed. A complete absence of Christopher's fingerprints would be strong evidence against Jeffrey, but it was now impossible to conduct further tests.

Could the clothes Jeffrey had been wearing the evening immediately prior to the killings, which were later found inside the house, be proof that Jeffrey never went to bed in the boatshed, but instead had waited in the house to stab his family to death, first removing his clothes to make sure he didn't get any bloodstains on them? As unlikely as it seemed that Jeffrey would choose to walk to his bed through the winter's evening dressed only in his boxer shorts, it was not impossible that he might have, so the discovery of his unstained clothes in the house didn't prove much.

That Christopher wasn't wearing his glasses when he died also gave rise to the suspicion that he may not have been the one who stabbed his parents to death, but what this fact actually proved was questionable. Christopher was short-sighted and always wore his glasses. His ex-girlfriend said he always wore them when walking around the house. However, his optometrist conceded it was possible for Christopher to move about without them in a familiar setting and with good lighting. It would make sense for Christopher to have worn them if he had gone upstairs to kill his parents, but it was arguable that he may not have. Also, at this stage his glasses seemed to have been lost. That also left open the argument that he may in fact have been wearing them, but they fell off and were destroyed by the fire.

Scientific testing of the carpets had shown that mineral turpentine had been the accelerant used to spread the fire, not petrol, so the fact of the jerry can with a small amount of petrol in it, the lengths of hose, and Jeffrey's explanation that he and his father had been siphoning petrol out of the car to use in their boat, was not going to shed any new light onto who lit the fire. The strong smell of kerosene on Jeffrey that his neighbours remember might arguably have been mineral turpentine, and the smell could have come from his being close to the fire his brother lit.

Despite the weight of expert evidence contradicting his assertion that his mother's body was set alight first, Jeffrey's account could still stand up as reasonable. My experience suggested that if pressed during a trial, the fire experts would concede the reasonable possibility of the immediate spread of fire from Jeffrey's mother's body to his father's body. Even though there was no proof of any accelerant on the carpet between the two bodies, the vapours from the accelerant surrounding each body may have been sufficient to cause the immediate spread of the fire from his mother's body to his father's if, as Jeffrey said, hers was set alight first.

Inconsistencies between the accounts Jeffrey gave neighbours, fire fighters and police about what happened were a questionable source of incriminating evidence. There were times he said he saw his brother holding the knife, other times he said he saw the knife on the ground, times he said he saw Christopher setting his mother alight, others when he said his parents were already alight when he came across Christopher; but all that could be consistent with Jeffrey being in shock. There were also problems with reading too much into whether Jeffrey could have seen his father while standing near his mother's body. When police walked Jeffrey through the scene, his mother's body had been removed, so there was no reference to exactly where he would have stood as he peered into his parents' bedroom.

Construing the pressure Jeffrey put on his grandmother over his parents' estate as revealing a motive of financial gain was unlikely to stand up. The vagaries of estate law could explain this unpleasant family argument. The evidence of tasteless jokes both brothers made about killing their parents for their money that family friends recalled, possibly inspired by the Menendez brothers' trial for the murder of their parents that was in the news at the time, appealed to many as an insight into a possible motive, but such speculation provided no evidence as to who the murderer was.

Claims by people who were not qualified psychiatrists that Jeffrey's calm demeanour not long after the event, his ability in the years that followed the deaths to successfully complete his education, have a career and get married was some sort of proof of an unnatural lack of feeling and devastation were opinions that wouldn't stand a chance of being admissible in criminal proceedings.

There was other evidence that added to the horror of the crime scene, but couldn't be explained at all. The axe beside Jeffrey's parents' bed, the syringes full of paracetamol, the document headed 'Evidence at the Scene of a Crime' found in a wastepaper basket that appeared to be part of Christopher's teaching materials, the knife being found under Christopher's arm. In the absence of new facts shedding light on what these things could mean, there could only be explanations based purely on speculation, and therefore not admissible as proof of the guilt of either brother.

Despite the finding of the second coronial inquest, the evidence capable of being admissible in a murder trial still couldn't conclusively prove Jeffrey murdered his parents. As the High Court explained in 1912, when the evidence is evenly balanced in a criminal case, it isn't a matter of members of the jury choosing the story or explanation they like best. Instead, the High Court explained that in such situations, 'It is the practice of Judges ... to tell the jury that, if there is any reasonable hypothesis consistent with the innocence of the prisoner, it is their duty to acquit.'

That Jeffrey could have been the murderer remained only a possibility. It was fair to say a jury would think it highly unlikely that two brothers would commit separate stabbing killings. If a jury accepted the neighbours' recollections of hearing frantic voices at around 4.00 a.m. then the inference could be made that Jeffrey's parents were murdered at around 4.00 a.m., not 4.30 a.m., which was when Jeffrey said his mother screamed at him through the intercom and he rushed to the house. If the jury accepted the murders happened half an hour earlier than Jeffrey claimed, it might follow that the doubts otherwise hanging over the rest of the admissible evidence would shrink. Instead, the jury would focus on Jeffrey having time to also kill Christopher, clean the knife that carried only his fingerprints, spread the accelerant, remove the accelerant container from the house and clean himself before running across to Mr and Mrs W's house while his house burned.

But what ultimately stopped this possibility from being proved beyond reasonable doubt was the possibility that his mother's blood was on Christopher's dressing gown, and this possibility supported Jeffrey's account of that night. The decision of the Crown to accept Jeffrey's plea to the manslaughter of Christopher in 1995, and no decisive new admissible evidence having been produced since that time, meant that even if a jury accepted Jeffrey's parents were murdered at around 4.00 a.m. rather than 4.30 a.m. and convicted Jeffrey, the conviction would almost certainly be overturned on appeal.

What's more, if Jeffrey was prosecuted for murder and found not guilty, there would be no second chance. Even if, after an acquittal, Christopher's dressing gown turned up without a speck of his parents' blood on it, or other new admissible evidence came to light, or Jeffrey decided to confess he was the murderer after all, the law at that time meant he could not be tried again for the murder of his parents. Rather than take that risk, on 21 July 2000 I decided that there was no reasonable prospect of a conviction and declined to proceed.

To say Jeffrey's uncle Tony was disappointed is an understatement. He had the words 'N Cowdery QC is protecting a mass killer [Jeffrey] from prosecution' neatly spelt out in large white letters on a sign on the rear window of his car, which he parked outside the Office of the Director of Public Prosecutions. Unfortunately for Tony, his car was illegally parked.

Chapter 3

WHEN PEOPLE ARE PUSHED TO BREAKING POINT: FATIMA AND BOBBY

Prosecutors are human, despite what some accused persons and their lawyers may think. So, too, are police. Of course they get upset; and there are particular problems for police and prosecutors when children and families are suffering.

People kill for a wide range of reasons, but alcohol, drugs, personal enmity, greed, emotional disturbance and the proximity of a weapon can all contribute. The most common implement of homicide in New South Wales is a kitchen knife and killers and victims are almost always well known to each other, if not related. (The lesson is to avoid drunken arguments with family or friends in the kitchen!) I think it's fair to say that most convicted killers are generally unsympathetic characters, but that is not the case for all and we should not lose sight of the circumstances that lead to any killing.

In 2003 the case of Fatima (pseudonyms are used in discussing this case) came across my desk. Fatima had killed her severely autistic ten-year-old son and then made a serious attempt to kill herself.

Fatima's son Bobby was diagnosed with autism at about 18 months of age. Despite their best efforts, Fatima and her husband Barry, Bobby's father, were not able to get Bobby the help he needed until he was six. Having finally obtained this help, Fatima and her husband were advised that the failure of local authorities to provide specialist help during Bobby's earlier years meant his ability to acquire better life skills had been lost. Unable to cope with Bobby's inability to feed himself, speak, take himself to the toilet or make friends, Barry had a mental breakdown. He was unable to work for two years. Fatima was left to care for Bobby and his sister alone while her husband stayed at home, drank too much and verbally and physically abused her.

In September 2001 the family moved from their coastal home town to Sydney with the hope of obtaining more support for Bobby. As they could not afford to buy a house in Sydney, they went from being home owners to renters. Also, the help they were hoping to find in Sydney wasn't there. Instead, Fatima lost the small amount of respite care she had previously been able to obtain back home. On the day before Christmas 2002, which happened to be Fatima's birthday, her father was diagnosed with a brain tumour and hospitalised. Meanwhile, Barry's drinking, gambling and abuse became too much. In January 2003 Fatima asked him to leave the family home, which he did. Not long after he left, Barry threatened suicide and was hospitalised for three days. Throughout, Fatima had to educate, feed, toilet, bathe, entertain and love Bobby and not neglect his sister as she navigated her teenage years. Even though Fatima's marriage was in tatters, she allowed her husband to come home around Easter 2003. Barry's behaviour did not improve and he still didn't help Fatima very much.

Things got worse. In June 2003 Fatima's father died. Her stepmother argued with Fatima over the details of the burial and her late father's estate. Then Fatima's grandmother became seriously ill and was hospitalised. Fatima was taking prescribed medication for depression and lost almost ten kilograms in weight in one month because of the stress. In late July, she and Barry went to a social function during which he behaved so badly that she came home feeling trapped in a relationship she hated.

On the morning of 4 August 2003, Fatima got up at 5.10 a.m. to start another day. She helped her daughter get ready for school. She also spoke with Barry about the ongoing problems they faced with Bobby, who was by this time ten years old. Bobby still had the habit of bending his teachers' fingers backwards when he didn't want to do what he was told, although this and his old habit of grabbing people's throats had diminished with constant supervision and correction of his behaviour at school and at home. Other problems Bobby had had since he was a very little boy had not changed. He still couldn't speak. His inability to understand what was being said to him, and his obstinacy, meant he only occasionally completed tasks set at his ability level in class. He made loud noises when frustrated, could not tolerate loud noises around him and often sang in a monotone. There was no reason to think he was going to get much better as he grew into a teenager and a young man. Meanwhile, on top of taking care of Bobby, helping other parents with disabled children and raising their daughter, Fatima worked three days a week. The extraordinary amount of stress she had been dealing with over the previous months meant she wasn't producing her usual standard of work, and her employer had spoken to her about this.

After about 8.30 a.m., by which time Barry had left for work and their daughter had left for school, Fatima got Bobby's clothes ready, had a shower and then tried to dress her son. He refused to cooperate and ran down the stairs into the rumpus room. Something in Fatima snapped. She followed Bobby and, once she caught up to him, held her hand over his mouth and nose. Bobby died by suffocation. Fatima then picked him up, carried him to his bedroom and laid him on his bed. She called her work, told them she wouldn't be coming in because she was sick, and placed some money, bank account withdrawal slips and written authorities on the table so her husband and daughter could access the money she had in her bank account. Then she went into the bathroom and slashed her wrists. The only reason her suicide attempt didn't succeed was because her mother let herself into the house and found her daughter bleeding to death in the shower.

Fatima's intense remorse over killing her son was obvious to everyone. She made it clear to the police who were first on the scene that she didn't want to live, telling them 'I don't want to get warm.' When police spoke to her as she lay in hospital, she made a full admission as to how she killed her son. She pleaded guilty when offered the charge of manslaughter (on the basis of the partial defence to murder of diminished responsibility, as it was called then).

Fatima's sentencing hearing included four psychiatrists, including one instructed by me, who all diagnosed Fatima as suffering a major depressive illness at the time of Bobby's death. Barry put aside his usual habit of abusing and blaming his wife to tell the court via his victim impact statement that she was a good mother who had taken care of Bobby for many years and didn't deserve to go to jail.

Given a fundamental purpose of the criminal law is to protect the sanctity of life, even in very difficult circumstances, the courts are bound to punish those who unlawfully take the lives of others. The endless scenarios that end up as manslaughter convictions, ranging from practical jokes that have gone wrong to actions just short of murder, or murder mitigated by a partial defence, mean judges need to have a wide discretion as to what the punishment should be in each case. A manslaughter conviction almost always results in a custodial sentence, but the sentences can range from under two years right up to the 25 years maximum. In very rare cases the sentence can be suspended. In even rarer cases, the punishment is a good behaviour bond.

So what was Fatima's punishment going to be? The sentencing judge knew of plenty of cases of people who were suffering in appalling circumstances when they killed others. However, even this rich history of misery didn't offer the judge the answer he would have liked. Almost all offenders were sent to prison, at least briefly. One rare case where the offender was not sent to jail involved a diligent and caring mother who was severely depressed to the point of near insanity when she killed her young child. The mother planned to commit suicide but killed her child first so he would not be left behind when she died. She was one of the exceptionally rare cases of manslaughter that was punished by a good behaviour bond.

The prosecutor in Fatima's case suggested to the judge that something other than full-time custody could be appropriate for Fatima. The sentencing judge not only agreed but also thought a suspended sentence was too harsh. On 2 June 2004, the judge sentenced Fatima to a five-year good behaviour bond, which essentially involved her giving an undertaking to the court that she would continue getting professional help with her depression, accept being supervised by the Probation and Parole Service plus a few other things – or face the possibility of being sent to jail for up to 25 years. Fatima was free to leave.

Before her sentencing hearing, the media were sympathetic. While not shying away from the fact that Fatima had been allowed to walk free from court despite killing her ten-year-old son, media coverage emphasised the lack of support from authorities as Fatima cared for Bobby.

Within two weeks of receiving the good behaviour bond, Fatima obtained an apprehended domestic violence order against Barry. She also obtained custody of their daughter and moved away from Sydney to the north coast. Around this time Barry had a very public change of heart about what punishment Fatima should face.

'I cannot forgive her for what she has done,' Barry said on national television. 'My wife should be in prison … The fact is my wife held my son down, placed a hand over his nose and mouth and held him there until he did not struggle any more. And there is absolutely no way my son did not struggle … To go through a loss like this and have it turned around that I now have an AVO on me. What more does my wife want to extract from me?'

Fatima had indeed moved on with her life. She and her daughter quickly made friends in their new home. The daughter began dancing classes and playing touch football, as well as seeing a counsellor once a week. Fatima kept in regular contact with her domestic violence counsellor and her psychiatrist, and was confident of being able to find work using her computer skills and experience as a trained bookkeeper.

Quite separately from Barry's call for Fatima to be put in jail, senior officers within the ODPP began to consider whether Fatima's sentence was too light. No one within the ODPP wanted her to go to jail. Nevertheless, as sorry as everyone felt for Fatima, her case was one of intentionally killing a vulnerable member of the community, one for whom she had a duty of care. Even though there was psychiatric evidence at her sentencing hearing that there had been times Fatima had contemplated murder and suicide as a way out of her family's dreadful situation, there was no suggestion that she was suicidal before attacking Bobby, only afterwards. Chasing and then manually suffocating a physically healthy ten-year-old boy would have required a degree of determination and persistence against his struggling. Bobby's death was not instantaneous.

As Fatima was not suicidal before she killed Bobby, the decision to not send her to jail was taking the law in a new direction and departing from precedent. For her to not even be given a suspended sentence was pushing the limits of judicial discretion, I thought. Fatima would certainly not be the last person who had suffered extreme misfortune to appear in front of a judge, and judges needed to know just how much mercy they could show. I decided it was time for the NSW Court of Criminal Appeal to make its views known on this important issue. On 25 June 2004, I directed that Fatima's sentence be appealed. She was legally represented in the appeal and there would have been discussions between counsel on both sides about the basis of the appeal.

In November 2004 the Court of Criminal Appeal handed down its decision. Two of the three judges thought the sentencing judge's understandable sympathy for Fatima meant he made a mistake in not sending her to jail, at least for a short time, for the manslaughter of Bobby. The Court of Criminal Appeal ruled that not only was the good behaviour bond too light a punishment, but that a suspended sentence would have been too light as well. In his efforts to show mercy to Fatima, the sentencing judge had failed to have sufficient regard to the court's responsibility to uphold the sanctity of human life. 'All human life is to be protected including that of the disabled, the handicapped, the criminal, the derelict and the friendless,' wrote one of the appeal judges.

But within the logic of justice, mercy could be found. Happily for everyone involved, even though the sentencing judge was held to have got it wrong, the Court of Criminal Appeal nonetheless decided my appeal should fail. Fatima had already faced court with the possibility of going to jail hanging over her head, so the Court of Criminal Appeal ruled it would be wrong to have her face court and the possibility of jail again for the same crime when nothing had really changed. Also, their Honours emphasised that the Crown had not requested a custodial sentence originally, so this would make the prospect of now imposing a prison sentence an even stronger breach of the principle against double jeopardy (as it was applied then).

This was really only a version of the operation of that principle – a form of double punishment or, more accurately, double liability for punishment. Its consideration in such circumstances in Crown appeals has since been removed by legislation. While it assisted Fatima to avoid imprisonment, hers was an exceptional kind of case and such assistance should probably not be available in the ordinary run of cases of more common criminal conduct. Nor would it be available to Fatima now.

Their Honours could not find any alternative punishment for Fatima. By law, home detention was not a sentencing option in cases of manslaughter. Periodic detention, for example spending only the weekends in jail, was not only inappropriate given Fatima's need to care for her teenage daughter, but it wasn't available for women where Fatima now lived. By law, suspended sentences were only available for terms of two years or less. Fatima's good behaviour bond was for five years, which was therefore too long to be neatly converted into a suspended sentence.

Justice had been served. Judges faced with the awful task of handing down sentences in such cases could look to the Court of Criminal Appeal's judgment for guidance as to how light a sentence they could give and in what circumstances, but the appeal had allowed that guidance to be given. Fatima and her family could get on with their lives.

Chapter 4

VOLUNTARY ASSISTED DYING: FRED AND KATERINA; SHIRLEY AND GRAEME AND CAREN

'Mercy killings' and people pushed by extreme misfortune into killing others (including so-called 'battered wives') evoke sympathy in most people. Of course it is against the law to intentionally kill someone: but what if that someone is a terminally ill loved one who desperately wants to die but is physically unable to commit suicide?

The temptation may be either to apply the letter of the law in a black and white fashion or, conversely, to sweep such cases under the carpet by choosing not to prosecute or by not looking closely at the sentence imposed by a sympathetic judge. But the DPP does not shape the law to his or her liking. Even if the DPP is deeply upset about how the law will deal with a particular case, the DPP must apply the law, as it stands, to everyone. If the DPP is unable to do that, the only option is to resign.

The issue of genuine 'mercy killings', when after careful and thorough scrutiny it is clear the killer honestly and reasonably believed their loved one wanted to be assisted to die but could not suicide, does not arise very often in the criminal justice process. We know it does occur, and probably quite widely with the assistance of medical professionals, but few cases come to official notice and usually only if something goes wrong. Nowadays the practice is termed 'voluntary assisted dying', a far more appropriate term than 'euthanasia' or 'mercy killing' because it describes the three elements of exactly what happens.

The great majority of Australians think that rational people who want to die but are unable to commit suicide, particularly the very old and the very ill, should be able to choose to die with dignity and with assistance.

As medical science develops, more ways are found to keep people alive through the ravages of disease and old age. I believe there is an increasing number of people being kept alive in circumstances where, if they had a meaningful choice, they might choose to end it. Because of the current, dangerously inadequate state of the law in New South Wales (a problem I speak about in Chapter 17), assisted voluntary deaths are technically unlawful acts that can attract very long jail terms, so they are kept hidden. I think I'm right in saying the two cases I'm about to describe were the only such cases that went for criminal hearings in New South Wales during my time as DPP. They made a big impact, and I believe they highlight why the law needs to be changed.

Nobody is publicly advocating that the choice to end one's life should be made by anyone other than the person whose life it is. It must be a free and voluntary choice by a person with the mental capacity to make it. There are real issues about people who are suffering from dementia, who are unable to reason, and protections should be in place for them, for juveniles, for the mentally impaired and for other people vulnerable to exploitation. The problem of how to allow people to end their lives when they want to, rather than passively allow medicine to extend lives that are reduced to mere existence, is one for lawmakers to address. There have been attempts to do so in Australia with success in recent times in Victoria and movement in Western Australia, Queensland and South Australia at the time of writing, but much to the frustration of the majority (surveys show 85 per cent of the population support such provisions), most politicians continue to dodge the issue. A bid to change the law failed in New South Wales in 2017.

Killings that hasten the inevitable end of life usually come to official notice when a carer 'plays God' and is found out (for example, a nurse in an aged care facility is discovered administering a drug, or something goes awfully wrong in the process) or something out of the ordinary occurs – such as a confession to police, as in the following sad case, which became a matter for me and my office in 2004.

Fred and Katerina's story

In late 2002, a 68-year-old retired plumber named Fred Thompson walked into a police station and made a confession: on 11 August that year, he had caused the death of his wife.

Fred and Katerina had married in the UK in 1960, when he was 26 and she was 21. They migrated to Australia in 1963. After the birth of their first child in 1965, Katerina was diagnosed with multiple sclerosis. The disease worsened as the years went by, and by 1986 she was in a wheelchair. In addition to multiple sclerosis, Katerina had cancer, resulting in her having a hysterectomy and her bladder removed. She needed around-the-clock care, but refused to go into a nursing home.

Around this time Fred, who was in his early 50s, retired so he could be Katerina's full-time, and only, carer. Their children were adults who loved their parents, but they lived overseas. Fred was a smoker and had health problems of his own. Their daughter said if Fred became unable to care for Katerina, she would be put into a nursing home.

Sixteen years later, in August 2002, Katerina was in the final stages of multiple sclerosis. She was a quadriplegic with no voluntary movement. She could speak and swallow, but was unable to sit properly or act for herself. Her mind was still sharp. Her doctor expected her to die at any time. Fred's health was also suffering. Katerina began to speak of her concern about what would happen to her if Fred were no longer able to care for her. In her last couple of weeks of life, she stopped taking her medications and constantly said to her husband, 'Please, darling, don't put me in a nursing home. Please speed me out of this place painlessly.' Fred often responded; 'OK my dear, if that's what your wish is.'

On 11 August 2002, Katerina asked her husband to send her 'to a better place … Could you please do a final thing for me?' When Fred asked her if that was what she really wanted, she answered; 'Well, I'm a Christian and I know I'm going to a better place.' She asked Fred to 'end it for her'.

Katerina's constant requests for help to die disturbed Fred. That evening, Fred gave Katerina six 2-milligram Valium tablets. The Valium had been prescribed for her, but this was a larger dose than usual. They told each other they loved one another as she swallowed them with water from a glass held by Fred.

After drinking some beer and smoking some cigarettes, Fred called a friend who was a retired clergyman to say he was going to 'finish it now'. Fred had spoken to this friend before about his desire to end his and his wife's lives. Concerned about what Fred had said on the phone, the friend visited Fred and Katerina's home at about 11 p.m. The friend saw about five white tablets near a beer bottle. Fred talked about having the tablets 'ready', that he had already given some to his wife, and was thinking about giving her more. However, after talking further, Fred assured his friend that suicide was not the way. The friend then went into the bedroom and saw that Katerina looked alive, but asleep.

Sometime after the friend had left, Fred tried to rouse Katerina but couldn't. He then held a pillow over her face until he couldn't feel a pulse or detect her breathing. In the early morning Fred called their doctor but didn't tell him what had happened. The doctor certified death by multiple sclerosis and complications.

There was no suspicion surrounding Katerina's death, but Fred was not at peace with what he had done. After Katerina's funeral, Fred visited his family overseas and told them the truth about how Katerina had died. They were horrified. Once he was home he spoke to a clergyman and said he was going to make a full confession to police.

Officers at the police station listened glumly as Fred made his confession. Even though the majority of Australians thought terminally ill people who are mentally alert but unable to kill themselves should be able to ask others to help them end their lives, not even a doctor could help Katerina die without committing a criminal offence. Fred was the one left to deal with his wife's pleas. With the way the law stood, the police had to charge Fred with murder. He was released on bail.

After reviewing the police brief in July 2004, I agreed with police that they had no option but to charge Fred with a criminal offence – murder. Fred had caused the death of his wife by suffocation, or by the administration of Valium, or both, that night in August 2002. There was evidence he intended that she should die when he did these things.

As I would say over a decade later, the law that applied to Fred and Katerina's case was brutally simple. No one, including Katerina, could ask someone to kill them without that person facing very serious criminal charges.

In Fred's case a charge of murder was the obvious conclusion, but I wanted to see if an alternative course could be taken. I considered the offence of aiding suicide. While committing suicide was and is not illegal, aiding suicide, in other words helping someone to commit suicide, was and is a criminal offence. Aside from the evidence that Fred acted to intentionally kill her, there was also evidence that Katerina wanted to die at the time but was physically unable to take her own life without assistance. In particular, she had stopped taking her normal medications and had made a direct and very recent request, repeating many such earlier requests, to her husband to help her take her own life painlessly. Katerina also voluntarily swallowed the Valium with Fred's help. I decided Fred could be charged with two criminal offences: murder, with an alternative charge of aiding suicide.

In a move that I would later describe as a 'creative' construction, or at least a creative application of the law, I took the following steps. I reasoned that this tally of two criminal charges gave this terrible situation a glimmer of hope for justice to be done. If Fred were to face only the charge of murder, a jury properly instructed as to the law would likely find itself with no proper alternative but to convict him of murder (unless it returned a merciful but unreasonable verdict of acquittal or failed to agree). It would then be up to a judge to decide what penalty should be imposed. However, given the jury's almost certain horror at having to convict of murder, a jury faced with the choice of having Fred convicted of that charge or of aiding suicide would likely choose aiding suicide. The judge would be better able to be more lenient in such a case. Given this reality, there was therefore little point in pursuing the charge of murder. After all, there was a reasonable prospect of a conviction under the lesser charge of aiding suicide and nothing in the public interest to be gained by proceeding with murder. Although a conviction for aiding suicide attracted up to ten years in prison, such a conviction didn't have to result in a jail sentence and could be heard in a Local Court. The law, which did not allow anyone to help Katerina die, would be upheld without Fred having to face a Supreme Court trial and punishment for murder.

In the time between first being charged with murder and ultimately being charged with aiding suicide, Fred had met Kep

Enderby QC, president of the NSW Voluntary Euthanasia Society (and former attorney general of Australia and judge of the NSW Supreme Court), at a meeting of the society in 2003. The Voluntary Euthanasia Society saw Fred and Katerina's story as the perfect example of why the law should change. It supported Fred throughout his involvement with the criminal justice system and its members were confident of positive media coverage for his case.

On 25 January 2005, Fred pleaded guilty in the Local Court to aiding the suicide of his wife Katerina. Fred didn't help his wife kill herself in order to make his life easier, with the magistrate noting there was 'no indication whatsoever that the defendant … had in any way tried to end the misery that his life had become'. Instead, Fred's motivation was his love for his wife and his desire to help her with her wish to die at the end of so much suffering. The magistrate gave Fred an 18-month suspended jail sentence, meaning that as long as he didn't break the law again, he didn't have to serve a day in prison, and ordered him to pay $63 in court costs.

The media were kind, describing Fred in prominent stories as a 'mercy killer'. Despite the media's judgment that the general public had a lot of sympathy for Fred, not a single politician in a position of real power said a word about his story or the issue of mercy killings.

Fred walked from the court a free man, but he was devastated. He had helped the love of his life kill herself and his children were no longer talking to him. Three days later he was in hospital after trying to poison himself.

Shirley and Graeme and Caren's story

In 2006 two women decided to take the law into their own hands. Shirley Justins and Caren Jenning knew each other through Graeme Wylie. Shirley had been Graeme's de facto partner for 20 years. Caren was a long-term close friend of Graeme and a friend of Shirley.

Graeme was a man with a singular personality. A retired commercial pilot, he had a life-long fascination with electronics. He was also particularly determined to get his way in relationships. Prior to his relationship with Shirley, he had been married twice and had two daughters. He threw his second wife out of their home when she, knowing he didn't want to have more children, expressed a desire to do so.

Beginning in late 2000, Graeme's mental faculties started to deteriorate. In March 2003, 69-year-old Graeme was diagnosed as suffering from Alzheimer's. He remained at home with Shirley, but was monitored by a hospital for the next two years.

Between the year before his diagnosis and the time he switched in 2005 from being supervised by hospital staff to being supervised by a GP, Graeme's quality of life sharply declined. He lost his fascination for electronics and stopped reading newspapers. His topics of conversation became very limited and at times he appeared disoriented. He also became increasingly depressed. By January 2005, testing indicated severe cognitive impairment.

One day in September 2005, when Shirley was out, Graeme attempted to cut his wrists. His GP confirmed the wounds were superficial, but it was obviously a sign of Graeme's accelerating unhappiness. Not long after this, he expressed an interest in travelling to Switzerland to Dignitas, an organisation that lawfully assists and supervises people who wish to take their own lives. Graeme's adult daughters knew about their father's desire to die with the assistance of Dignitas. They had some reservations, but were nonetheless supportive. Graeme's two sisters, who lived in Tasmania, also knew and had spoken to him about it. They indicated their support to Shirley as they believed it was what their brother wanted.

Shirley and Caren started gathering material to support Graeme's application to Dignitas. Shirley obtained medical records from a doctor who had given him care at the hospital and told hospital staff that she and Graeme needed reports and a prognosis as they planned to travel overseas. In late 2005, while Shirley completed the application and paid a fee of 1000 Swiss francs to Dignitas, Caren approached Graeme's GP for a report on his mental health. As was later revealed in the trial relating to Graeme's unlawful death, it was unclear whether Caren told the GP about the true purpose of her request for such a report.

In 2001, Caren had attended her first workshop with pro-euthanasia group Exit International Australia. In the year following Graeme's diagnosis, Caren became an office holder in the group. In November 2005, Shirley approached the founder of Exit International Australia, Dr Philip Nitschke, for help with Graeme's application to Dignitas. Despite the fact Graeme couldn't remember his date of birth or whether he had any children, Dr Nitschke advised Dignitas that Graeme had sufficient insight into his condition to be able to make the application. At about this time, Caren, who was still heavily involved with Exit International Australia, warned Dr Nitschke about one of Graeme's daughters, Ali (a pseudonym), believing she would cause trouble.

In early December 2005, Dignitas rejected Graeme's application on the basis of doubts about his ability to freely make the decision to end his life. Graeme was deeply disappointed. He spoke to his sisters about his feelings and indicated he would have to look for other means to end his life. Shirley unfairly accused Ali of interfering and swaying Dr Nitschke against supporting the application, even though this was not the reason for the application's failure.

In January 2006, Caren and Shirley began to consider what members of Exit International Australia called the 'Mexican Option'; that is, obtaining Nembutal from Mexico. Nembutal is a brand of the drug Pentobarbitone, which is used by vets to euthanase animals. In Australia it is not available to members of the public, but in Mexico anyone can buy it over the counter at chemists.

Things were getting very grim in Shirley and Graeme's household. In February 2006, Graeme, who suffered mild to moderate dementia by that time, fell in a shed under his house. This happened during a failed suicide attempt. He had tried to poison himself with fumes from a lawnmower bought especially for that purpose, but only succeeded in hurting himself. While he recovered in hospital, Shirley and Caren met with Dr Nitschke to discuss another application to Dignitas. He was not enthusiastic.

Shirley and Caren secretly decided it was time for the Mexican Option. The day after Dr Nitschke expressed his reluctance to support another Dignitas application, Caren booked a flight to Los Angeles, departing on 13 March 2006. Neither Caren nor Shirley said anything to Dr Nitschke, Graeme's daughters, his sisters, or anyone else, about their new plan to end Graeme's life via Nembutal.

It was known amongst Exit International members that Nembutal is so foul-tasting that it is impossible to not vomit after swallowing. To combat this, it was recommended to take an antiemetic (a drug that prevents vomiting) for a few days before swallowing the Nembutal.

Four days after Caren booked her flight to Los Angeles, Graeme was discharged from hospital and returned home. He could walk only with the assistance of a walking frame. Three days later, Shirley visited his GP to say Graeme was suffering from nausea since leaving hospital. Without examining or speaking to Graeme, the GP prescribed Maxalon, an antiemetic.

Before Graeme's failed suicide attempt with the lawnmower, when the two women first contemplated the Mexican Option, Shirley had contacted a solicitor about Graeme's will. A week or so after obtaining Maxalon from the GP, Shirley made an appointment for Graeme to see his solicitor.

Graeme had made his will in 1995, well before his dementia. In it he left half of his estate to Shirley, and a quarter to each daughter.

There was also a provision to sell the house where he and Shirley had lived for nearly 20 years one year after his death. On 3 March 2006, without the knowledge of Graeme's daughters, Shirley and Graeme met with his solicitor in order to change his will. The solicitor was not made aware of Graeme's Alzheimer's or of the plan to end his life. Graeme told his solicitor he wanted to leave nothing to his daughters. Shirley suggested to Graeme that he might want to leave each daughter $100 000. He changed his instructions to his solicitor as suggested by Shirley.

On 13 March 2006, Caren began her trip to Mexico via Los Angeles. In Tijuana, Mexico, she bought Nembutal. Not long afterwards she flew back to Australia, illegally bringing the Nembutal with her.

On the same day Caren bought the Nembutal in Tijuana, Shirley visited Graeme's obliging GP again. This time she asked the GP for a certificate stating Graeme was 'capable of making decisions and understanding the nature of those decisions'. Despite later telling the court he did not know the purpose of the certificate, Graeme's GP provided it to Shirley.

Two days later, Shirley and Graeme settled his new will in his solicitor's office. It left the entire estate to Shirley, save $100 000 for each daughter. The GP's certificate was not used, nor was the solicitor informed about Graeme's severely limited ability to make decisions. Instead, a charade took place. Graeme could no longer read, but he sat there looking at the document before signing it. Shirley, knowing Graeme could not read a word of the document he was signing, said nothing.

Three days later, Shirley, Graeme and Caren had dinner together. Having already given Shirley the bottle of Nembutal, Caren reminded them both that Graeme would need to take Maxalon for a few days before drinking the drug that would kill him. Caren also handed Shirley a copy of a newspaper she had picked up in the US that featured an article about the dangers of a drug Graeme had been prescribed for his Alzheimer's. The two women then made plans for Graeme to die the following Wednesday. Shirley would be the one to give Graeme the lethal drug. She would then leave, hand the empty Nembutal bottle to Caren, who would be elsewhere the whole time and would then dispose of it and whatever vessel Shirley used to give Graeme the Nembutal.

The women also discussed the need to avoid an autopsy, given one would almost certainly reveal the Nembutal in Graeme's body. They decided that once he had died, a doctor who had never treated Graeme would be called to issue the death certificate. Shirley and Caren thought such a doctor would be more likely to do so without asking awkward questions.

During the morning of the following Wednesday, 22 March 2006, Shirley gave Graeme a glass with Nembutal in it and watched him drink it. She later told the court he died within a few seconds. She then left the house, taking the bottle and glass with her, and went shopping with a friend. At some stage, she gave Caren the bottle and glass, as planned. At about midday, Shirley returned home. Instead of calling Graeme's GP, she called a local doctor who had never treated him to come over to issue a death certificate.

It was at this point that Shirley and Caren's plan fell apart. The local doctor refused to issue a death certificate as she hadn't been treating the deceased. The police arrived. So did Caren, who showed the police officers the US newspaper article about the dangers of an Alzheimer's medication Graeme was taking and suggested this is what killed him. Two days later, the autopsy that Shirley and Caren were so keen to avoid was performed. It clearly showed what really killed him. When interviewed by police, Shirley and Caren denied any knowledge of or involvement in Graeme's death.

The secret plan to kill Graeme began to surface once Shirley informed his daughters of his new will. Surprised by how radically different it was from the one their father had had for over ten years, they lodged a caveat against it. Shirley replied with legal action to allow administration of the new will to go ahead.

The argument over the brand-new will of an Alzheimer's sufferer led police to further investigate whether Shirley and Caren were lying when they said they didn't know how Graeme came to die by Nembutal.

In February 2007, Shirley and Caren were charged with the murder of Graeme and refused bail.

As the ODPP geared up to prosecute the two women, Caren set about courting media coverage in order to portray herself as a blameless victim of unfair laws. She let it be known that she was an office holder with Exit International Australia, and also revealed to journalists that she was dying from breast cancer. Her efforts were successful. The *Sydney Morning Herald* decided to portray the prosecution of Caren and Shirley as a test case for the need for euthanasia or mercy killing laws.

*

On 12 November 2008 Shirley stood alone in the dock, waiting to be sentenced for manslaughter. Both Shirley and Caren had been tried in June for Graeme's unlawful death.

The trial began with Shirley charged with murder, with an alternative charge of aiding and abetting Graeme's suicide. Caren was charged with importing an illegal drug and being an accessory to murder, with an alternative charge of aiding and abetting suicide. The alternative charges gave scope to the jurors to render merciful verdicts if they were so minded. As the trial progressed and evidence emerged, Shirley decided to plead guilty to the charge of aiding suicide and Caren pleaded guilty to the importation offence. They hoped that would mean the murder and accessory to murder charges would be dropped. However, it was becoming clear that Graeme did not have the ability to decide anything for himself at the time of his death, including whether he wanted to commit suicide, so the trial continued. This distinguished the situation from that of Fred and Katerina.

At the beginning of the trial both Shirley and Caren denied outright that they had anything to do with Graeme's death. This was despite police phone taps and emails showing the two were discussing Nembutal, the drug that had killed Graeme. Also, there was evidence to show Caren had concocted a plan to pretend that Graeme was lucid enough to make his own decisions at the time of his death as a ploy to avoid responsibility for it. This involved pretending he discussed the news headlines of the day when she had returned from Mexico with the Nembutal. Her lies exposed, Caren told the court she did this in order to fabricate evidence for the court hearing over Graeme's will, which his daughters were contesting after learning it had changed radically a week before their father's death. To say that the judge was unimpressed with Caren is an understatement.

The trial revealed that Caren, who had been diagnosed with breast cancer many years earlier, didn't make the trip to Mexico to purchase Nembutal solely for Graeme. The judge wrote:

> I have no doubt that the Mexican option was [Caren's] idea, to some extent motivated by her desire to obtain the drug for herself, even though she swore to the jury that she had purchased only one bottle.

His Honour also described Caren as the moving force behind the events leading to Graeme's death after the rejection of the application they had made on his behalf to Dignitas in Switzerland.

Very late in the trial the senior crown prosecutor Mark Tedeschi QC indicated that he thought manslaughter by gross criminal negligence was a more appropriate charge for Shirley, who had handed the Nembutal to Graeme to swallow. This was an unusual move, but by this time the prosecutor thought it appropriate that Shirley not be liable to be convicted of murder. He also asked that the charge for Caren be changed to accessory before the fact of manslaughter, rather than murder. The jury found both women to be guilty of these new, lesser charges.

After the verdict Caren took her own life. Tragically, it was discovered that she had not been suffering from inoperable cancer, as she had thought – she had adhesions from previous surgery that were causing symptoms.

A few days after her suicide, Philip Nitschke read out her suicide note to a voluntary euthanasia conference in Sydney, which was in turn reported by the media.

'I have no trust in the outcome of this matter and have decided to impose upon myself the penalty of death ... in a way that I choose and at a time I select,' Caren wrote, adding she felt harassed by the prosecutor and a police sergeant who worked on her case.

One of Graeme's daughters also spoke to the media. 'I don't agree with what they did,' she told a tabloid after both women were found guilty. 'They broke the law,' the daughter said, adding that she believed her father, 'died a lonely death surrounded by those who put their own interests and beliefs first'.

Whatever the views of Graeme's daughters, his long-term friend Caren, his partner of nearly 20 years Shirley, the police officers involved, the prosecutor, the judge or Graeme himself about assisted suicide, the law was clear.

'It is a criminal offence carrying a maximum penalty of imprisonment for ten years to aid or assist a suicide,' stated his Honour. 'It is for parliament to change the law.'

Judges can't make new law. Politicians elected to parliament can. By the end of 2008, the NSW Parliament had made a huge number of new criminal laws and changes to the existing laws. These changes and new laws created hundreds of new offences. Some of the new laws dealt with very serious criminal offences. Most, such as the *Graffiti Control Act 2008*, dealt with minor offences. Not a single new law dealt with the problem of how sufferers could end life voluntarily and with dignity and assistance. Parliament chose to do nothing about changing the law so doctors could legally end the lives of patients who wanted to die but who were physically unable to end their lives themselves. Parliament also remained silent on how such end of life issues could be planned for while someone like Graeme was still capable of making such decisions.

The judge was left to sort out a situation that parliament kept putting in the too-hard basket. Shirley had pleaded guilty to assisting suicide, but this offence was overshadowed by her being found guilty of Graeme's manslaughter, a more serious offence with the possibility of a maximum of 25 years behind bars. His Honour said:

> Of course there are extremely sad cases of offences committed by persons pushed beyond endurance by concern for a loved one in never-ending pain and suffering without hope of remedy. In those circumstances the court can take a very merciful view of the criminal conduct especially when it occurs without significant planning … But this was not such a case.

Shirley and Caren had planned Graeme's death for months.

> On the other hand it is not at the upper limit of seriousness such as where the offender operated a commercial enterprise in assisting the deaths of members of the community for gain.

In other words, Shirley and Caren weren't running an illegal business helping people die for a fee. Nor did Shirley do it so she could get her hands on Graeme's money. Despite the radical change in his will just before his death, during the trial it became apparent that Shirley was not motivated by financial gain. Ultimately, while she was relieved that the change in Graeme's will meant she could continue living in their home after his death, she was motivated by what she thought Graeme wanted. His Honour also thought that Shirley was in the habit of doing what Caren told her to do:

> Although [Caren] was charged as being an accessory to the actions of [Shirley], to a significant extent she was more criminally liable for the death of [Graeme]. It is one of those, perhaps rare, cases where an accessory would have deserved greater punishment than the principal.

However, it was just Shirley left standing in the dock.

Some people knew that what had happened was against the law but thought Caren and Shirley had done no wrong. Shirley's lawyer suggested his client shouldn't be punished in any way except for having a manslaughter conviction attached to her name. His Honour thought this would not do. He feared the manslaughter conviction might be seen as a badge of honour by those frustrated with the law as it stood. Others thought what had happened was an affront to the sanctity of life. The law reflected this view. Both views existed within Graeme's family. His daughters were devastated that Shirley deliberately denied them the chance to say goodbye to their father. His sisters held a very high opinion of Shirley and made sure the court knew this. His Honour thought Shirley was trying to help Graeme, the man she loved.

Shirley was 60 years old. She had been employed in bush regeneration work for the National Trust for years. She had never been in trouble with the law and was held to be of good character. People who knew her described her as reliable and trustworthy with little interest in monetary reward.

His Honour ruled:

> The offender is sentenced to a non-parole period of 22 months with a balance of term of eight months. The sentence is to be served by way of periodic detention. The sentence is to be served at the Tomago Periodic Detention Centre and is to commence on 21 November 2008. The offender is to be released to parole on 20 September 2010.

Shirley was going to spend every weekend in jail for the next two years.

Chapter 5

THE LAW APPLIES TO EVERYONE: THE CROWN PROSECUTOR

I was attending a conference of the International Society for the Reform of Criminal Law in Brisbane on 4 July 2006 when I received an alarming phone call from my deputy DPP in Sydney. One of the crown prosecutors, Patrick Power SC, had child pornography (now called child abuse material) stored on a computer he kept at home. The computer had crashed, so Power had brought it into the office to be fixed. An office computer technician examining the hard drive of the faulty computer that afternoon found videos of adult men engaging in sexual acts with children and immediately told his supervisor.

Mindful that the video files could be evidence in a case that Power was working on, Deputy Director Greg Smith SC and I discussed what should happen next. We decided written statements should be obtained from the computer technician and anyone else involved with the computer, so they could be handed to police if appropriate. The deputy DPP then asked the technician to return to his workstation to do that, while Power's hard drive and any copies of it were brought up to my chambers for safekeeping. The deputy then called me again. We agreed I would try to contact the attorney general (which I was able to do by telephone) while the deputy asked Power to come into the deputy's chambers as soon as possible.

Within an hour or so, Power arrived. In the presence of two

other crown prosecutors, the deputy director outlined what was found on his computer, said that it was evidence of the crime of possessing child pornography and warned Power not to comment unless he wished to do so. The deputy director also told Power that he had told me about what had been found on his computer. Power was visibly shaken. He said he had been away for a while and offered the explanation that two other people had been staying at his home. He did not claim the videos were evidence in a case he had been working on. Deputy DPP Smith then asked Power to voluntarily step down from his position as a crown prosecutor, which he did. Once Power had left, Deputy DPP Smith again called me. We agreed that he should contact the police commissioner's office to arrange for police to become involved in the investigation.

The next day, 5 July, I returned to Sydney (while keeping the attorney general informed of events) and to the office. Police officers executed search warrants by taking possession of Power's computer and drives from my office and a number of computer disks and other items from Power's home. An examination the following day revealed 31 video files, 433 still images and one novel that consisted of child pornography. One of the seized computer disks held 20 files of child pornography. Power was arrested that afternoon. He had been present while police searched his home and was then taken to a police station where he was charged.

A police examination of Power's computer showed that when it crashed, it contained a drive F. Although the computer remained off until the computer technician turned it on, drive F was not attached when police took possession of it. The search of Power's home and office by police did not find it and Power said nothing to police about it. The scientific examination was able to reconstruct much of what would have been on drive F, which included files with names strongly suggestive of child pornography. In the time between Power being told by the deputy DPP what had been found on his computer and the police search of his home, Power had an opportunity to make sure police wouldn't find drive F and see the actual content of these files.

But despite some missing evidence, Power could see the writing on the wall. He did not intend to fight the charges. Instead, he would have to break the news of his child pornography possession to everyone in his life, accept that his career as a lawyer was over, accept that he was going to jail and prepare for the sentencing hearing in the midst of a media storm.

That media storm began on 5 July with a late afternoon media conference I conducted at the office after the police searches. All the circumstances were explained in a very tense session and the media went into overdrive.

In one of life's bitter ironies, I was then required to return to Brisbane the next day to be presented at the closing conference dinner with the medal of the International Society for the Reform of Criminal Law (which was a great honour): 'In Recognition of [My] Contribution to the Goals of the Society'.

In May 2007 Power was sentenced to 15 months jail with a non-parole period of eight months. The case was deeply shocking for all of us at the ODPP, and assumed a political dimension when it was used to attack the ODPP in parliament later that year and to attack Deputy Director Smith when he became shadow attorney general (see Chapter 7).

Chapter 6

THE LAW APPLIES TO EVERYONE: THE MINISTER OF THE CROWN

Not long after the scandal broke of a crown prosecutor possessing child pornography, a similarly shocking case emerged in 2006.

In August 2006, an office manager named Gillian was working in the electoral office of the state Minister for Aboriginal Affairs, Milton Orkopoulos. She was about to share serious allegations about her boss to see if others were suspicious that something terrible had been going on.

Nearly a year earlier Gillian had taken a call from a distressed young man, who claimed Minister Orkopoulos had sexually abused him when he was 15 years old and had supplied him with drugs. The young man, who was crying, told Gillian he decided to call the minister's office in order to move on with his life. Not sure what to make of the stranger's claims, Gillian made written notes as he spoke. After the call finished, she called the minister and told him about it. She would later tell the court that, having listened to what she said, Minister Orkopoulos replied, 'After all I have done for him', before hanging up. When he called her again to tell her he had contacted police, Gillian thought she heard Minister Orkopoulos say, 'I'm a Minister of the Crown for God's sake … Oh, anyway, he wasn't 15.'

The police superintendent Minister Orkopoulos spoke to that day recalled the minister saying he knew the troubled young man who had called his office, that he had made the mistake of giving him money a number of times, and now this young man was hassling him and his staff for more money. Minister Orkopoulos did not say a word about the allegations of sexual abuse and supply of drugs. The superintendent asked the minister if he would like the matter recorded on COPS, the police computer system. The minister said no, adding 'I'm sure it will be all right if you talk with him.' Not long afterwards, a police officer called the young man to say they had heard he was harassing Minister Orkopoulos for money and told him not to call the minister or his family.

On this day in August 2006, Gillian showed the written notes she had taken while speaking to the young stranger nearly a year earlier to a fellow staff member. Instead of being shocked that anyone could make such allegations about the minister, the staff member, who was male and in his late teens, had his own complaints about Minister Orkopoulos.

When he was 16, he had approached the minister and told him about his interest in politics. The minister, who at that time wasn't a minister but had been a member of parliament for about four years, arranged for the teenager to attend a Labor Party conference in Sydney. He also arranged for the two of them to share a hotel room. Minister Orkopoulos sent an email to the teenager saying he didn't need to pay for the room or for meals, but to bring spending money for 'little things, newspapers, menthol (yuk) cigarettes, condoms, etc'.

The young staff member said when he and Minister Orkopoulos arrived by car at Parliament House, the minister asked the youngster to bring up a small bag that was in the glove box. It contained condoms and cannabis. Minister Orkopoulos gave the teenager some cannabis, and together they smoked it in the minister's office the night before the Party conference. The hotel room Minister Orkopoulos had booked for them had two separate beds in it. During their first evening in the shared room, the teenager went to bed as Minister Orkopoulos went to the bathroom to take a shower. He soon emerged from the bathroom still dressed in his clothes, said 'I don't trust myself. I'm going back to Parliament House' and left the room. However, the young staff member recalled Minister Orkopoulos did visit him in a hotel room one other night during that conference, and told the teenager, 'I would love to have you,' and rubbed the 16-year-old's chest and neck.

Just over two years later, the young man had a job in politics. When he attended Minister Orkopoulos's office to pick up a pay cheque, he claimed the minister again rubbed his chest and neck. The young staff member told Gillian he was so incensed by the minister's behaviour that he had decided to write a letter to the Independent Commission Against Corruption about it. Having heard his story, Gillian decided to approach police with her notes about the distressed young stranger's phone call that had bothered her boss so much.

A month or so after Gillian and the young male staff member compared notes and she contacted police, Minister Orkopoulos called the police a second time. He complained that the young man who police had rung at his request a year ago – who the minister now described as a drug addict – had started making demands for money again. This time, Minister Orkopoulos made reference to the young man's allegations of sexual abuse while talking to police:

> When I became a minister he began making allegations and Michael [the first police superintendent Minister Orkopoulos spoke to] got someone to ring him and told him he can't start making allegations and blackmailing people. He needs money or he's going to start spreading allegations again … I don't know where to turn, I'm up for re-election … I helped him with an apprenticeship because he lost his job. It was a normal

> constituent relationship. Then he kept coming back and I found out he was a speed freak. I don't give money to anyone any more, desperate people make wild allegations …

By then the police were suspicious about Minister Orkopoulos. They again contacted the troubled young man, but this time he made two statements outlining a history with the minister, of drugs in return for sex that began in 1997. He told police that when he was 15 years old, he was waiting at a bus stop one night after working his shift at McDonalds. Minister Orkopoulos, who happened to be driving by, offered the boy a lift home. He told police that once in the car, Minister Orkopoulos offered him marijuana. That night was the first of many occasions where the teenager would meet up with the politician to smoke marijuana. He told police that once, after he had become stoned, the politician started to fondle him. On subsequent occasions, more sexual activity was initiated by Minister Orkopoulos, and imposed on the boy, who was in Year 10 at school at the time, while ignoring the boy's pleas to stop. Still, the boy kept meeting up with Minister Orkopoulos, telling friends about the marijuana and lifts the politician had supplied to him. He also said the drugs the minister offered him included amphetamines, which they often took together.

The young man admitted to police that by the end of 2000, a year after Milton Orkopoulos became a member of parliament, he had begun to hassle him for money, and threatened to expose their relationship if he didn't give him what he wanted. The politician regularly gave him money, either cash or, once he no longer lived with his parents, deposits into his bank account or the bank account of a person he lived with. The young man told police the two continued this relationship until 2004, when he was 22 years old. He told police that in October 2005, at his request, he and Minister Orkopoulos met. The young man told the minister that he needed money, was struggling generally and was thinking about telling people everything about their past relationship. He told police that on hearing this, Minister Orkopoulos laughed. He handed the young man $50, the two agreed not to see each other again and the minister prepared to drive away in his government car. The young man told police he then decided he wanted Minister Orkopoulos to wait and banged on the car window. The minister instructed his driver to get out of the car and deal with the young man, who was essentially brushed aside. The car then drove away. The next day the young man called the minister's electoral office, which was how he came to speak with Gillian.

As police looked into whether his story could be verified, another accusation surfaced of Minister Orkopoulos offering a teenage boy drugs for sex. In 1995, another 15-year-old boy was introduced to Orkopoulos (then a member of a local council, before he became an MP) at a Party function. One evening the teenager had a meal with Orkopoulos. He told police that after the meal, Orkopoulos invited the boy to come with him into a garden shed, where he offered the boy marijuana. After they smoked it together, the boy told Orkopoulos that he was molested as a child. Orkopoulos told the boy he could trust and confide in him. The boy told police that as a teenager he met with Orkopoulos and obtained marijuana from him on several subsequent occasions, usually in a park, which he told a school friend about.

He also told police that around this time, Orkopoulos introduced him to heroin. According to him, one day he met Orkopoulos in the park, where they drank alcohol and talked. After a while, Orkopoulos asked the boy if he had 'ever tried H'. The boy replied that he didn't know what Orkopoulos was talking about, after which he said Orkopoulos sprinkled some heroin into a marijuana joint and told the boy that it would relax him. The boy, after smoking some of it, sat in a car feeling sick and said Orkopoulos imposed sexual acts on him. The boy had a strong aversion to the sexual activity, but a heroin habit had started to take hold. He subsequently would meet with Orkopoulos in order to obtain more heroin, but would avoid meeting him at night in an effort to avoid attempts by Orkopoulos to engage in sex. He told police that one time when they met in the park, Orkopoulos produced heroin and injection equipment, showed him how to use it and held the boy's arm as he injected heroin. He told police it wasn't an isolated incident. He said he was in Year 10 at school at the time.

Within a few months, police had enough evidence to lay over 30 charges relating to the supply of prohibited drugs and sexual offences, namely sex with underage boys, indecent assault and aggravated indecent assault. During their investigation, police also discovered that Minister Orkopoulos possessed child pornography, so he faced one charge of that as well.

On 9 November 2006, as campaigning for the state election was in full swing, the story broke. The *Daily Telegraph* published details of the police brief against Minister Orkopoulos, which dominated TV news programs that evening. His colleagues couldn't distance themselves from him fast enough. Orkopoulos was sacked as a minister and expelled from his party, with Premier Morris Iemma publicly declaring he would make sure Orkopoulos was forced out of parliament altogether.

As with Power's colleagues within the ODPP, Orkopoulos's colleagues, both within his own party and in the Opposition, had no idea about these alleged crimes. Their reaction wasn't one of fear of a petty scandal or embarrassing gossip as they went about the business of trying to win the upcoming state election, which was less than four months away: it was one of horror. Despair came on top of the horror within Parliament House. Unlike Power, who had fairly promptly admitted his offending, Orkopoulos was going to deny the charges against him, meaning all the sordid details were going to be aired in court in full view of the media and the public when the trial was held a year or two later.

In February and March 2008, Orkopoulos faced trial for multiple sexual and drug offences. He pleaded guilty to one count of possessing child pornography and one count of supplying cannabis to the teenager whom he invited to attend a Party conference, but maintained his innocence in relation to all other charges.

He elected to give evidence. Throughout his time on the stand, Orkopoulos told obvious lies and frequently criticised the prosecutor rather than answering questions. A year after he was found guilty on almost all charges, he unsuccessfully tried to appeal his convictions. The chief judge in the Court of Criminal Appeal observed that Orkopoulos's conduct during his trial 'would not have endeared him to the jury'.

There were also difficulties for Orkopoulos's former staff member Gillian, the woman who had contacted police about the awful stories she had heard about her boss. She was reported to have been made redundant from her government job on the day she gave evidence against him.

Chapter 7

POLITICS AND THE LAW: MANDATORY SENTENCING

I think there are at least three ways of doing the job of DPP. One is to go to work each day, roll the arm over and professionally attend to what is necessary and go home. Another is to do that job and also apply oneself diligently to improving the way we do things, but to carry out the processes of reform without public exposure, in the corridors of power. (I suspect that my predecessor operated that way, and very effectively.) A third is to do all that but also to agitate the reform process in public, in view of the community. I tried to do that – and I think succeeded, by and large (although not every reform was achieved). And I am not saying that there is anything wrong with doing the job in the other ways.

Why should I have chosen to make life difficult in that way? I think it began in reaction against the 'law and order auction' that accompanied the 1995 state election, soon after my appointment as DPP – each side preying on the community's fears by talking up law and order issues and pretending that the answers lay in ever more draconian law enforcement and punishment. Then later there were threats to introduce mandatory sentences or some form of grid sentencing, and it seemed to me that somebody should be publicly putting forward the opposing view. These wouldn't be the only times that I and other senior members of the legal profession had to battle over issues of principle, and the contest continues.

In March 2007 the state election was held. Another member of the government's party stood for Orkopoulos's seat and won it, and the government was returned to power. It was also another 'law and order auction' election. In the lead-up, politicians from both major parties promised to force judges and magistrates to pass tougher sentences.

New South Wales politicians weren't the only ones to regularly promise and attempt to pass such laws. Politicians in two other states knew that shopkeepers were sick of shoplifters and the general public were sick of nuisances committed by the town drunks. In the late 1990s, those states had passed laws that forced judges and magistrates to impose more, and longer, jail sentences for petty theft and property damage.

The effects of these new sentencing laws in those two states were immediate. A 24-year old Aboriginal mother was sentenced to the mandatory 14 days in prison for receiving a stolen $2.50 can of beer. A 20-year-old man with no prior convictions was sentenced to 14 days in prison for the theft of $9.00 worth of petrol. Two 17-year-old girls with no previous criminal convictions were each sentenced to 14 days in prison for the theft of clothes from other girls who were staying in the same room. Two young apprentices were each imprisoned for 14 days for first offences. One of them broke a window and the other broke a light worth $9.60. Legal observers noted the mandatory sentencing laws were harshest on the young and vulnerable and Aboriginal persons, particularly those who stole food and clothes because they didn't have families who cared for them. What's more, the effect of the mandatory sentencing laws on the crime rate was zero.

I had made my opinion of mandatory sentencing laws known on many occasions since becoming the DPP in 1994. Through academic papers and media interviews, I regularly stressed that mandatory sentencing laws stop judges and magistrates from doing an important part of their job – making the punishment fit the crime and the criminal and achieving justice.

Much to the annoyance of some within the NSW Government, I repeated my criticism of mandatory sentencing laws in a book I published in 2001, *Getting Justice Wrong: Myths, media and crime*. I gave the examples of a wildly reckless drunken driver who runs down and kills a child on a pedestrian crossing and a submissive woman who, in a fit of despair, grabs a kitchen knife and stabs and kills the aggressive husband who has beaten her and made her life a misery for years. Both have committed the same crime, manslaughter, but they did not deserve the same punishment. As I wrote:

> [J]ustice means the courts considering what penalties to impose following such convictions ... to take all of the circumstances of the offences and the offenders – their conduct and history – into account before fashioning suitable sentences, and not simply look up the prescribed penalty for manslaughter and apply the same sentence in both cases.

At other points in my book, my frustration with politicians appealing to people's usually unjustified fear of crime to win votes was more pointed.

> Elections cause crime waves. They must – just listen to the candidates! For months before elections it becomes unsafe to leave your homes – or even to stay in them. We could obviously go a long way towards reducing crime by not having elections. Alternatively, we could achieve the same result by having lots of elections because once the election is over, the crime wave miraculously disappears ... In the months leading up to the March 1999 New South Wales election there was much hysterical talk on both sides about mounting crime ... Barely three months later, in June 1999, the Bureau of Crime Statistics and Research (a part of the Attorney General's

> Department) published the results of research it had been carrying out ... there was no increasing crime rate. Where were the politicians getting their information?

I wasn't pretending that judges always got sentencing right. I knew that as state governments around the country joined the trend of passing mandatory sentencing laws, there were legitimate concerns about judges and magistrates struggling in isolation to impose consistent punishments for similar convictions of like offenders.

The criminal justice system took action. Between 1998 and 2004, the NSW Court of Criminal Appeal issued seven guideline sentencing judgments to help judges and magistrates give more consistent sentences for offences such as dangerous driving, armed robbery, break, enter and steal, high range PCA (prescribed concentration of alcohol) and for taking other matters into account on sentencing. The bottom line was they had to have the freedom to decide sentences on a case-by-case basis. The alternative, mandatory minimum sentences, meant an irresponsible drunk driver and a desperate abused wife risked getting the same sentence for taking a life.

But the horse had bolted. Politicians were convinced that promising to pass mandatory sentencing laws made them sound tough on crime and that the electorate somehow accepted that they had solutions and approved. Some thought it was none of my business. When I publicly criticised the government's policy to make life sentences mandatory for certain serious offences in 1995, some members of parliament called for me to resign.

'He has entered the political fray on a policy issue,' the minister for police said in October 1995. 'My advice to him is that he should give up his position and run for parliament.'

Premier Carr explained that I couldn't be made to resign because by law the position of director of public prosecutions was independent of the government. Politicians couldn't sack me for saying things they didn't like. What's more, short of being declared insane or bankrupt or committing a criminal offence or going AWOL, I had the job for life.

Nonetheless, there was a push to punish me. In 1995 there was an attempt to establish a committee of politicians to watch over me and control the ODPP's budget. Those pushing for the committee promised that they would be careful not to tell me which cases to prosecute or how. After all, from time to time politicians, including ministers, found themselves facing criminal charges, and it was obviously not acceptable to have fellow politicians able to make such prosecutions disappear. The proposed committee didn't happen despite eight attempts to introduce legislation for it over the years – until the party pressing for it became the government.

A similar plan was again put forward in 2001. In order to put even more pressure on me, the tabloid media launched attacks over my travelling to international law conferences and meetings.

This international travel included a series of workshops held in China over five years. Chinese mid-level prosecutors with promising careers from many different provinces attended sessions that addressed the rules of evidence in criminal procedure and their place in the protection of human rights, the rights of suspects, victims of crime, juveniles and defendants in court hearings, the role and responsibility of the prosecutor, the discretion to prosecute, the place of victims in the prosecution process, summary prosecutions, committal proceedings, the investigation and prosecution of a serious criminal offence, the rights of suspects in police custody, accused persons on remand and sentenced prisoners. These workshops took place under an Australia–China governmental program and included other distinguished practitioners from Sydney. As part of the program Chinese prosecutors and judges also visited Australian jurisdictions.

Information about my expenses on my trips overseas to attend such law conferences and meetings of international organisations in criminal justice and prosecution (all approved in advance by the attorney general at the time), were reported by the tabloid press, who labelled me as 'globetrotting' before reporting the plan to take control of the ODPP's budget from me. (The *Daily Telegraph* even ambushed me at the airport to take a photograph of my return from one trip.) Despite this, the plan didn't have enough politicians supporting it and failed to be implemented.

Mandatory sentencing and fearmongering over crime rates weren't the only government policies on which I made my views known. My 2001 book *Getting Justice Wrong* made headlines when I expressed my frustration with the war on drugs:

> There will always be a demand for mood altering drugs, and there will always be a supply of them. So whether we like it or not, let us accept those as facts and work from there. We must be realistic ... The approaches we have been adopting for decades are based on wishful thinking and wilful blindness ... How can we keep drugs out of the country if we cannot even keep them out of maximum security prisons? ... Research also shows that increasing penalties, particularly for drug related crimes, has no demonstrable effect on offending. Drug users do not stop to consider the possible criminal justice consequences of their acts.

I also suggested an alternative to making drugs illegal and jailing addicts:

> Make heroin available free to addicted users on prescription by licensed medical practitioners. This is not heroin on demand, available from the corner store. This measure addresses the needs of those who presently prostitute themselves, steal or find other buyers in order to buy unknown substances to inject

> into their veins in unsanitary conditions. It would be a safety valve, for when earlier influences have failed.

As far as I was concerned, this radical change – even to the legalisation, regulation and taxation of all presently illicit drugs – was a better alternative to criminal gangs making astronomical amounts of money from the illegal sale of highly addictive drugs and reinvesting it in other crime. Eighteen years later I hold the same views and it is interesting to note that parts of Australia may at last be moving slowly and cautiously to more rational policies on some aspects of drug use, catching up with the world at large. But we still have a long way to go.

The resentment against me among some politicians in 2007–2008 and beyond was intense. Even if they privately agreed with my views, their political instincts told them the general public would vote them out if they ever supported anything like what I was proposing. I was known to be very good at deciding what cases should be prosecuted and when and how, but I was too opinionated and outspoken on criminal justice policy matters. In the minds of some, I had crossed the line and was playing politics. Others just couldn't stand such disobedience from a public servant, no matter how often it was explained to them that, just like judges, the DPP is supposed to be indifferent to the opinion of the government.

My political enemies soon had something to smile about. When ex-crown prosecutor Power was facing jail for possessing child pornography in May 2007, it was said the ODPP was not looking so squeaky clean now. What was more, the deputy DPP who had handled the discovery of child pornography on Power's computer, Greg Smith, had resigned and become a politician. He was a member of the Opposition and held the position of shadow attorney general. Despite police having found plenty of evidence to convict Power, and Power pleading guilty and being sentenced, the government fully intended to make life as hard as possible for the new shadow attorney general.

The day after Power's sentencing hearing, amid calls for points of order and general uproar in parliament, the minister for police accused Shadow Attorney General Smith of tipping off Power before contacting police.

> The simple fact is that an officer from the Office of the Director of Public Prosecutions told [Power] about the child pornography before he notified New South Wales police. That person's actions have put vital evidence at risk … The person responsible for that tip-off now needs to come clean and explain why he tipped off his friend before telling police … The former holder of that office needs to explain why he put the protection of an alleged child porn suspect ahead of his duties to the community as a senior prosecutor.

Shadow Attorney General Smith told parliament that he had wanted to clarify whether the child pornography was part of a criminal case Power was working on before calling police, but the government smelled blood. The government passed a motion of censure against Smith, which is a formal way of parliament expressing its disapproval, accusing him of misleading the parliament in his personal explanation over his handling of the Power matter. As Shadow Attorney General Smith defended his actions in parliament, he and members of the Opposition mentioned the criminal charges against Orkopoulos. It turned into an argument, with one government MP daring Smith to say Orkopoulos, who was yet to face a trial, was guilty of anything. The instinct amongst politicians to fight along party lines, no matter the issue being fought over, runs very deep.

There was plenty of mud being thrown around. The *Daily Telegraph* published a list of the 50-plus prominent citizens who provided positive personal references for Power for the judge to consider when deciding his sentence. It was done within two stories, one titled 'Pervert and his 59 Mates' and a second that included photos of some of the referees with the caption 'Named and shamed'. There were those who wanted the mud to stick to me, too. The day after the censure motion against Smith was passed, Attorney General Hatzistergos asked a retired High Court judge to investigate and report on whether I should have spoken to police before telling Power that child pornography had been found on his computer. Four days later, Attorney General Hatzistergos had his answer. The retired High Court judge thought that as soon as I and then Deputy Director Smith took the view that this was a police matter, then Power should not have been told about the discovery of child pornography on his computer. Attorney General Hatzistergos sent the advice with a 'please explain' letter to me the next day.

A week or so later I replied, telling Attorney General Hatzistergos that I hadn't actually taken the view it was a police matter on that fateful day because I wasn't sure whether the child pornography was part of a case Power was working on. But Hatzistergos wasn't satisfied. On 21 June, he told parliament the day child pornography was found on Power's computer must have been difficult and confronting for the ODPP. However, it was Hatzistergos's predecessor, Bob Debus, who received my calls from interstate nearly a year earlier as I prepared to return to Sydney. The new attorney general could see decisions had had to be made quickly, but told parliament 'the judgment needed to handle them however, was not, in my view, arduous'.

My political enemies were not hiding their intention to put as much pressure on me as they could muster. But as the gloves came off, there was an unexpected episode of high farce.

Chapter 8

THE CHASER

In September 2007 the NSW Government was involved in Australia's hosting of the Asia Pacific Economic Cooperation [APEC] conference in Sydney. The president of the United States, plus heads of state and leaders from China, Russia, Japan and many other countries arrived in Sydney under the glare of the international media spotlight. This was a chance for Sydney, and the NSW Government, to shine.

Security was a high priority. It is an unfortunate reality that there are people who are keen to inflict violence on others, including those who claim moral, religious or political ideals as some sort of justification for their desires. The terrorist attack on New York's Twin Towers on 11 September 2001, seared into the public imagination forever as 9/11, is an obvious example of this reality, and it loomed large in the minds of everyone involved in the 2007 APEC Conference.

It was also on the minds of a group of comedians. A satirical group called The Chaser were known for making provocative comedy about those in power. They decided to pull a prank involving the APEC Conference.

On 6 September, one of the days on which the APEC conference was held, members of The Chaser created a fake motorcade, which at a glance looked like the sort of motorcade a head of state attending the conference might travel in. The comedians had hired two large black 4WDs, one black sedan and had access to two motorcycles. The 4WDs and the sedan travelled slowly, at walking pace, flanked by five men on foot and two motorcycle outriders. Hidden behind the tinted windows of the sedan sat comedian Chas Licciardello, dressed like terrorist leader Osama Bin Laden.

Canadian flags flew on the vehicles, and though Canada was a member of APEC, anything more than a glance would reveal the motorcade was a fake. The identification carried by the five men on foot and the identification stickers on the vehicles were deliberately, and obviously, bogus. The words 'It's pretty obvious this isn't a real pass,' 'Insecurity,' 'Joke' and 'Chaser's War' were printed on them, as well as photos of the well-known comedians not wearing any disguises. One of the motorcyclists wore jeans.

The NSW Parliament had passed special security legislation for the APEC conference, making it a crime for anyone to be within certain areas (two levels of restricted zones) near conference meeting venues and accommodation unless permitted by a police officer. Gates and fences physically marked out and blocked access to restricted zones and the streets immediately near them. Police were stationed at gates and along the relevant streets to stop any unauthorised vehicles or ordinary members of the public from being there.

The Chaser members were aware of these security measures. They weren't planning to raid the conference or fight with police. The carefully considered and rehearsed plan was for 'Osama Bin Laden' to hop out of the car when it was near, but outside of, a restricted zone.

At about 11.30 a.m., with a number of cameras capturing their prank, the fake motorcade drove along a fenced-off street outside a restricted zone. They pulled up to the gate, but to their surprise, the police guarding it waved them through. The comedians drove on towards a second gate leading into a more restricted zone.

The leader of the prank, Julian Morrow, who was also one of the fake security men on foot, was starting to feel nervous. He was no longer confident the police would stop them before they got into the second restricted zone. He also knew snipers were in position to shoot unauthorised people found within it. He made radio contact with others involved in planning the prank, seeking exact information on where the nearest part of the second level restricted zone began.

The street was becoming narrower, lined with extra fencing and barriers. Morrow feared they may have already entered the second restricted zone. It was necessary to travel further in order to get to a part of the route wide enough for the fake motorcade to turn around. Without revealing they were not authorised to be there, Morrow told a nearby police officer there had been a change in plan and asked if it was all right if they turned around at the upcoming intersection.

'You can do what you want, matey,' the unsuspecting police officer cheerfully replied.

While turning in the intersection inside the second restricted zone, which happened to be right in front of the hotel where the president of the United States was staying, Morrow decided to go ahead with the prank. Licciardello jumped out of the sedan and began to walk down the street. Police realised the motorcade was fake and arrested 11 members of the group on the spot. The two on motorcycles had already driven away.

The whole episode, including police waving the comedians through security gates and the cheerful response of the unsuspecting officer, was captured on camera and broadcast around the world. News presenters on outlets such as CNN, America's ABC, Fox News, NBC and CBS smiled, or raised eyebrows, as it played. Everyone got the joke. In the years since 9/11, conspicuous security measures in public places had become common, particularly in airports. People all over the world wondered why something insisted on in one airport, such as all passengers taking off their shoes, simply didn't matter at all in another. In the eyes of many, The Chaser's APEC prank highlighted the question of what security measures actually mattered and which ones, while appearing impressive, made no real difference.

The NSW Police were deeply humiliated. They expressed their fury as concern for the safety of those who made them look so foolish in the eyes of the world.

'I'm very angry that this stunt happened, it was a very dangerous stunt,' the NSW police commissioner told a press conference. 'We have snipers deployed around the city. They weren't there for show, they mean business.'

The unrepentant comedians rubbed salt into the wound. The day after their arrest, a number of them walked up to an outer security gate carrying cardboard cut-outs shaped like cars, as if this might also fool police into letting them pass.

The special APEC legislation was one of strict liability. This meant physically being in the restricted area on that particular day without approval meant the comedians had committed an offence, even if they didn't plan to do any harm. The offence was a summary one, meaning that it was minor enough for police themselves to prosecute in the Local Court. The police set about building their case against The Chaser team. Before too long, senior police wondered if, given the high profile of the case and the issues involved, it might be better to hand its prosecution over to the ODPP. And so it came to me.

Some in the wider community were asking themselves what the comedians were actually guilty of. It was clear the police had been embarrassed. If that was the real driver behind the prosecution, there was a problem. In a free society, it shouldn't be a crime to expose the shortcomings of those in positions of authority or to question the amount of power in the hands of police.

On the face of it, it seemed an offence for the comedians to be where they were during the APEC conference, inside the second-tier restricted zone. However, it could be argued the police actually gave the comedians permission to enter by waving them through a part of the prohibited zone and into the intersection in the second restricted zone where they would turn around. Under the *APEC Meeting (Police Powers) Act 2007*, police permission constituted special justification or excuse for entry. By their own embarrassing actions, the police had let The Chaser off the hook. The Prosecution Guidelines supported withdrawing the charges; going to the expense and effort of a prosecution was impossible to justify. Julian Morrow, the comedian in charge, had no previous criminal convictions and was otherwise of good character. The others involved were employees doing their job. The operation had been planned and rehearsed with videorecording the night before. Even if only Morrow was successfully prosecuted, odds were the magistrate hearing the matter would choose not to record a conviction, something magistrates have the option of doing for offenders of good character who are not dangerous and are found guilty of minor offences.

In late April 2008, much to the State government's fury, I dropped the charges against The Chaser team.

Chapter 9
UNDER PRESSURE

Behind the scenes as The Chaser story unfolded in 2007, there were those who continued their campaign to silence me.

In March 2007, a few weeks before the state election, I gave a speech that made some determined to do whatever it took to get rid of me. I addressed the Sydney Chamber of Commerce and referred to a cartoon depicting a premier giving a lesson on how to stay in power. When dealing with any situation, so the lesson went, use smears ('exhaustive public consultation'); lies ('clarification'); phoney figures ('statistics'); and distraction ('let's change the subject'). When dealing with a really big problem, '[r]ather than attack the federal government, attack your DPP. Nobody likes them and you can't sack them. Perfect arrangement.'

I told the audience:

> DPPs are known throughout the common law world for their independence – we like to think of ourselves as both frank and fearless in the execution of our functions. For many of us there is little downside once we become accustomed to the incessant public abuse by some politicians and some media commentators … [T]he attorney general gets frank and fearless advice from me.

Further, I said that I was worried other senior public servants didn't have the same job security I did. I reeled off a list of those previously employed by the state government who had lost their jobs after giving advice their political masters didn't want to hear, or after refusing to appoint political hacks to important posts, or who were made scapegoats for mistakes made by politicians. My concerns extended to well-informed and effective bureaucrats being demonised by their political masters or having their careers unfairly damaged by being moved to areas outside their expertise.

What allowed me to do my job was how hard it was to get rid of a DPP. As I told the Chamber of Commerce:

> I can be dismissed by the governor, on advice, if I become mad, bankrupt, criminal or absent without leave or moonlight – or nominate for parliament … Premiers and chief ministers cannot just sack us.

I made it clear I was going to stand my ground.

In the meantime, I had a job to do. On top of my usual workload of making decisions in relation to hundreds of alleged murders, manslaughters, sexual assaults, child abuse and armed robberies, there were plenty of incidents to make an already toxic situation worse.

There were also moves afoot to strip some power from me while I still had the job. But how? It was very hard to find fault with the decisions I made about if, when and how to prosecute. No matter how difficult or upsetting a case was, and no matter how much I disliked the relevant law, the law was the chief authority that guided me. That meant those in power had no control over me and that is why some despised me. The only sort of control left was attack. Saying nasty things about me in the media didn't stop or influence me. The next weapon of choice was criticism of how I handled the ODPP budget.

Just like any other government department, every financial year the ODPP was required to identify ways costs could be cut. The

ODPP had an annual budget then of just over $90 million, most of which went to pay the salaries of prosecutors and support staff. Crime never takes a holiday and prosecuting is highly skilled work performed by professionals. After much searching, I concluded the only way a budget cut could be made was if someone else did some of the prosecutions. There would be no real financial saving to government if this happened, just to the ODPP. The work had to be done and the government would end up having to pay whoever did it.

I provided this advice to the government in April 2007. However, almost a year later, Attorney General Hatzistergos found my report unacceptable. He referred the matter to the treasurer, who expressed the view that this raised 'serious questions as to the financial management within the (ODPP)' and asked the auditor-general to conduct a review.

In March 2008, the auditor-general handed down his report. No fault was found with the quality of the work done by the ODPP. However, the report stated that over the past five years the ODPP's budget had been increased by 40 per cent while its caseload had fallen by 30 per cent.

Caseload, of course, is not the same as workload. However, the figures in the auditor-general's report gave the strong impression that the ODPP was inefficient. But despite such damning figures, the report stopped short of actually declaring the ODPP inefficient. Instead, it found the ODPP had failed to demonstrate it was efficient.

The president of the NSW Bar Association was not impressed, stating:

> The problem, according to the report, was not that the office was inefficient, but that the auditors were unable to decide whether it was efficient or not because of the insufficiency of measures to assess efficiency.

To put it simply, senior members of the legal profession thought the report was bureaucratic double-speak. There were also grumblings that some cases, such as deciding if, when and how to prosecute Jeffrey Gilham for the murder of his parents, took far more time and effort than other cases, something the auditor-general's report overlooked. It should have been measuring workload, not caseload.

The government was deaf to such complaints. It quickly announced the auditor-general's report cleared the way for it to place someone of their choosing in the ODPP to manage its finances. What's more, this government-appointed person would report to the government, not to me, and have the same status as a deputy DPP.

I was enraged. In an interview with the *Sydney Morning Herald* I had a rare outburst of anger, describing the state government as 'ruthless' and 'grubby' and saying that putting a government appointee in such a powerful position could compromise the ODPP's independence. Some politicians will always be tempted to cover up truly dreadful scandals. Politically sensitive cases such as the conviction of a government minister for drug and child sex offences could only be properly handled when the DPP and prosecutors working within the ODPP were out of the reach of powerful politicians. In a piece for *The Australian* I put it this way:

> [It] adds an outsider to the prosecution process with the capacity to direct resources to prosecution services. The risk of even indirect influence in prosecution decisions is obvious, especially if driven by a government that is intent on getting its own way, regardless of principle.

I noted the ODPP from time to time gave 'advice and conduct[ed] prosecutions concerning both friends and enemies of the government in power'. In tricky situations like that, there were no prizes for guessing to whom a high-level government-appointed person paid to report to the government was going to be loyal. As it happened, after an appointment was made we managed by careful application to avoid any such scandal and eventually the unneeded position was abolished.

There had been so many attempts by different politicians to put people they controlled within the ODPP. Prior to this, there had been the attempts in 1995 and 2001, and in 1997 and 2003. None of these attempts succeeded, but I and other senior members of the legal profession had to divert to fight them every time. There was also plenty of talk. Desire to directly control the budget of the ODPP had been discussed openly in parliament in 1997, twice in 2002, in 2003 and 2005. It was even part of one party's policy going into the 2007 state election. Time after time, these attempts to keep the ODPP on a shorter leash failed, only to be resurrected in ongoing efforts to beat me into submission.

*

In October 2007 a law to limit the number of years a future DPP or crown prosecutor, public defender or solicitor general could serve passed in state parliament. The media, lawyers and politicians debated the problem this law posed for the proper functioning of the rule of law. The whole point of life tenure for such positions is to take politics out of the prosecution (and other legal) processes. How could a DPP, especially, resist political pressure if politicians were the ones deciding whether to renew the DPP's contract? The need to have contracts limited and renewed would surely make it more difficult to attract senior, talented lawyers to the ranks of prosecutors and DPPs.

In fact I had persuaded the government to increase the term of engagement of future DPPs and solicitors general from the proposed seven to ten years (or to age 72) and to make that term non-renewable in the case of the DPP. For the other officers the term was to be seven years (or to age 65), renewable.

The new law did not apply to existing prosecutors or to me as DPP, only future ones. But there was something lurking in the fine detail of this and earlier legislation. I still had my position for life but, by an accident of legislative drafting in amendments over the years, if I didn't retire by my sixty-fifth birthday, I would lose my pension. The implications for me were overlooked as debate over the more obvious problems of the new law continued. However, I quietly saw the trap that was now waiting for me in only a few years, and sought independent legal advice.

I didn't have a problem with DPPs having to step down once they turned 72 years of age. That was the age Supreme Court judges had to retire at that time. The problem I, and I alone, had was the choice of either continuing my job for life with no possibility of a pension if I retired at some point, or retiring before 65 and receiving a pension. I would turn 65 in March 2011.

The grim nature of a DPP's work and the stress it involves would conceivably make some DPPs happy to step down sooner than I would choose to. Even so, legislation to limit the tenure of DPPs did have real potential for unacceptable consequences.

Those championing limits on tenure had to be persuaded that the problem of DPPs having to please politicians in order to keep their jobs could only be solved by DPPs being able to serve one ten-year maximum term, non-renewable – and I was able to achieve that. As they couldn't reapply for the job, there was no danger of their inappropriately trying to please politicians while doing it. But the same safeguard would not apply for future deputy DPPs, crown prosecutors and public defenders, whose tenure would be both limited (to seven years) and also renewable under the new law. Never fear, the limited tenure champions argued, this wasn't a problem because of general professional standards and the establishment of anti-corruption watchdogs such as the Independent Commission Against Corruption.

In late 2007, politicians told the media about the new laws they would like to pass. At the top of the list was a mandatory minimum sentence of 25 years for convicted child murderers. Anyone who said this was a bad idea would sound like someone who was soft on child murder. Politicians in favour of mandatory sentencing laws congratulated themselves on creating a sure-fire vote winner and outsmarting me.

*

By 2007–2008 I think I had become fairly well practised in dealing with political pressures, even indirect political pressures, and media pressures. I had developed a way of addressing them by relying on the facts and on the fundamental principles that should underpin a criminal justice system in any civilised society. I was able to fall back on those principles when the pressure mounted.

Three years later, when the ABC dedicated an episode of its flagship program *Australian Story* to me at the end of my tenure as DPP, Mark Tedeschi, the senior crown prosecutor said, 'In terms of any attack from the media, in terms of politicians, [Cowdery] bears the brunt of that and allows us to get on with doing our jobs … There have been times when I don't know how he's withstood the pressure because there has been immense pressure on him.'

I identified these sorts of pressures as belonging very much to the work environment rather than belonging to me. I think that is a useful coping mechanism. My wife has always said that I never brought it home with me. I made a point of that. One habit that I had been able to develop was to leave the work in the office when I left in the evenings. I had also reclaimed my weekends (which I had always worked when at the Bar), so I had recovery time.

Very importantly, I also had the support of the deputy directors, the senior crown prosecutor Mark Tedeschi, the deputy senior crown prosecutors, barristers, solicitors and the staff in the office. If I had not had their support, if I had been white-anted or attacked from within in any way, it would have been much more difficult.

Chapter 10

DEFINING INDECENCY: THE BILL HENSON CASE

Around the time I dropped the charges against The Chaser team in late April 2008, storm clouds between me and the state government quickly gathered again. Richard Jinman, the arts editor at the *Sydney Morning Herald*, received an invitation to the opening of a new exhibition. He regularly received such invitations, and those who sent them knew how hard it was to have theirs stand out. This particular invitation, for an exhibition by the internationally celebrated photographer Bill Henson, certainly made an impact. It featured a photo of a naked 13-year-old girl, her budding breasts revealed for all to see. 'That's a bit off,' Jinman thought.

The photo on the invitation was like a number of others in the planned exhibition. Dark and moody, just like teenagers, they captured both the last rays of childish innocence and the dawn of sexual maturity. The teenagers were nude.

The day before the exhibition was due to open was the day Orkopoulos was to be sentenced. Naturally, all major media outlets would send reporters to court to cover it. During discussions about what else the *Sydney Morning Herald* should cover, the Henson exhibition invitation came up. One of the paper's prominent columnists, Miranda Devine, decided to write a stern condemnation of the photos of naked teenagers.

The next day, as reporters prepared to descend on the courtroom where Orkopoulos would receive his sentence, the column appeared.

> Opening tonight … is an exhibition of photographs by Bill Henson, featuring naked 12 and 13 year olds. The invitation to the exhibition features a large photo of a girl, the light shining on her hair, eyes downcast, dark shadows on her sombre, beautiful face, and the budding breasts of puberty on full display, her hand casually covering her crotch … The effort over many decades by various groups – artists, perverts, academics, libertarians, the media and advertising industries, respectable corporations and the porn industry – to smash taboos of previous generations and define down community standards, has successfully eroded the special protection once afforded childhood.

As with any other day, radio shock jocks scanned the papers for topics they would discuss that morning. The topic for 22 May 2008 was obvious. As condemnation of the photos blared from people's radios, and people realised they could easily view them online, police received a call from Hetty Johnston of Bravehearts, a child sexual assault awareness group in Queensland. She wanted the police to take action. Premier Morris Iemma, who was overseas, issued a statement declaring the photos 'offensive and disgusting'. That day the police visited the gallery, which decided to postpone the exhibition.

The Orkopoulos sentencing was being rapidly overshadowed. The judge remarked that the former minister's actions were premeditated, predatory, manipulative and had a lasting effect on his victims. The judge also said there were no reasons to believe he felt any remorse for what he had done to those teenage boys. Orkopoulos was jailed for a minimum of nine years and three months, with a maximum of 13 years and 11 months. A friend of one of the victims yelled at him after he was sentenced: 'You're not so big and tough now.'

'This man is now in jail where he belongs,' said Premier Morris Iemma in a statement that day. 'His repugnant double life has been exposed and he has been prosecuted for his vile acts, the sentencing decision today brings a welcome closure to the case.' Outside the courtroom, one of Orkopoulos's victims told reporters he was relieved by the sentence. 'It's been a long road but we got justice in the end,' he said.

The Orkopoulos sentence was still big news, but the growing media storm over the controversial photographs was becoming much bigger. The next day, Friday, 23 May 2008, police went back to the gallery with a warrant. They seized ten photographs from the exhibition of 31 photographs, two from an office area in which four photographs were displayed and 20 from storage. The police made a public statement about the seizure of photos and their intention to prosecute:

> The child depicted in the image is female. We believe that the child is 13 years of age. The information is that the child … is not a resident of New South Wales and we have referred liaison through our child sex crime unit to liaise with the State where the child is believed to live.

While making an unrelated appearance on national morning television, the prime minister was asked what he thought of the controversial photographs. 'I find them absolutely revolting,' Kevin Rudd answered, amid doubts that he had actually seen them. Police soon announced that charges would be laid.

There were those prepared to swim against the rising tide of moral outrage. A prominent owner of a different gallery was reported as saying:

> It's a dark day for Australian culture in my view. It is an indictment of a culture when an artist of the integrity and stature of Bill Henson isn't free to show his work.

David Marr, a senior writer and journalist who published a book about the media-driven storm a few months after it erupted, was the target of ongoing attacks for his opinion that the photographs were beautiful.

Late on Friday, 30 May, the police prosecution brief on the photographs was delivered to me. The photos, some of the naked girl featured on the invitation, others of a naked boy, included images where the breasts and genitalia were visible or partly obscured. The police were seeking legal advice about two possible charges, one of producing, disseminating or possessing child pornography, the other of publishing an indecent article.

To legally qualify as child pornography (as it was known then – now called child abuse material), the depiction of a child under 16 years of age had to be in a sexual context. Attorney General Debus, the predecessor to Attorney General Hatzistergos, once explained in parliament that under the relevant law, 'sexual context' was a term broad enough to cover not only situations depicting children engaged in sexual activity, but also situations where a child is depicted in an indecent pose or watching another person engaged in sexual activity. It is the duty of police and others in the criminal justice system to deal with such hideous material, so these upsetting guidelines had to be made.

I noted that in the photos before me, with the exception of a few photographs of the boy taken from storage, whose age was unknown at that time, the teenagers were not shown in proximity to any other human or animal. None was depicted engaging in any sexual act. They were simply nude. As I would later advise police, in my view 'mere nudity is not sufficient to create a "sexual context".'

There were other considerations for the possible charge of child pornography, including whether the person who took the photos was a reputable artist. Over the decades Bill Henson's photography had won critical acclaim in Australia and overseas. His work, which was often concerned with capturing adolescence, had been exhibited in highly regarded galleries all over the world. His credentials helped me reach the conclusion that 'a genuine artistic purpose could well be established'.

The possibility of an indecency charge was less clear. Such a charge would have to reflect what the general community would think was so beyond the pale that it should be illegal. There was plenty of heated debate in artistic and media circles about whether the photos, even with their artistic merit, were decent, but the loudest voices weren't the only ones that counted. Was mere nudity enough to attract a criminal charge of indecency in the modern world of popular culture? Putting aside my personal taste and opinion of the photos (which was irrelevant), I relied on case law and judged mere nudity to not be indecent in the legal sense.

On 6 June 2008, I advised police that the charges against the photographer would be dropped. And braced myself for the inevitable backlash.

Meanwhile, real criminal trials were being held. One of them was the trial of Shirley and Caren for the death of Graeme. Two others, the trial of Gordon Wood for the murder of his girlfriend Caroline Byrne, and the second trial of Jeffrey Gilham for the murder of his parents, had been in the criminal justice system for over a decade apiece. All these trials occurred in 2008 and would be argued over for many years to come.

Chapter 11

GORDON WOOD AND THE DEATH OF CAROLINE BYRNE

In late 2008, a jury was listening to a closing address from the state's senior crown prosecutor, Mark Tedeschi QC. It was the trial of Gordon Wood for the alleged murder of 24-year-old model Caroline Byrne, who had been found dead at the bottom of a cliff 13 years earlier.

The cliff, known as The Gap, was well over 20 metres high. It looked out over the sea near South Head. Before the cliff dropped away completely, there was a shelf of rock with holes in it that the sea pushed through. The view from the top made it a popular picnic area. There was a footpath that in places allowed an uninterrupted view of the sea, enclosed by a fence that at its closest point was just over a metre from the edge of the cliff. Unfortunately, it was also a notorious suicide spot.

In the small hours of 8 June 1995, a police officer stood at the base of The Gap. It was cold and dark that night. Water kept surging over the rocks. To avoid being swept away, the police officer positioned himself behind a large rock and waited for another officer to join him.

Not long before, a tall, athletic man named Gordon Wood had come into a nearby police station saying, 'I'm pretty sure my girlfriend has jumped off The Gap ... I'm pretty sure I know where she is.' Police officers carrying torches followed Gordon to The Gap.

Gordon's girlfriend was Caroline Byrne. Her father Tony and brother Peter were at The Gap, waiting in the dark. Caroline's car, a Suzuki Vitara, was parked nearby. Police checked the car but found nothing of significance. The Police Rescue Squad arrived together with a helicopter and a patrol boat.

As police searched for Caroline, Gordon told them he could identify Caroline and that he would be able to recognise the clothing she was wearing. He told a constable Caroline had only one pair of joggers, four pairs of tights and one denim jacket.

It was not until 4.40 a.m. that the police officer who ultimately retrieved Caroline located her body using his light at the top of the cliff. He then rappelled down the cliff to the shelf of rock below. As the officer swept his light across the rocks at the base of The Gap, he heard a male voice say: 'That's her. That's the clothes she was wearing.'

Caroline's body was about the tenth body this officer had helped retrieve from the bottom of The Gap. As he waited for assistance, he observed its position. It was unusual. He had not seen one that had gone into a hole in the rock shelf on any of his other retrievals. The police officer formed the opinion that she had gone directly in, head first. He was surprised that there was no damage from her waist to her feet. He tried to work out the point at which Caroline left the cliff top. He observed her feet pointing to the corner of a fence on the edge.

A second police rescue officer joined this officer at the bottom of The Gap and Caroline's body was retrieved soon after. The police assumed it was a suicide. In an omission that would have consequences for decades to come, the police took no photos and made no records of where Caroline's body was found. Given the condition she was in, it was decided to take her body to the morgue before asking Gordon to formally identify her.

At about 5 a.m. Gordon phoned Peter. Peter recalled Gordon telling him, 'It was where we were looking, Pete, it was the spot where we were looking. That's where they found her.'

A few hours after Caroline's body had been retrieved from the bottom of The Gap, an ex-boyfriend of Caroline's named Andrew, who happened to be a police officer, was at the morgue for unrelated police matters. While there he received a call from a friend and fellow police officer, who told him that Caroline was dead, having been hit by a car. Andrew said he went straight to the morgue admission book to look for Caroline's name. He found one of the last entries, stating an unidentified woman's body, believed to be Caroline, was in the morgue awaiting dental records. Not long afterwards, Gordon went to the morgue to identify Caroline's body.

There was a man who lived in an apartment very close to The Gap. The day after Caroline's death he told his neighbour he had heard a scream the previous evening in the context of 'somebody going off The Gap'. Afterwards, at about 1.00 a.m. to 2.00 a.m., he heard a helicopter.

Gordon's employer, Rene Rivkin, was curious about what had happened. Gordon met with him for breakfast that morning and apparently said that Caroline's father didn't want people to know that his daughter had committed suicide, and asked Rene to tell his wife that Caroline had died from being hit by a car.

At about 3.00 p.m., Gordon went to Tony's apartment. Tony recalled Gordon saying, '[T]he police have found receipts in Caroline's wallet which show … that she was out there that day and the day before, and the receipts show that she had left a trail.'

Sometime that day Gordon stopped Andrew on the side of the road and told him that Caroline was hit by a car and had died. Andrew recalled saying, 'That is absolute bullshit … I am going to find out what happened.'

Gordon would later say, '[F]or a period of time I told people that she got knocked over by a car.'

The next day, Gordon told Tony he had traced Caroline's steps. 'After I left her at lunchtime she would have got up out of bed, not long after I had left to go back to work. She's got dressed, gone over and got the car, and then she's virtually left a trail. She's used her card at Paddington and then she has used her card again at Vaucluse, virtually leaving a trail. She's then hung around out at around Watsons Bay and then at about 6.00 p.m., she's taken her own life.'

He also told some people that Caroline was at The Gap the night before she died, or two nights before she died, contemplating suicide. His then associate Donald recalled Gordon telling him this when, on the Saturday after Caroline's death, he, Gordon and Caroline's work colleague Rupert drove to The Gap. The three stood at the top of the cliff while Gordon told them where he had stood on the night she died and seen her ankle, shoe and some of the lower leg of her trouser. He also pointed to the spot where Caroline's body landed. A number of Caroline's friends recalled Gordon making similar claims of what he had seen from the cliff top.

Caroline's father Tony and brother Peter declined to make a statement to police on the night of Caroline's death. But years later, they did.

Tony and Peter told police that at about 12.30 a.m. on 8 June 1995, they were woken by a phone call. It was Gordon, calling from a public phone. He explained that he feared something terrible had happened, and arranged to pick up both Peter and Tony and bring them to The Gap, where he was calling from. Peter recalled Gordon being 'frantic', 'emotional, speaking quickly' and 'driving way too fast'. When Peter asked Gordon how he knew where to find Caroline, Gordon apparently said, 'I don't know, Pete. I don't know. I just had this feeling.'

Peter said that when they arrived in Gap Lane, Gordon 'appeared to be opening the door [of Caroline's car] with a key … he bent down into the car … and when he came back up he had Caroline's wallet in his hand'.

When they moved away from the streetlight in Gap Lane, Tony recalled, 'It became so dark and so black that I could not see the ground in front of me.' The three men then found two nearby fishermen who reluctantly lent them a torch. Gordon used it to look over the edge. Peter said Gordon pointed down towards the rocks and said, 'Look Pete, down there. I can see legs and a body. It looks like legs and a body.' Peter responded, 'I can't see anything down there, I can't make out anything.'

It was Tony who suggested they call the police.

Caroline had been an unusually attractive young woman. Aside from working as a model, she also had a part-time job at a finishing school with deep connections to the modelling world. Her employer was a highly distinguished woman, June Dally-Watkins, recipient of an Order of Australia Medal and founder of the school that bore her name.

June was among the many people to whom Gordon gave different accounts of what had happened after Caroline died. One of the comments she recalled him making was that Caroline had gone missing for five hours on Tuesday, the day before she died. He told her he thought she was at The Gap contemplating jumping at that time.

June suspected that Gordon knew more about Caroline's death than he was telling her. What's more, June decided to take matters into her own hands. She suggested to Gordon that he have his photo taken by Rupert (a pseudonym), who was a professional photographer. Gordon agreed, but he didn't realise the reason behind her suggestion. That same day, June went to The Gap and its surrounds. She noticed a café. About a week later, accompanied by one of Caroline's friends, June spoke to the two owners of the café. She showed them a photo of Caroline and asked if they had seen her. The two conferred, then said they thought they had, and that she had been with two men. One was 'tall and fair', the other a 'much shorter person, who was dressed in all black and had black hair tied back into a kind of ponytail'. Mention was also made of a Vitara car as June, Caroline's friend and the café owners discussed what they might have seen.

Four days after Caroline's death Gordon made a statement to police in which he claimed, 'I saw what I thought was shoes at the base [of] the cliff however Peter said that he didn't believe they looked like shoes.' He didn't mention the conflicting comments he made to Caroline's friends and work colleagues about what he knew of her whereabouts the night before she died. Gordon told the police about the two fishermen. Police tried briefly and unsuccessfully to find them.

Caroline's memorial was held on 21 June 1995. June attended and saw Gordon and an associate of his there. June thought the two fitted the exact description of the men seen by the café owners. She took photographs of Gordon at the service. In one of those photos, a green Bentley thought to be owned by Rene Rivkin was in the background. Within a week of the memorial service she took these photos to the café near The Gap and showed them to the two café owners.

By law, violent, sudden and unexplained deaths are among those that must be reviewed by a coroner. The primary purpose of a coronial inquest is to inquire into the manner and cause of death. The investigation remains open until the coroner makes a finding. If it is a finding of a crime, the inquest is suspended while prosecution is considered by the DPP. If it is an open finding, the investigation remains open.

Police made a video in 1996 in preparation for the inquest into Caroline's death. In the video, an officer who had helped the officer who ultimately retrieved Caroline's body pointed to the hole where Caroline's body was believed to have been found. The video was then made available to the media, the idea being to maximise the chances of seeking out persons who may have seen her death or have witnessed other incidents at the time that could assist the police in putting together an account of what happened.

In mid-1996, Gordon Wood was again interviewed by police. When asked how he knew to go to The Gap, he said, 'I can't tell you exactly why I went to The Gap … I suppose maybe subconsciously or instinctively I picked up that Caroline wasn't her normal self for the last few days …' When asked how he found Caroline's car, Gordon said he 'just had a feeling … I believe in spirituality and all that and I think the kind of connection Carol and I had was very strong … I think there was some kind of spiritual communication to me that was occurring to me subliminally to go there.'

Gordon was asked about his movements the day Caroline died. He said that Caroline, who was normally an early riser who exercised first thing in the morning, had found it really hard to get out of bed as she was feeling depressed. While Caroline stayed in bed, he set out for the day with the plan they would have lunch together. Gordon said that he came home between 12.45 p.m. and 1 p.m. after dropping off his employer, Rene Rivkin, at a restaurant for a lunch engagement. In Gordon's recollection, the lunch engagement was with a business associate of Rene's, former senator Graham Richardson. He said he found Caroline still in bed, and when he went to wake her, she stirred and smiled. He asked her if she wanted to get up and come and have lunch and she indicated she didn't. Did she want to stay in bed? She nodded. He said he felt that 'this was not normal Caroline behaviour'. He said that he entered the bathroom and opened the cupboard to find '3 or 4 Rohypnol sleeping tablets in a little cut-off piece of silver foil'. He said that the tablets were left over from his recent overseas trip with Rene. Gordon said that he returned to the bedroom and asked Caroline if she had taken the Rohypnol. She said, 'Yes, I've had some for the last few nights 'cause I haven't been able to sleep.' He said he then went to lunch with two friends, Rupert and another man, at a place not far from where his boss was lunching. Before he had a chance to eat, however, Gordon said he was paged by his employer and had to leave. He then picked up his boss's luncheon guest from the restaurant.

Gordon said he came home at the end of his day and noted that Caroline wasn't there. He said he went straight to the couch and, just as the ABC's evening news bulletin was starting, fell instantly asleep. At around 11.00 p.m. to 11.30 p.m., Gordon said he suddenly woke up in a panic. He had given a similar account in his first police interview, but had previously told police he had woken up at 12.40 a.m.

'Caroline wasn't home and there was something seriously amiss,' said Gordon. He knew something was wrong because 'she would never ever ever ever ever go out without telling me where she was going'. He said he tried to ring her but her mobile phone did not answer and then he realised he had told her to turn her phone off. He said that he left a scribbled note at home saying, 'If you come home, call me on mobile.' He said that he then went down to the car park where they usually parked their car. When he could not find the car, he ran down to the street and took one of Rene's cars, an F100 utility, which he used on occasion.

Gordon said he went to Tony's apartment to see if Caroline's car was there. He drove around the outside of the building and did not see her car. He did not go into the building's car park where he knew Caroline normally parked when she visited. Gordon said that he then went up a street and then to Bondi, 'once up to South Bondi round the cafés and once back'. He said that he then went to Camp Cove, which he described as 'where we used to go for our picnics'. He did not find Caroline. He said that he then drove back through Watsons Bay and saw Caroline's car in Gap Lane. He could not remember whether he went up the lane or not. He said that he saw her car parked at the bottom of the steps and said 'at that point I felt sick and I thought, "Well, she's jumped off The Gap."

Gordon said that he ran up the stairs towards The Gap in the pitch black and saw two fishermen. They did not mention this to Gordon, but both had heard a woman's scream about an hour earlier. He asked them if they had seen a girl and they said no. After searching for a while and shouting out Caroline's name, Gordon said he called Caroline's father and brother from a public phone booth as his phone battery had died.

Now accompanied by Peter and Tony, Gordon again approached the fishermen, who this time told them they had heard a woman's scream. Gordon asked to borrow a torch.

'Well, I don't think I could see her with that torch,' Gordon told the Inspector. 'When I – when Pete was holding the torch over the edge, I said to him, I think there's something there, and he held the torch and between he and I we decided it wasn't anything. And that, because of the weak torch … I think he said, it can't be because it's too big for a foot to be at the bottom of the Gap. It's, you know – he dismissed it like that. So I don't think I did see her with the weak torch but I certainly did see her legs with the powerful [police] torch … where we were looking with our little torch was like right against the cliff face but where she was was, like, substantially away from where I thought we were looking.'

The time Gordon said he woke up had changed, and phone records would sit uncomfortably with a number of his claims, but these anomalies were just the tip of the iceberg. His claim to have fallen into a deep sleep without any worry as to Caroline's whereabouts but to have woken in a panic, his claim that a spiritual connection led him to look for Caroline at The Gap and find her car there, his decision not to call home to see if she had returned but to bring Caroline's father and brother to The Gap in the middle of the night, all created a deep suspicion in the minds of police. Was Gordon, despite his habit of telling fanciful, and at times false, stories, someone close to Caroline who correctly suspected she was suicidal that night; or was he a killer trying too hard to cover his tracks?

Towards the end of 1997, Inspector Wyver asked Associate Professor of Physics Rod Cross and another expert to provide an opinion as to whether Caroline may have been pushed off the cliff or may have jumped. Both experts came to the conclusion that Caroline may have jumped. Associate Professor Cross's report stated 'the most likely cause of death was that Caroline … ran over the edge of the cliff in the dark at a point 8 metres south of the safety fence. There is a 20-metre long approach to this point from the west fence where the cliff top is flat and level and relatively free of obstructions.'

The coronial inquest into Caroline's death was held in November 1997. There had been no suicide note and apparently no witnesses to her death. The two café owners attended one day. Both recognised Gordon. By this time they had been shown photographs of him by June and the matter had received coverage in the media.

While watching the 1996 police video being played during the coronial hearing, the police officer who retrieved Caroline's body realised the spot identified as the place where her body landed was incorrect. He would later say he didn't tell anyone until he spoke to Associate Professor Cross in January 2006.

The coroner made an open finding. This meant the coroner was not satisfied Caroline's death was a suicide or a homicide or a misadventure and unanswered questions about her death remained. The open finding did nothing to dampen police suspicions that Gordon Wood had something to do with it.

The question mark over the death of a beautiful model had all the mystery and glamour of a crime novel. High-rating shows on television were keen to follow it, and Gordon was keen to tell his side of the story. In 1998, not long after the coroner's open finding, Gordon appeared on the national TV program *Witness*.

'I'd be a bit of an idiot, wouldn't I, to point to everybody about where she was if I had killed her,' he told the interviewer. When asked how he knew what she was wearing, he responded, '... after I dropped her father and brother back I went to the apartment specifically to find out what she was wearing'. He said it was easy to work out what she was wearing because Caroline 'only owned one denim jacket, she owned one pair of runners and she had two pairs of black tights. Simple.'

In June 1998, police began a third investigation into the death of Caroline Byrne.

The police spoke to Caroline's and Gordon's friends, family, workmates and acquaintances. Years had passed and the story of Caroline's death was by now a media sensation. Rumours were flying alongside genuine recollections. Some recalled snippets of conversations that indicated she was happy in her relationship with Gordon and excited when he came back from his overseas trip with Rene in the days prior to her death. During lunch the day before she died, one of her friends recalled Caroline saying that she and 'Gordy' were 'having a moment', but assumed she was talking about the sort of tiff all couples have from time to time.

Family members recalled discussions about marriage. Gordon's family remembered his desire to marry Caroline and have children before he turned 35. Gordon confirmed this was so. Caroline's family recalled conversations where she talked of him pressuring her, that he wanted her to give up work once they were married and that she was too young (she was 24 years old when she died) to make this commitment.

There were also dark recollections. Aryan (a pseudonym), one of Caroline's friends at the gym she and Gordon frequented, recalled her talking about how possessive and jealous Gordon was, adding that she wanted out of the relationship and sometimes feared for her life. Bo (a pseudonym), who worked as a sales assistant at the gym, recalled Caroline cowering in distress as Gordon berated her, probably on the Friday night before she died. Bo recalled this happened while a fellow employee of Rene's, a man named Tom (a pseudonym), was present. Another friend in the gym recalled seeing Caroline run out crying afterwards. Caroline's family and some of her other friends, including a teenager, thought the number of calls Gordon made to her mobile was excessive, bordering on obsessive and controlling.

Odd facts and claims mounted. On the Monday following Caroline's death, Gordon told the proprietor of a car park Caroline regularly used that he had to obtain a copy of the movements of Caroline's Vitara to and from his car park for the coroner. Having confirmed that his manager had indeed printed out and highlighted the movements of Caroline's car, the proprietor, suspicious of the request, told the manager not to provide any more information to Gordon. Whatever Gordon's intentions were, his claim that he was gathering the information for the coroner was a lie.

On closer inspection, one of the receipts that Gordon told Tony left a trail showing where Caroline had been did not have the merchant's name on it. However, Gordon's claim of where it came from was correct. Also, Tony did not remember seeing any receipts when Gordon produced Caroline's wallet after opening her car, yet Gordon somehow had them and somehow knew where all of them were from.

Contrary to Gordon's claim that he was easily able to deduce what she was wearing the night she died by looking in her wardrobe, Caroline had too many clothes to make such an easy deduction possible. She was a keen shopper and a professional model. Her regular gym visits meant she had several variations of the type of clothing Gordon identified.

Different accounts of Gordon's whereabouts that day began to emerge. One of the friends he was just about to eat with before claiming he was paged by Rene recalled their luncheon being an hour earlier than Gordon told police. This was Rupert, the friend who took Gordon's photo for June Dally-Watkins. Also, the phone records showed no call from Rene to Gordon at that time. Graham Richardson denied Gordon's claim that he had had driven him to lunch with Rene that day.

The owner of the restaurant where Rene had lunch recalled seeing Gordon and Rene having a heated exchange at about 3.00 p.m. in the presence of Tom. The restaurant owner told police he was later approached three times by Gordon and 'threatened not to say anything about having been seen at the restaurant that day. And also offered a share deal in the UK if he kept quiet.'

The man who lived in an apartment very close to The Gap had been travelling extensively between June 1995 and early 1998. Upon his return, his neighbour showed him a newspaper article that contained photographs of Gordon and Caroline. Ten days later he told his neighbour his recollections of the night Caroline died. As he told police, these included seeing a young woman sitting in a gutter, slurring her words as if she was drunk or under the influence of drugs, arguing with two men, one who was standing under the awning below his apartment and the other sitting on a wall just up from where the young woman was sitting. As they continued arguing, the man who lived in the apartment said he 'looked out once more and the three people were together on the far side of the road … the girl was in the middle of the two men and they were walking north towards The Gap park … they just became shadows as they walked up the road'. He described the man who had been under the awning as being about six feet tall, while the other man was much shorter and wearing dark clothes. At about 10.30 p.m., he recalled hearing another argument coming from a pathway near The Gap and he thought he recognised it as a continuation of the argument he had heard earlier. At about 11.30 or midnight, he heard a woman scream.

Shortly after talking to his neighbour, this man watched Gordon's interview on *Witness*. He thought the man he remembered standing under the awning the night Caroline died looked like Gordon, with a similar build and head shape. He made a statement to police in April 1998.

Aside from Gordon's movements the day Caroline died and what he did and said afterwards, police also investigated what was going on in Gordon and Caroline's life generally.

The couple had met at a gym about four years before Caroline died. He worked as a casual fitness instructor and she was a full-time model. The two of them lived together for about six months in an inner city flat. Before too long, Gordon was without a job and his future prospects were uncertain, so Caroline ended the relationship.

In early 1994, Gordon got a job as driver for Rene Rivkin, a high-profile investor. Gordon and Caroline got back together and moved into an apartment in upmarket Elizabeth Bay.

Rene and Graham Richardson both had interests in a business, Offset Alpine Printing Company. There were rumours the fire that destroyed the company's printing plant on Christmas Eve 1993 had been deliberately lit so insurance money could be collected. At the time of writing, such claims are unproven and remain mere rumours.

From 7 to 27 May 1995, Gordon Wood and Rene Rivkin travelled to Zurich and London on business apparently related to Offset Alpine. Prior to their departure, an official inquiry was announced into the Offset Alpine fire. There had also been unfavourable press coverage of the controversy and of Rene around this time. There was evidence that Gordon had encouraged others to buy shares in Offset Alpine because its insurer was about to pay out on a claim for the destruction of the premises in a fire.

On Tuesday, 6 June 1995, the day before Caroline died, the authorities interviewed Gordon and Rene about the Offset Alpine fire. A journalist covering the investigation recalled Gordon telling him it was difficult for Caroline as he 'couldn't tell her or explain to her what was going on'. In 1998, during the third investigation into Caroline's death, Rene told police, 'I've only met her six or seven times. I don't know what she knew.'

Caroline's father, Tony, didn't like or trust Rene. In about March 1994, Caroline and Gordon had dinner at Tony's home. Tony recalled that Caroline went into the kitchen and began to prepare the meal. He and Gordon were in the nearby dining room when Gordon produced a share price indicator, which was a device about the size of a mobile phone. Tony then recalled Gordon saying he had recently bought shares in Offset Alpine Printing, that the company's share price was going to go up because '[t]he fire was a set-up' and the insurance company was going to pay out on the insurance claim. Tony also recalled that 'I looked at Caroline at the end of that conversation and she looked up at me.'

Gordon and Caroline decided to buy an apartment, but they couldn't afford to. Tony and Rene considered helping them financially. Tony only agreed to assist if he alone was on the title and his solicitor did the conveyancing, conditions which Rene did not accept. As a consequence Tony withdrew his offer and Rene purchased the apartment for Gordon and Caroline in his own name. These events soured the relationship between Gordon and Tony. Gordon was confident that working for Rene would mean he would soon be able to own the apartment in his own right.

Further investigations revealed that Gordon never did buy shares in Offset Alpine Printing. Tony made this and other negative, incriminating statements about Gordon to police years after Caroline's death. As the Chief Judge at Common Law, presiding years later in Gordon's appeal against his conviction, noted, Tony was consumed with grief over the death of his daughter, which he first thought was a suicide but then, along with so many others, he heard the growing whispers that she had been killed and Gordon might have been involved. Gordon was a man given to bragging and big-noting himself. Tony might have really heard Gordon make a claim about owning shares and how they were going to go up in value, but well before the trial for the alleged murder of his daughter began, Tony clearly suspected Gordon.

His daughter did have a history of depression. For reasons Caroline never fully explained at the time and were the subject of contention for many years to come, her depression surfaced again just before she died.

Having been a full-time model when she first met Gordon, in the final weeks of her life Caroline was facing the reality that her full-time modelling career was coming to an end. For some time she had combined her modelling with a part-time teaching job with June's finishing school. Approximately three weeks before her death, Caroline received an offer to work in a full-time marketing role with the school. As she discussed with her many friends, her father and her siblings, she was conflicted about the offer of full-time work as she thought it might have an adverse effect on her modelling career. Nonetheless, Caroline accepted the offer and began her full-time job on 29 May 1995. Only days later, she was complaining that her new role was harder than she thought it would be.

Despite her angst, modelling work was still coming her way. On 2 June 1995, the Friday before she died, Caroline had a modelling assignment. The person who gave her a lift back to the city recalled overhearing Caroline call Gordon on her mobile. He said it sounded like a happy conversation. She had apparently decided to not persist with her new full-time job. Around this time, her father recalled Caroline telling him she had spoken to her agent, who said she would never be a top model, but she still had several years of work as a model ahead of her. He also recalled her saying that, having spoken to her agent, she intended to cease working full-time, but would work part-time and continue her modelling career.

The one dampener that Friday was that Caroline was coming down with the flu. This was the night that, some eight years later, her friends and acquaintances at the gym claimed to have seen Gordon berating her to the point of tears while Tom stood watching. These claims were the subject of intense scrutiny both in the trial and years later in the Court of Criminal Appeal. What is agreed is, despite not feeling well over the weekend, Caroline went to work that Sunday.

On Monday, 5 June, Caroline visited her GP, who described her as 'very depressed' that day and noted Caroline had been depressed for about a month. The GP recalled Caroline couldn't quite 'put her finger' on why she was feeling depressed. An appointment with a psychiatrist was made for the following Wednesday, 7 June.

That same Monday, Caroline took a call at 12.30 p.m. to book a modelling job for late in the afternoon the next day. This was the day on which Caroline had said 'Gordy and I are having a moment' during lunch with her friends. She also mentioned her work dilemma. Caroline didn't mention her appointment with a psychiatrist or seem depressed to her friends.

The reality of not in future being one of the tiny number of full-time models weighed heavily enough on Caroline's mind for her to visit her modelling agency that day to again seek advice. The booking agent told her that while she should still be able to do some part-time modelling, the amount of work she could expect would be 'nothing compared to the leading models' and that working another job full-time would be more stable.

Gordon had issues of his own. The next day, Tuesday, 6 June 1995, he and Rene were to be interviewed by the authorities about the Offset Alpine Printing fire.

While Gordon was being questioned, Caroline rang the modelling agency twice. It seems she withdrew from the modelling job which had been offered to her on Monday and scheduled for that day at 5.15 p.m. The job was allocated to another model. Instead, Caroline carried out her marketing role at June's school until about 2.15 or 2.30 p.m.

Early that evening, Gordon called his doctor to ask for a medical certificate to excuse Caroline from work. The doctor declined. Later that same evening, Gordon rang June's finishing school and left a message stating Caroline was sick and wouldn't be able to work for a while. An employee soon rang back. Gordon told her Caroline would not be returning to work. He said he then suggested to Caroline that she turn her mobile off.

The following day was Wednesday, 7 June 1995, the day Caroline died.

The world that admired Caroline hadn't always been kind to her. Caroline's mother had committed suicide, something Gordon mentioned during his *Witness* interview. Caroline had made a suicide attempt soon after her mother's death, something Gordon also mentioned on TV. Caroline was prescribed medication when she was about 21 and made a successful recovery.

Despite Caroline's history of depression, the more police combed through the lives of Caroline and Gordon and the details of her final days, the stronger their conviction that Caroline had been killed and Gordon was involved. But suspicion isn't proof. To prove that Gordon murdered Caroline, no other reasonable explanation for her death could exist. One obvious explanation for how Caroline ended up at the bottom of The Gap was suicide. Unless the Crown could rule that out as a reasonable possibility, Gordon could not be convicted of Caroline's murder.

Although he originally concluded that Caroline could have jumped from the southern ledge at the top of The Gap to where police originally thought she landed, Associate Professor Cross changed his mind.

In 2003, during a walk-through interview with police eight

years after Caroline's death, her brother Peter said Gordon was pointing in the direction of a large pyramid-shaped rock at the base of The Gap when he nominated the spot in the darkness where she landed that night. It was a different spot from where the police had pointed in their 1996 video. In January 2006, the police officer who retrieved Caroline's body told Associate Professor Cross that he thought they had the wrong hole and that he realised this during the 1997 coronial inquest.

The police officer now nominated a new hole, 5.4 metres away from the original hole, near a large pyramid-shaped rock and further away from the cliff, as being where she was found. Photos were taken. When Detective Inspector Jacob was compiling the police brief for me two days later, he noticed that the hole featured in the new photos wasn't the same hole police had previously nominated as the spot where Caroline was found. In April 2004, the day before Associate Professor Cross was due to take measurements at The Gap, Detective Inspector Jacob and Associate Professor Cross spoke about this.

The problem of not knowing exactly where Caroline landed was here to stay. All that could be done was to acknowledge it. The original spot was labelled 'Hole B' while the second spot near the pyramid-shaped rock was labelled 'Hole A'.

One of the reasons why Associate Professor Cross ultimately dismissed Hole B, the original spot, was his opinion that if Caroline had gone head first straight into Hole B 'her shoulders would have impacted the sides at 80 kilometres an hour'. The injuries such an impact would create were not present.

Having decided Caroline had landed in Hole A, there was a question mark over whether she could jump or propel herself that far. After finding out about Caroline's athletic ability, which was average to below average, and carrying out further experiments, Associate Professor Cross decided she couldn't have. Those experiments included women jumping and being thrown by strong men into a swimming pool.

Associate Professor Cross also changed his mind about where Caroline left the top of the cliff. Part of the police brief was a photograph of the northern ledge at the top of The Gap. It showed bushes that confined the run-up to the edge to four metres. This photo had the date '1996' written on the back. Associate Professor Cross decided this was where Caroline left the cliff. The police officer who retrieved her body recalled that Caroline's feet were pointing to the corner fence post. Associate Professor Cross ultimately dismissed the corner fence post and the area around it as it was inaccessible from the footpath, there was a much smaller run-up there compared to the northern ledge and the area slopes downwards, meaning just standing there would risk toppling over.

Associate Professor Cross concluded that the only way that Caroline could have ended up in Hole A was if she was thrown by a 'spear throw' from a strong man. He understood that Gordon could bench press 100 kilograms. He believed that under ideal conditions such a person would have been sufficiently strong to have thrown Caroline the necessary distance. Once Associate Professor Cross had reached this conclusion, it was decided to prosecute Gordon for murder.

Gordon had gathered photos from the Department of Lands and had a photo from a surveying company that indicated the bush in the photo marked '1996' did not exist in 1995.

In the months leading up to the trial, police became aware of Gordon's legal team's back-up plan should the jury not accept that Caroline's death was a suicide. In memoirs he was drafting, Gordon suggested that Caroline's ex-boyfriend Andrew should have been considered a suspect. There was evidence, including from Tony and friends of Caroline's, of arguments between her and Andrew in the months before her death. Otherwise, there was not much to back up this very serious allegation. Andrew, who had resigned from the police force a few years before the trial, had encouraged police to keep investigating Caroline's death. What's more, Gordon had reason to wish Andrew ill as Andrew had displayed animosity towards him before Caroline's death.

This was to be an unpleasant surprise for Andrew, who first learnt of the plan to paint him as a suspect when he was being cross-examined by Gordon's lawyer during the trial.

There was another surprise, but this one would remain hidden until well after the trial ended. In his second report dated 2004, Associate Professor Cross assumed that the run up on the northern ledge was restricted to four metres by vegetation. He relied on the photo showing bushes limiting the run-up to four metres marked '1996'. In 2006, two years before the trial, Associate Professor Cross learnt that the photo marked '1996' was actually taken in 2003. For unknown reasons, he didn't tell the senior crown prosecutor Mark Tedeschi.

The Crown case at trial in late 2008 was that at approximately 11.30 p.m. on the night of Wednesday, 7 June 1995, Gordon, acting either alone, or jointly with a second man, threw Caroline off The Gap at Watsons Bay.

In his opening address, the prosecutor offered a motive for why Gordon would want to kill Caroline. It had two parts. The first was that Caroline was not happy in the relationship and wished to end it and, rather than lose her, Gordon had killed her. The second was that, thinking that she knew too much about business dealings that his boss Rene didn't want others to know about, Gordon decided to kill her in order to protect Rene.

The prosecutor said Gordon was in a situation where:

> … the woman of his dreams was the subject of paranoia by the employer upon which his whole self-esteem was based.

> [Gordon] had confidential information about powerful people, including people in government. He had told people things, including Caroline and Tony and [Aryan] that you might think would have horrified [Rene] if he knew. So [Rene] had every reason to be paranoid about Caroline and Tony.

The prosecutor described Gordon as controlling, and stated:

> … by the time [Caroline] spoke to [Aryan], when [Gordon] had become abusive to her, she realised that his attention to her had a very negative side. It was very dark and unwanted and verging on being stalking …

He submitted that the jury should conclude the relationship between Caroline and Gordon was unravelling:

> … that she was scared; that she didn't know how she was going to get out of the relationship cleanly; and, that things were going from bad to worse … [Gordon] stood to lose everything: love, employment, money, future fortune, self-esteem, the façade of prestige he had built up with others. His whole life was about to unravel [sic] we would submit to you that she must have intimated to him that she wanted out, and it must have been obvious to him that this time it was going to be forever.

The Crown's case was that, as depressed and sick with the flu as Caroline might have been, on the day she died:

> … he [Gordon] decided to make one last desperate attempt to woo her back into their relationship, and that's why he made arrangements for her not to be at work on 7 June 1995. When

> he failed to convince her to stay in their relationship, he killed Caroline rather than losing her and losing everything else in his life.

According to the Crown, Gordon had told 'a tissue of lies about where he was during the course of the day' Caroline died. He didn't leave Caroline in bed that morning, leave lunch before he had the chance to eat because he had to pick up Rene's business associate, go back home to find Caroline still in bed, fetch a Rohypnol for her before going back to work, then come home to fall asleep on the couch just as the 7.00 p.m. TV news was starting, wake up in a panic about Caroline late at night, then, without calling anyone and driving around a bit first, was led by some spiritual connection to The Gap, where he found Caroline's car, then decided to abandon his search for Caroline, not to alert police but to call Caroline's father and brother and bring them to where he was able to make surprisingly accurate guesses as to where Caroline was and the position of her body.

Instead, the Crown alleged Gordon had met up with two associates between 12 and 1.00 p.m. and dropped his boss Rene at the restaurant where he was to have lunch before 1.00 p.m. The Crown alleged that between this time and approximately 3.00 p.m., Gordon was with Caroline and another, unidentified man at Watsons Bay, presumably having lunch. At that stage, everything was friendly.

Shortly after 3 p.m., following lunch at Watsons Bay, Gordon and Tom reported to Rene at the restaurant. Rene became agitated. Between 3.30 and 4 p.m. Caroline's card was used to do some shopping or banking transactions. At some stage around 4.30 to 5 p.m. Caroline drove her Vitara back to Watsons Bay for some unknown reason.

By 5.14 p.m. Gordon had switched off his phone. By 5.30 p.m. Caroline's phone was switched off and her diversion was switched off. Around the same time, Gordon's diversion was switched off. At

5.48 p.m. Gordon made his last mobile phone call for the day until 4.44 the next morning. He ignored some pager messages from Rene and his son around 7.30 p.m. to 8.30 p.m.

At some stage in the evening, Gordon and a second male joined Caroline at Watsons Bay. At around 8.00 p.m., the man who lived in an apartment that was very close to The Gap saw Gordon and Caroline and a second man arguing in Military Road. By that stage the situation had become very ugly, with Gordon berating Caroline in a very similar manner to the way that he had berated her at the gym the previous Friday. Caroline was cowering in exactly the same way that gym employee Bo had seen her cowering at the gym the previous Friday. She was still answering him back in a combative manner.

They continued arguing from about 8 p.m. for about three and a half hours until Caroline's death at 11.30 p.m. The argument went right up until the scream. The scream was most likely Caroline being rendered unconscious or incapacitated. Her death was not a suicide but a murder.

The prosecutor submitted that over the days following Caroline's death Gordon carried out a 'relentless pursuit to try and convince Tony and Peter that Caroline had committed suicide'.

There were issues with some of the evidence the Crown relied on for this narrative.

Both café owners recognised Gordon from the coronial inquest. Both also identified Gordon as he sat in the dock, and gave evidence of having seen a Bentley motor car at The Gap. They said it was a two-door vehicle and, both being car enthusiasts, described it in detail. It was apparent that the only relevance of that observation was that Rene owned a Bentley. However, it emerged during the trial that the Bentley Rene was thought to have owned at the time was a four-door model.

The trial judge, Justice Barr, told the jury the café operators' claims to have seen a Bentley on the day of Caroline's death 'ceased to have any consequence' and that he wasn't 'going to say any more about it'.

Both café owners claimed to be able to identify the 'second man' as the person June saw at Caroline's memorial, who they thought fitted the description they had given her. They were all proven wrong. The prosecution accepted their identification of the 'second man' was not correct.

Given the honest but shaky evidence of the two café owners, the prosecutor asked the jury whether they could believe it was just 'an amazing coincidence' that they could be describing Caroline and Gordon.

When it came to the evidence of the man who lived in an apartment that was very close to The Gap, the trial judge told the jury the identity of the second man was unknown. The trial judge also told the jury that the Crown would submit 'that if the deceased [Caroline] were there, then the accused, her partner [Gordon], was more likely to be there as well. So you can use the evidence in that way as well.'

A problem with the man in the apartment's evidence was that Caroline's friends and family told the court they had never seen her drunk, sitting in a gutter and being argumentative.

The prosecutor said to the jury:

> That doesn't mean that that woman was actually drugged or drunk. We submit to you that Caroline … at that stage had been subjected to the most concerted attempt by [Gordon] to convince her to stay in her relationship; they were arguing and arguing and arguing and continued to argue until the time of her death. You might think that she had been so harangued in such a vociferous way by the accused that she was just totally and utterly distressed, not wanting to go, not wanting to be there, wanting to be out of the relationship, not knowing how

> to cleanly end it, as she told [Aryan] and that is why she was slurring her words and sobbing.

The autopsy revealed no alcohol in Caroline's body. It also revealed no Rohypnol in her bloodstream, only some in her urine, suggesting she had taken some in the recent past, but not at lunchtime. The prosecutor used this to suggest Gordon had made up the scenario of handing her a tablet while she lay in bed, depressed, in the middle of the day to 'enhance his fabricated suicide scenario'.

Tom gave evidence at the trial. He denied being at Watsons Bay on the day Caroline died, or any other day with Gordon, Caroline or indeed anyone.

Nonetheless, Tom featured a number of times in the prosecutor's submissions, which reminded the jury that Tom was 'standing shoulder to shoulder' with Gordon when he was allegedly berating Caroline at the gym on Friday night, adding '[Tom] … was also a weight-lifter at the time.'

> This argument must have been something very serious, and it must have had something to do with [Gordon's] employment with [Rene]. That's why [Tom] was standing next to him. I mean, would you have a rip-roaring row with your spouse or partner with one of your fellow employees from your work standing next to you? Of course you wouldn't. Neither would the accused if it was something purely personal. It must have had something to do with [Rene] for [Tom] to be there.

Tom also featured in the prosecutor's submissions about the meaning of Gordon speaking to Rene at the restaurant:

> If [Gordon] had attempted to isolate Caroline that day, to provide him with an opportunity to convince Caroline to stay

> in their relationship, and … [if] the accused [Gordon] had failed to convince Caroline to stay … that would account for why [Gordon] reported back to [Rene] at the … restaurant at 3 p.m. and why [Rene] appeared to be agitated and was throwing [his] arms around when he spoke with [Gordon].

The restaurant owner observed Gordon arrive with Tom.

Gordon's lawyer was concerned that the Crown was planning to prove that Tom was the second man the café owners and the man who lived in the apartment very close to The Gap saw with the man and woman who looked like Caroline and Gordon. He and the trial judge both thought the prosecutor was trying too hard to make up for the fact that both café owners had already wrongly identified someone else as the second man.

Throughout the trial, the prosecutor emphasised Gordon's strangely accurate predictions as to where Caroline's body was, head first and feet up, on the rock ledge in the dark of the early morning:

> How would he possibly know that she's feet up? He couldn't possibly have known that … [I]f you suspected that a loved one had jumped off The Gap, you would think that their body was splat on the rocks. You would not think, 'I can see her feet, I can see ankle skin, I can see the end of the trousers.' The only rational explanation for the [Gordon's] knowledge is that [Gordon] was there when she went over the cliff.

The prosecutor also described this as the 'bottom line' and 'killer point' of the Crown's case.

The Crown submitted Gordon had a motive to kill Caroline, and he had the requisite strength to throw her to her death, either on his own or in combination with the second unknown male. The

Crown submitted Gordon caused her death, either on his own or in combination with the second unknown male.

Gordon's lawyer was unhappy that the prosecutor was allowed to talk about a joint criminal enterprise, meaning a situation where if two or more people work together to commit a crime, such as murder, they are as guilty as each other, no matter who did the actual deed.

The trial judge also spoke to the jury about how the legal concept of joint criminal enterprise fitted into the Crown's case, namely that Gordon alone threw Caroline off the cliff or that the criminal activity that took place at the cliff top was carried out jointly by Gordon and an unidentified man. The trial judge explained that as a general principle, the understanding between two or more people needed to create a joint criminal enterprise 'need not be arrived at by any particular words, written or spoken. The existence of a joint criminal enterprise may be inferred from all the circumstances including anything said.'

Gordon's lawyer was also unhappy that details of the Offset Alpine fire scandal, the issue Gordon and his boss Rene were questioned about the day before Caroline died, were allowed into evidence to support a motive for Gordon to kill Caroline. After considering the defence's objections, the trial judge allowed these facts to remain. However, the judge did direct the jury:

> You will need to ask yourselves how, in June 1995, one year after the claim had been paid and the problem with the fire and the share price because of it had gone away, those things could bear upon the mind of [Rene] and, in turn, the accused [Gordon] … how they could motivate anybody to do anything? … He [Rene] did not care what the deceased [Caroline] knew … You might wonder really whether she knew anything …

Associate Professor Cross told the court it was his theory that Caroline was thrown from the northern ledge into Hole A, and that he imagined:

> … if they [two men together] practised many times they would be able to coordinate their actions and then actually get a higher speed throw, but when I filmed them, the two men's spear throw technique resulted in a lower throw speed …

Besides Associate Professor Cross, there was another physics professor, called by the defence, two biomechanics experts (one called by the Crown, the other by the defence), and four medical doctors (two called by the Crown, two called by the defence).

Professor Elliott, who was called by the Crown, agreed that 'the most logical conclusion from the data present is that Caroline … was spear-thrown from the top of The Gap.' However, Professor Elliott told the court he seriously doubted a struggling person could be thrown from the northern ledge to Hole A. All of the experts agreed that a struggling person would be more difficult to throw.

Professor Pandy, who was called by the defence, agreed with the calculations of Associate Professor Cross, but not with his assumptions. According to his experiment with females of average athletic ability, Professor Pandy thought Caroline may have been able to jump to Hole A from the northern ledge. Associate Professor Cross was critical of the speeds predicted by Professor Pandy, saying that they were only possible for an elite athlete. Mr Rosemond, a senior biochemist at the Australian Institute of Sport, stated that Professor Pandy's results would not have placed his subjects in the category of elite athletes.

Associate Professor Ness, who was called by the defence, said he 'could not make up his mind' whether Caroline died as a result of a throw of any kind, or a running jump, or a jump that turned into a dive resulting in her landing head first. Dr Duflou, who was called by the defence, said that the injuries or lack of them on Caroline's body were consistent with her being unconscious.

The senior crown prosecutor told the jury 'in all probability, Caroline … was unconscious or at least incapacitated when she was thrown off the cliff at The Gap'. He relied on Caroline's broken humerus (the bone running from the shoulder to the elbow) and the fact that she had a compound fracture of the metacarpal (the bone in the hand) as well as the evidence of a single short scream from the fishermen and the man who lived in the apartment close to The Gap. The Crown also relied upon the expert evidence of Dr Hilton and Dr Duflou that injuries to the knuckles of both hands and a missing fingernail could be consistent with defensive injuries from an earlier struggle, although the prosecutor told the jury that it wasn't necessary for them to decide whether or not she was unconscious or incapacitated when deciding what their verdict would be.

'[T]he most persuasive evidence that she did not commit suicide is that she could not have committed suicide to end up in Hole A. That really is the be all and end all of it,' he said.

Before closing his case, prosecutor Tedeschi posed 50 questions for the jury to consider while they listened to Gordon's lawyer make his closing address. He had originally wanted to give each member of the jury a written copy of these 50 questions, but Gordon's lawyer objected and the trial judge ruled against it. With no other objections, the prosecutor listed the questions orally for the jury and invited them to take notes.

Some of the key questions were:

> How would anybody, athletic or not, do a running dive from the top of The Gap in almost total darkness and on uneven ground into either hole A or hole B?

Would Caroline have voluntarily gone over the fence onto the rock at the cliff line if she was having a severe argument with two men during which she had been sobbing?

Why did Caroline purchase some petrol and a Freddo frog and get $50 out of the bank between 3 and 4 p.m. on the 7th [the day she died]?

Why was it that [Gordon's] employment with [Rene] was under such a threat in about March 1995, and what was the plan that he devised to get around this?

If the accused [Gordon] had been advising people to buy Offset Alpine Printing Company shares at a time when he knew that the price was going to massively increase, was this insider trading information? If so, had he disclosed such insider trading information to Caroline and Tony … and, indeed, to others?

If the ASIC inquiry was important enough to cause [Rene] to go on a three-week overseas trip to speak to bankers, was the accused [Gordon] under any pressure at being called before the inquiry on Tuesday, 6 June?

Was Caroline concerned about [Rene's] intentions towards [Gordon]? And did those concerns heighten during the overseas trip?

How did [Gordon] get it so wrong about having driven [Graham Richardson] before and after lunch on 7 June when he spoke to his friends just three days later on the Saturday?

After finishing his list, prosecutor Tedeschi said:

> Now ladies and gentlemen, there's something very important that I should say to you about those questions. The accused [Gordon] is not under any obligation at all to prove anything in this case. My learned friend [Gordon's lawyer], has no burden of proof at all. We submit that the answers to those questions have been provided in the evidence, and that they all point to the guilt of [Gordon].

Gordon's lawyer then got to his feet to deal with the 50 questions in his closing address, but it was to no avail.

The jury decided Gordon was guilty of murdering Caroline.

Chapter 12

ONE BROTHER, TWO MURDER TRIALS: THE GILHAM CASE RETURNS

Expert opinion evidence plays an increasingly significant role in the criminal justice process, particularly with the development in recent years of DNA evidence and other scientific advances in many areas.

I think expert opinion evidence can be extremely valuable in the search for the truth, but there's a risk of the opinions of experts being simply accepted as fact, which is not right. During a trial, the expert witness gives an opinion based on certain facts (proven or assumed) that is taken into account with all of the facts and other opinions that need to be considered. An expert does not determine the issue, but can be very influential. It is therefore important that experts be properly qualified in particular fields of learning and give evidence within their own areas of expertise.

In late November 2008, Jeffrey Gilham was found guilty of the murder of his parents. Expert evidence played a large role in the two trials that led to his conviction.

Fifteen years had passed since Jeffrey's neighbours had answered a knock on the door to find Jeffrey, wearing only boxer shorts, saying his family was dead and his house was on fire. In 2001, when I first considered the possibility of putting Jeffrey on trial, the whereabouts of the glasses Jeffrey's dead brother Christopher needed to see beyond an arm's length were unknown. Since then, they had been located in the downstairs bathroom near Christopher's bedroom, where his body was found, and had remained in the custody of police. However, since Jeffrey's guilty plea to the manslaughter of Christopher 13 years earlier, other major pieces of evidence had gone missing and were no longer available for DNA testing, which had improved markedly since the time of the deaths.

These missing pieces of hard evidence underlined the fundamental problem at the heart of this case – a real life horror with no obvious way of discovering beyond reasonable doubt which brother was the murderer.

It was this lack of definitive, hard evidence that had led me to shut down the attempts by Jeffrey's uncle Tony to have Jeffrey tried for murder in 2001. Tony continued to push for a closer examination of Jeffrey's claim that Christopher was the murderer. That closer examination could only be done by experts.

Expert opinion evidence helps juries and judges to interpret a crime scene and to see if the evidence of the facts has anything more to reveal about the crime. For someone to be accepted as an expert in a court of law, able to express opinions in evidence, they have to show appropriate qualifications and practical experience in a specialised area. This requirement takes forensic experts to places few would otherwise willingly go. Dr Lawrence, who performed all three autopsies of Jeffrey's family, was also an expert on gunshot wounds and their comparison.

The similarity of the stab wounds inflicted on both of Jeffrey's parents and, as Jeffrey openly admitted, inflicted on Christopher by his own hand, featured prominently in the renewed police investigation that his uncle Tony had campaigned for. Dr Lawrence, Dr Oettle (who spoke on *60 Minutes*), Professor Cordner and Dr Cala (who both gave evidence at the 1999 coronial hearing), were joined by Dr Culliford.

Dr Culliford was approached by police in June 2005 to report on whether the stab wounds on the three deceased were likely to have been inflicted by one perpetrator rather than two. After cautioning that stabbing to the chest is common in homicides, she stated:

> The similarity of the grouped wounds was such that I cannot believe that the violent acts required to stab three people virtually the same number of times in such a similar manner could be perpetrated by two different people.

Her opinion echoed those of Dr Cala and Dr Oettle. This additional evidence was considered by police and in February 2006, Jeffrey was charged with the murder of his parents.

Jeffrey was going to fight this all the way. In September 2006 he sought from the court a permanent stay of the proceedings against him, which would stop a murder trial from being held.

His legal team said there were three reasons why Jeffrey shouldn't face a trial. The first and the third dealt with the fact it had been so long since the stabbing deaths of his family. During that time there had been nearly a decade of public and media speculation, such as the *60 Minutes* TV story, about Jeffrey's role in the horror of that night. His legal team argued it would be vexatious and oppressive to subject Jeffrey to a murder trial after he had been through so much already.

The second ground related to Jeffrey's 1995 conviction for Christopher's manslaughter. That it was manslaughter rather than murder was due to the court accepting Jeffrey's claim that, having learnt that his brother had stabbed their parents to death, Jeffrey was provoked into stabbing Christopher to death. Jeffrey's lawyers argued it shouldn't be an option to now seek verdicts that assumed the reasons why Jeffrey was convicted of Christopher's manslaughter were false, especially given that Jeffrey had pleaded guilty to manslaughter rather than waste the court's time by pretending Christopher hadn't died by his hand.

As both sides waited to learn if Jeffrey would be made to face a murder trial, the lawyers considered Professor Cordner's opinion that it was wrong to suggest there was any sort of pattern in the stab wounds pointing to a single perpetrator. The prosecutor had decided not to include his evidence on the basis that Professor Cordner was a 'plainly unreliable' witness, and Jeffrey's legal team demanded to know why.

The month before the High Court made its decision regarding the stay of proceedings, Jeffrey's lawyers were notified of the prosecutor's decision not to call Professor Cordner.

'Professor Cordner has openly expressed that his opinions are based upon a complete acceptance of [Jeffrey's] account of what happened', wrote the prosecutor, who added: 'Professor Cordner's opinions are often argumentative.' The prosecutor's letter also quoted Professor Cordner in his 1999 report:

> I do not regard it as my function to try and describe any defects in Jeffrey's story other than those which, if demonstrable, show that he killed his parents or that Christopher did not kill his parents … mistakes or lies … are generally outside the province of the forensic pathologist and are best evaluated by the decider of fact [in other words, a jury] … I start from the premise that Jeffrey's account is given in good faith.

Years later, the Court of Criminal Appeal correctly assumed this decision by the prosecutor was made without any regard to what I would have thought had I known this was happening.

In February 2008 the High Court dismissed Jeffrey's application for a permanent stay of proceedings. His first murder trial began soon after.

If several doctors or professors (or other properly qualified experts) give the same opinion, it's safe to assume that a reasonable person would accept that opinion as fact. No competent trial lawyer could ignore the powerful effect of several stab wound experts giving the same opinion to a jury. Jeffrey's lawyer was keen to avoid this, so a mini-hearing in the absence of the jury between the lawyers on both sides and the trial judge, known as a voir dire, was held.

Any opinion an expert can give in court has to be based on their specialised knowledge. An eye doctor can't tell a jury what they think about feet. But as this trial would show, real expertise is by definition very narrow and defined. The voir dire allowed Jeffrey's lawyer to demand to know each expert's qualifications and to put their opinions under intense scrutiny before they could utter a word in front of the jury.

Dr Cala obtained his qualification as a pathologist in 1994, a year after the stabbing deaths and post-mortem examinations of Jeffrey's family. By the time of the trial he was an experienced forensic pathologist, having performed 4100 autopsies, of which between half and one-third had involved stab wounds. He did not, however, claim to have had any exposure to multiple homicides where multiple stab wounds were inflicted.

Dr Lawrence, who was also a forensic pathologist, had performed somewhere between 3000 and 4000 post mortems by the time Jeffrey was tried for murder.

Dr Culliford was a forensic physician. Her experience was limited to either attending the scenes of crime or assisting forensic pathologists as they carried out post mortems. Her only previous experience of multiple stab wounds inflicted on a number of victims in the one incident was where there was no question that all wounds had been inflicted by the same person. She openly admitted that her exposure to multiple homicides didn't qualify her to make her claim of a discernible pattern of stab wounds in this case.

Instead, she backed up her 1999 claim of the similarities in the stab wounds pointing to one stabber, using the post mortem findings, diagrams and overlapping transparencies of the stab wounds of all three deceased members of Jeffrey's family prepared by Dr Lawrence.

The experts acknowledged there were some differences, particularly in some of the defensive wounds, but Dr Culliford, Dr Cala and Dr Lawrence all agreed the differences paled in significance compared with the similarities, in particular between Jeffrey's father and mother, who were on any view killed by the same person, be it Christopher or Jeffrey. The prosecutor intended to rely upon Dr Culliford's opinion that from a scientific perspective the similarities were 'extraordinary' so that the jury would reject the idea that '… two people … by coincidence, happen to inflict almost identical wounds to different victims on that night in the same household using the same knife'.

Having dismissed Professor Cordner's opinion as unreliable, the prosecutor hadn't spoken to him further. However, Professor Cordner wasn't excluded entirely.

Jeffrey's lawyer made sure he gave evidence at the voir dire. Professor Cordner said that there was no database kept in Australia or overseas relating to patterns of wounds caused by knives. He also confirmed that there was no scientific comparison of patterns of wounds other than references to signature, or 'Mark of Zorro' patterns of mutilation inflicted by mentally disturbed or psychotic offenders. It was obvious that this was not one of those cases. He also said the infliction of a large number of stab wounds, be it 14, 16, 19 or more, is not uncommon. While he conceded some of the stab wounds were similar, he was adamant that the science of stab wounds couldn't offer much in this case.

'I do not believe there is an area of expertise that enables a person to say that injuries are similar as between numbers of victims to allow a conclusion that there may be one or more assailants,' he told the judge and the lawyers for both sides.

Professor Cordner's views didn't win him any friends during the voir dire.

'I don't care what this witness's opinion is on that matter [the conclusion as to the number of assailants] at the present time,' said an exasperated trial judge. 'I am simply asking whether [fellow expert Dr Culliford] has sufficient expertise to say whether these injuries are similar full stop, nothing more ... Are you suggesting that Dr Culliford cannot, as a matter of expertise, tell me that these injuries or these wounds are similar? Is that what you're saying, professor?'

Professor Cordner eventually agreed Dr Culliford could do so.

Jeffrey's lawyer didn't argue with the prosecutor's decision not to put Professor Cordner in front of the jury, nor did the trial judge comment on it.

During the voir dire, Dr Culliford said Professor Cordner was absolutely correct about there being no scientific database relating to patterns of wounds caused by knives, but stressed that when forensic medical practitioners spoke about injury interpretation, they 'talk persistently about patterns of injuries, and from determining patterns of injuries you draw conclusions'. It was going to take a concerted effort not to use the term 'pattern' in front of the jury.

Despite not insisting Professor Cordner give his views to the jury, the trial judge accepted Professor Cordner's observations about the limits of science in this case. He ruled that neither Dr Cala, Dr Culliford nor any other expert would be allowed to express an opinion as to whether the wounds sustained by the three deceased were probably, or even possibly, inflicted by one killer or that they thought the similarity was so great that it was really a pattern. Given this, Jeffrey's lawyer wondered why the experts should be allowed to testify at all to the jury about how similar the stab wounds were and argued to that end, but the trial judge dismissed his attempt to stop

Dr Culliford, Dr Cala and Dr Lawrence saying in front of the jury that the stab wounds were similar.

The trial judge also ruled on what the experts could say about any expectations there would be blood on the knife used for all three stabbings and on Jeffrey himself.

Under intense questioning from Jeffrey's lawyer about Dr Culliford's qualifications in blood splatter, the trial judge ruled she was qualified to offer her opinion about the blood she expected to be visible on the knife, but that she was only qualified to talk about her expectations of blood being on Jeffrey's hand, not the rest of his body. A similar ruling was given in relation to what opinions Dr Cala could express. Before they gave their opinions to the jury, the trial judge warned that any expectation by any expert that there should have been visible blood on the knife needed to be balanced against such things as the fact the knife had been handled by police at the crime scene without ensuring that any blood that might have been on it was preserved, the fact that the knife was not tested for blood and the fact that the knife, having been lost, was no longer available for forensic testing.

The potential fifth expert, Dr Oettle, who had appeared on *60 Minutes*, also gave evidence at the voir dire. The Crown dropped him. His views that it was somehow weird that most of the stab wounds on all three deceased were to the chest and that Jeffrey should have been covered in blood, may have made good TV viewing, but when tested in a court of law, they were easily dismissed. They simply weren't properly qualified expert opinions.

Even with the evidence of three stab wound experts with similar views, the trial ended with a hung jury, meaning the 12 members of the jury couldn't agree whether Jeffrey was guilty or not guilty. Another trial had to be held.

The second trial began on 13 October 2008. The same trial judge presided, Justice Howie, and Jeffrey was represented by the same lawyer, but there was a new prosecutor. Jeffrey was to now be prosecuted by a deputy senior crown prosecutor, Margaret Cunneen SC.

It was the Crown case that a neighbour heard Jeffrey's mother's voice as she defended herself from Jeffrey after he had attacked his father in the bedroom with such brutality that he had no time to defend himself; the male voice heard by the neighbour was Jeffrey's father in the throes of death. The Crown submitted that Jeffrey was a calculated killer who said nothing at all as he stabbed first his father and then his mother. It was also the Crown case that there was an interval of at least 20 minutes after Jeffrey killed his parents and then his brother before he raised the alarm, during which time he took steps to destroy any evidence that might point to him as the murderer. These included finding accelerant, be it petrol from one of their cars or the mineral turpentine that scientific testing had shown was ultimately used, and setting fire to the house, washing himself to remove any blood transferred to him during the knife attacks, and washing the knife to remove his fingerprints. Central to the Crown's case was a timeline fixed by reference to such things as the neighbours' evidence about hearing frantic voices, the evidence of Mr and Mrs W (the neighbours whose door Jeffrey knocked on), the emergency call from the Ws' home and the arrival of the firefighters.

Just like the prosecutor in the first trial, deputy senior crown prosecutor Cunneen in the second trial decided to leave out Professor Cordner, a decision the Court of Criminal Appeal would ultimately find contributed to a miscarriage of justice. Both sides had agreed to be bound by the ruling given during the first trial regarding expert stab wound evidence. Despite renewed objections by Jeffrey's lawyer, Dr Culliford was again allowed to give a modified version of her expectations of blood on the lost knife and on Jeffrey in front of the jury. Dr Cala was not asked. Instead, another expert, Dr Raymond, a blood spatter expert and the chief scientist in the Forensic Services Group of the NSW Police Force, was the second expert to do so.

The trial judge warned the jury that Dr Culliford's expectations about visible blood on the knife were 'of little weight':

> … don't put too much weight on expert evidence even though it can sound very dramatic from the witness box. Just accept at the end of the day you are going to have to assess the expert's opinion based upon the facts that you will find or are unable to find, and there are two major issues here, as I understand it: one, the presence or otherwise of blood on the knife, and two, the question of the amount of blood on the accused. They are two matters which are very much open to debate and open to a conflict of evidence.

As the trial judge said, the evidence went both ways. Sergeant Ahern, who was at the scene, gave evidence that he had attended several multiple stabbings over the course of his career and had never seen a knife used in a stabbing without visible blood. The area where the knife was found had been doused with water by firefighters. Another crime scene officer, when asked if he thought that water might have washed the knife, said, 'My thoughts would be that it would have been washed in the sink, not just have water dribble on it.' Sergeant Reynolds, who was also at the scene, gave evidence that it was not impossible that any visible blood on the lost knife had been washed off by that water. Dr Raymond agreed. Dr Raymond also said the small amount of blood on Jeffrey was not inconsistent with him having stabbed Christopher, but added that he would have expected Jeffrey to have had blood on his hand after stabbing a body 17 times. Dr Culliford gave similar evidence. However, both Dr Raymond and Sergeant Reynolds agreed there was little projected blood where Christopher was found, which was consistent with there being minimal blood transferred to his killer, Jeffrey. Sergeant Reynolds also gave evidence that he had seen other cases where considerable violence had been inflicted with very little blood on the offender, even though there was a vast amount of blood at the scene and on the victim.

People close to those who had died also gave evidence, and a lot of it pointed towards Jeffrey being the murderer.

Jeffrey told police the piece of cut garden hose found at the scene had been cut in order to siphon petrol from a family car with the knowledge of his father. One of Jeffrey's father's good friends gave evidence suggesting this was unlikely. Jeffrey's father was an instrument maker by trade who made his living installing traffic counter boxes by the sides of roads. This friend said Jeffrey's father was a precise man who wouldn't cut up a perfectly good garden hose, especially as the friend believed Jeffrey's father had the proper equipment in his garage to siphon petrol.

All of the evidence about Christopher's aggressive behaviour towards his parents originated, either directly or indirectly, from Jeffrey. Christopher may have been quiet, but the jury heard evidence that he did have a life. Far from being an angry loner, his former girlfriend said that Christopher was:

> … just a calm, gentle, sincere person … I remember him as being very interested in everything. As I mentioned before, we just spoke about practically anything really and he spent so much time on public transport, and whenever he was interested in something he would just go and borrow a book from the library and read all about it. I think he would have made a wonderful teacher. He had a good sense of humour. As I mentioned before, he was very interested in jazz and we went out and saw many sort of jazz bands in that way. I always found him very mature. He was certainly older than me at the time, but he also seemed very, very astute, very perceptive, and someone who … was able to say what he was thinking

> and say what he was feeling. He wasn't a, you know, he wasn't a repressed person or anything like that, just a calm, gentle person really.

The prosecutor wanted the jury to hear and see evidence from fire expert Mr Munday, who was the principal of a company that specialised in investigating fires, so as to contradict Jeffrey's claim that he was unable to assist his parents when he first entered the house.

Mr Munday told the jury:

> If there were mineral turpentine present, then the fire would develop relatively slowly at first and would gradually accelerate as the fire became larger. But certainly for the first 15, 20 seconds, maybe up to 30 seconds, the fire would remain relatively small and would gradually increase in size and then would increase more rapidly in size as the fire size grew.

He added that he thought it was likely the flames would have remained under 30 centimetres high for the first 10 minutes. Mr Munday had carried out a series of experiments to assess how quickly the fire might have spread, which he filmed and saved on a DVD. Jeffrey's lawyer objected to this DVD being put in front of the jury.

Another voir dire took place.

There was no challenge to Mr Munday's expertise. However, as Jeffrey's lawyer questioned him about the experiments he had filmed, Mr Munday openly admitted there was no way of making an exact re-enactment of the fire in the Gilham home that night. The nature and type of carpet and underlay was unknown. The house had floorboards, whereas his experiments were conducted on a concrete floor. It was not possible to know where the ignition point of the fire was. PVC pipes had been used to represent

Jeffrey's mother's legs during the experiments. It was important to know if there was a trail of accelerant between Jeffrey's mother and father, but there was no evidence – and no way of knowing – if one existed that night. Despite Jeffrey siphoning petrol from one of the family cars that night (if he did), it was accepted the accelerant was mineral turpentine. However, there was no way to determine how much was used to spread the fire. The list of variables and unknowns went on.

'What I am minded to do is to allow this jury to have some idea of how the lighting of the substance [mineral turpentine]: it's effectively up to the 10 to 15 [seconds] build up,' said the judge, who ruled that the jury should be shown an edited version of Mr Munday's DVD.

He told the jury:

> [Y]ou should understand that it is not necessarily what would have happened on this particular night … So just understand this is a very limited experiment, it gives you limited assistance. Don't put too much weight upon it as being an exact replica or even a very close replica of what had occurred on this particular night …

Someone facing trial does not have to give evidence. It is up to the Crown to prove they are guilty. It is never up to the accused to prove they are innocent. However, even though he was perfectly entitled to say nothing, Jeffrey decided to step into the witness box. While Jeffrey was being cross-examined, the prosecutor presented him with a knife similar to the one used in the murders that had been lost by police and questioned him about ways of holding such a knife for different tasks.

As impressive as expert evidence can be, it is opinion, not fact, and opinions can change. By the time of the second trial,

Dr Culliford had changed her mind. She no longer thought the concentration of stab wounds on the chest or trunk of each deceased and the number of stab wounds meant much.

'But in relation to the grouped wounds that you have described, 14 for Christopher, 13 for [Jeffrey's mother] and 15 for [Jeffrey's father], were you able to notice any similarity between that pattern of wounding in each case?' the prosecutor asked, phrasing her question in a way that perhaps reflected the mood in the courtroom at the time but attracted criticism years later in the Court of Criminal Appeal (especially for using the word 'pattern').

'You have to be careful not to put too much importance on the fact that the chest was chosen,' answered Dr Culliford. '[W]hen you stab someone and wish to kill them, you will tend to, I believe, go for an area where it is likely to kill the person; that is what they are trying to do … that if you stab somebody in the heart and lungs they are going to die. So in homicides, in Australia and all around the world, it is a very common place to kill somebody … I don't think that can be particularly correlated as being anything particularly special.'

'What about the sheer number; is it common that there is a large number of stab wounds in homicides involving a knife?'

'I don't think any particular significance can be correlated from that either,' answered Dr Culliford.

After a few more questions the deputy senior crown prosecutor asked, 'Are there any other similarities upon which you wish to comment, doctor?'

'Only in summary that they had grouped – they each had grouped stab wounds. Christopher had 14 in the front chest and [Jeffrey's mother] had 13 in the back chest and [Jeffrey's father] had 15 in the front chest, a single possibly fatal wound on the side of the chest opposite to the grouped injuries; Christopher in the back, [Jeffrey's mother] in the front and [Jeffrey's father] in the back. There were other random injuries and defence injuries, as I have already described, that may be explained by the randomness of the initial assault. And there were defence injuries in two victims, Christopher and [Jeffrey's mother].'

Dr Culliford wasn't the only expert to have changed her mind since the first trial earlier that year. So too had Dr Lawrence. But unlike Dr Culliford, Dr Lawrence was more convinced than ever that the similarities between the stab wounds pointed to there being only one assailant that night.

The prosecutor asked him, 'Doctor, what do you say about [the] comparison of the grouped stab wounds to these three victims?'

In the first trial, Dr Lawrence had answered, 'I think they're similar.' Faced with exactly the same question in the second trial, he answered, 'Well, when I first prepared it [the transparencies], I was surprised how similar they looked.'

By now, the jury had worked out the fundamental issue. Before Dr Lawrence was cross-examined, the jury asked the trial judge (as juries may do in trials), 'Is the pattern of chest stabbing in the three victims a common pattern for multiple stabbings?'

Having asked their question, Jeffrey's lawyer asked the trial judge to send the jury out of the courtroom. Once they were gone, Jeffrey's lawyer told the trial judge he thought Dr Lawrence's use of the term 'surprising' ignored what the judge had ruled could be said about the wounds. He also wanted to know in advance what Dr Lawrence would say in answer to the jury's question. Dr Lawrence outlined the features of the stab wounds that he thought were similar and said he was aware there wasn't much data regarding one person stabbing multiple people.

This was another point on which the three experts had different views. Earlier in the trial, Dr Culliford had said the number of stab wounds on each deceased wasn't of any particular significance. Dr Cala, the last expert to give evidence in the second trial, had a different answer again. He said '[m]ore than ten stab wounds would be uncommon'. To make things even more confusing, Dr Cala also thought the number of stab wounds on each deceased was one of the major reasons they were similar.

There was, however, one more expert opinion. It was to be the most powerful in its contribution to Jeffrey being convicted.

Jeffrey had always maintained that his mother made a frantic call over the intercom to his boatshed bedroom that night, so he entered the house to find his brother had stabbed both his parents and had already started the fire that would engulf the house. The prosecutor argued Jeffrey was lying. She said that having stabbed both his parents and brother to death, Jeffrey was the brother who set fire to the house before going to his neighbours' house to raise the alarm.

Dr Lawrence had measured the carbon monoxide in the blood of all three deceased when he performed the post mortems just hours after their deaths. Carbon monoxide, a by-product of fire, is part of smoke. The prosecutor used the carbon monoxide levels measured by Dr Lawrence to see if Christopher was alive and breathing when the fire had started to take hold, as Jeffrey said, or whether Christopher was dead before this happened and could not have inhaled carbon monoxide.

Dr Lawrence told the court that the levels of carbon monoxide in the bodies of Jeffrey's father, mother and brother Christopher were four per cent, three per cent and six per cent respectively. He also told the court that all three were within normal limits. In other words, all three were dead when the fire was lit and had not been able to inhale carbon monoxide in the smoke.

The prosecutor used Dr Lawrence's expert evidence to establish that, like his parents, Christopher was dead when Jeffrey, who wanted to destroy all evidence that he was the only killer that night, lit the fire on the upper level of the house, near where his parents' bodies lay.

Any avenue of reasonable doubt seemed closed.

Before the jury left to decide whether Jeffrey had been proven guilty of the murder of his parents, the trial judge said to them:

> The scientific evidence is that there is no scientific basis for assuming that people who have the same type of wounds, similar wounds, had the same perpetrator. But you put that in context. It may be the case that, if there were three people killed, one each week, over different parts of the city, that had the same wounds to them generally as these three persons had, that you could not on the scientific basis conclude that it was the same person who inflicted those wounds. But you have to look at this question in this particular context, that is, of three people in the one family being killed roughly at the same point in time …

On 28 November 2008, after eight days of deliberation, the jury found Jeffrey guilty of the murder of his parents.

Jeffrey's wife sobbed and clutched Jeffrey's hands before he was led from the dock to the cells below. Jeffrey's uncle Tony, who had campaigned relentlessly to have Jeffrey tried for murder, was shocked but happy.

'It's slowly sinking in, what's happened,' Tony told the media. 'I've hit so many brick walls along the way … I feel relieved that I have cleared Christopher's name, that's why I did this. He went to the grave as a convicted killer, [sent] by the person who murdered him.'

Three years later …

If the evidence changes then a prosecutor has to change his or her view. You've got to keep at the back of your mind that a prosecutor's job is to ensure justice is done. If the facts change, and the conclusions to be drawn from the facts change, then justice is going to have to be done in a different way.

Jeffrey lodged an appeal against his conviction. During the appeal there was a very substantial about-turn in relation to one important aspect of the evidence. It certainly put a totally different complexion on the sequence of events the night Jeffrey's family was stabbed to death and changed the inferences that could be drawn from the now available evidence. It required a complete reversal of the decision. Being scientifically based, the new expert evidence was something that was objectively established and not subject to the vagaries of direct personal observation. It had to be accepted. It wasn't a case of making a difficult choice about anything. The evidence had suddenly become very different and the consequences had changed.

It had been nearly 20 years since the stabbing deaths of Jeffrey's brother Christopher and both of his parents. By the time of the appeal hearing in 2011, Jeffrey had spent over three years in prison, serving the two life sentences he had received in 2008.

The jury didn't believe Jeffrey's account of the night his parents and brother died. Jeffrey had always admitted to the stabbing death of his brother Christopher, but claimed he did this after discovering Christopher had stabbed both of their parents and had set them, and the house, on fire. For 15 years there had been no way of disproving Jeffrey's version of events, and Christopher, whom Jeffrey had killed, was deemed to have been the murderer of their parents. In 2008 the Crown claimed expert evidence, particularly about whether Christopher had inhaled smoke before he died, proved that it was Jeffrey who had stabbed all three members of his family. The jury in Jeffrey's second trial agreed and convicted him of the murder of his parents.

His uncle Tony thought justice had been done. Since deciding it was Jeffrey, not Christopher, who had murdered his brother and sister-in-law, his 16-year obsession with seeing Jeffrey convicted had cost him his marriage, his job and his health.

Jeffrey was now a convicted murderer, but he still had the loyalty of his wife and friends. While he was in prison, Jeffrey's supporters set about collecting new evidence for his appeal. They hunted down his old university timetable and confirmation from one of his lecturers that Jeffrey would have been at a lecture on the afternoon when his mother left work two hours earlier than usual, indicating to her workmates that she was worried about one of her sons. Those workmates told police they didn't know which son she had been referring to. The judges of the Court of Criminal Appeal held this new evidence pointed towards Jeffrey's mother going home early to deal with Christopher, not Jeffrey. However, this still didn't prove Christopher was the murderer.

Jeffrey's wife and supporters collected other evidence, but it wasn't as strong. After repeatedly studying police crime scene videos, they thought there was a bloodied fingerprint on the intercom unit, which could only have been put there by Jeffrey's mother. Jeffrey's story had always been that he came into the house from his boatshed bedroom after his mother had made a frantic call over the intercom. The intercom was one of many pieces of hard evidence that had been lost before both of Jeffrey's murder trials. This fact, plus the judge's view that there was, at best, only a theoretical possibility the police would have overlooked or ruined such a big potential clue, meant it didn't make much of an impression at the appeal. Neither did Jeffrey's supporters attempt to introduce more fire expert evidence.

What blew the Crown's case apart in the Court of Criminal Appeal in its judgment in 2012 was the new carbon monoxide expert evidence.

A new expert, Dr Green, had written a report in 2010 that dealt with how the smoke from the fire would have travelled through

Jeffrey's home and how long Christopher would have had to inhale smoke to have the level of carbon monoxide Dr Lawrence had recorded during the post mortem.

'The conditions in the house prior to the explosion of the windows, did not allow smoke and carbon monoxide to move against the ventilation flow that was coming from below,' wrote Dr Green. 'It was not possible that carbon monoxide from the upper level was responsible for the raised carbon monoxide level in Christopher if he had been downstairs at all times.'

Carbon monoxide, which is a by-product of fire, remains in the body for a very short period of time, leaving quickly when fresh air is inhaled. Bodies don't take up additional carbon monoxide once death has occurred.

Dr Green's report stated it was necessary to assume that Christopher was inhaling carbon monoxide from the fire over a two- to four-minute period, in order for the level of carbon monoxide in his blood to be six per cent. 'The raised level of carbon monoxide in Christopher's blood was compatible with his being in the vicinity of the fire in the upstairs lounge room.'

Professor Penney was a specialist toxicologist who had been studying the effects of carbon monoxide since 1974. He was the author of over 100 peer-reviewed articles published in respected scientific journals since 1963, most of which dealt with issues related to carbon monoxide inhalation, toxicity and poisoning. Professor Penney agreed with Dr Green's report.

Dr Lawrence had claimed during the second trial that up to 10 per cent of carbon monoxide in the blood was normal, but Professor Penny said that 10 per cent was a serious health risk seen only in a few of the very heaviest cigarette smokers.

'[N]one of these [carbon monoxide] levels [in the blood of the deceased] should be considered normal for normal, adult, non-smoking humans,' said Professor Penney. 'In my opinion, Christopher inhaled a significant amount of smoke before he died. This is in sharp contrast to the opinion of Dr Lawrence that he did not … the normal blood level of COHb in healthy non-smoking adults is 0.4 to 1.4 per cent … 10 per cent COHb is not normal.'

Both Dr Green's and Professor Penny's evidence put Christopher upstairs after the fire had been lit and was starting to take hold, just as Jeffrey had said all along.

There were clear signs before the appeal hearing that the new carbon monoxide expert evidence was very strong. In a highly unusual turn of events for a convicted murderer, Jeffrey had been granted bail before his appeal hearing. He arrived at the Court of Criminal Appeal with the threat of being sent back to prison hanging over his head. The Crown came to the appeal to argue that Jeffrey's murder convictions should stand. They were prepared to challenge and hoped ultimately to discredit the new carbon monoxide expert evidence; but after Professor Penney gave his evidence, there were no further questions from the Crown.

Crown witness Dr Lawrence, who had measured the carbon monoxide levels while he performed all three autopsies of Jeffrey's family and had given evidence at both of Jeffrey's murder trials, was called to give evidence on the appeal. He had read Professor Penney's report.

'[D]o you agree, generally speaking, that it was wrong to say that the CO level was not significant given what you know now?' asked Jeffrey's appeal lawyer.

'I think it's probably better to say I don't know what the significance of the level is,' answered Dr Lawrence, who now realised that he was not an expert in what carbon monoxide levels are normal for people who are still alive.

'In most of our cases we deal with either levels of zero or over 10 per cent,' Dr Lawrence continued. 'I deal relatively infrequently with cases between zero and 10 per cent because I don't mostly …

see live people and so my experience and knowledge of interpretation of that sort of level is small.' Dr Lawrence had admitted while giving evidence in the Court of Criminal Appeal that he was not qualified to give the expert evidence that had played such a central role in Jeffrey's conviction for the murder of his parents.

Two massive holes had been blown into the Crown's case: that Christopher had never been upstairs, and that all three were dead by the time the fire was most likely lit.

'It is inevitable from this that we reach the conclusion that [Jeffrey] has lost a fair chance of acquittal, and that a miscarriage of justice has occurred,' said all three Court of Criminal Appeal judges jointly.

Their Honours weren't saying that Jeffrey was innocent, or that it was their job to decide if he was innocent, but the new expert evidence was very powerful, supported Jeffrey's version of events and raised a reasonable doubt about his guilt.

Allowing Dr Lawrence, Dr Cala and Dr Culliford to say the stab wounds inflicted on Christopher and both of his parents were similar in front of the jury was also held to be a miscarriage of justice. '[I]t ought to have been rejected [by the trial judge],' wrote their Honours. They held that the risk of three experts saying the wounds were similar created an overwhelming danger of the jury thinking there must be a pattern that could only be explained by Jeffrey stabbing all three members of his family. Their Honours also held that Dr Cala did not have the practical experience necessary to be an expert in wounds on multiple victims.

The prosecutor's decision not to put Professor Cordner in front of the jury was also held to be a miscarriage of justice. Professor Cordner was correct to be adamant that there was no scientifically valid pattern to the stab wounds and he should have been heard. At least part of the reason Professor Cordner was left out was that he held a different opinion from the other expert witnesses the Crown intended to call. 'The Crown is simply not entitled to discriminate between experts, in particular between those whose views they have sought, calling only those that advance the Crown case,' all three Court of Criminal Appeal judges wrote. Their Honours also held the claim that Professor Cordner's opinions were argumentative, in other words arguing with other points of view simply for the sake of it, was 'baseless'.

The decision to exclude Professor Cordner was second-hand. The prosecutor in the first trial, which ended with a hung jury, was the one who first made it. Their Honours held prosecutor Cunneen's failure to make up her own mind about whether to call Professor Cordner in the second trial was a breach of her duties.

As high as the hurdles are for prosecutors, the Court of Criminal Appeal is not there to overturn convictions every time a problem is found. For example, their Honours agreed with some of the complaints by Jeffrey's legal team concerning the prosecutor's behaviour during the trial, particularly her presenting Jeffrey with a knife similar to that used to stab his family in front of the jury and making stabbing motions with it. This was a problem, but not a miscarriage of justice. Also, complaints concerning how the prosecutor spoke in front of the jury about how very similar the stab wounds were could have been solved by her doing things differently; but again this was a problem, not a miscarriage of justice.

But the new carbon monoxide evidence first revealed during the appeal was game-changing evidence that no one, including the prosecutor, saw coming. It suggested Jeffrey could have been telling the truth the whole time, even though that truth involved Christopher frantically stabbing both of his parents to death and setting fire to the house while not wearing his much-needed glasses or any pants.

Because of the new carbon monoxide expert evidence, slabs of expert evidence that led to Jeffrey's murder convictions were struck out. The Court of Criminal Appeal judges were faced with a difficult choice. Given they all had ruled that Jeffrey had been denied a fair chance of acquittal, should they order a third trial or set Jeffrey free once and for all?

Ordering a third trial didn't mean a new trial would automatically happen. It would mean the usual process of police and prosecutors working up the case, then presenting it to the DPP, who would decide if the case was strong enough to go to trial again in accordance with the Prosecution Guidelines. In effect, ordering a new trial was the Court of Criminal Appeal passing the decision whether to retry Jeffrey to the new DPP (as I had retired in March 2011).

Chief Judge McClellan had found an authority (meaning a previous influential judgment) where the Court of Criminal Appeal decided not to order a third trial where someone was twice tried for murder and had already been in prison for three years. This was a very similar situation to Jeffrey's, but the Chief Judge wanted to do the opposite. He wanted to order a new trial.

Chief Judge McClellan thought that the passing of nearly 20 years since the stabbing deaths of his family wouldn't cause any additional problems for Jeffrey because vital pieces of hard evidence such as the knife and Christopher's bloodstained dressing gown were missing. Both of the other judges completely disagreed.

'[E]vidence has been lost or destroyed. While it is true that was the case at the earlier trials, it does not for that reason cease to be relevant,' wrote Justice Fullerton. Justice Garling stated the problems such a long delay would hold for Jeffrey's defence in a third trial were 'a matter of common experience and common sense'.

If a third trial was going to be possible, the police and prosecutors would have to work out a new time frame that still had Jeffrey as the one who stabbed everyone to death and then set the house on fire but included the powerful new carbon monoxide expert evidence. While conceding the Crown case 'may not be as strong as was previously thought', Chief Judge McClellan held that, with some adjustments to the timing of events, a strong Crown case was still possible.

The two other judges, however, viewed the Crown case as already irreparably weakened and not sufficiently strong to justify a third trial.

The fact that Christopher was found not wearing his glasses and with no pants on was originally, and sensibly, thought to point to Christopher being roused from his sleep once Jeffrey had entered the house. But the powerful new carbon monoxide expert opinion evidence put the 'unusually attired' Christopher upstairs, as Jeffrey had always said. As one of the judges observed:

> [T]he Crown will be forced to concede not only that Christopher was upstairs when or after the fire was lit and that he remained there for two to four minutes, but to abandon the argument that he was unlikely to be the killer because he was unable to negotiate his way in the dark and without his spectacles.

This made the truth of what happened that night even more horrible, but criminal trials are there to deal with reality, which can be strange beyond belief.

There were other major weaknesses the two other judges could see.

'[T]he Crown will be forced to abandon the case that [Jeffrey] killed his parents and his brother and then set about siphoning petrol from the car only settling on mineral turpentine because the siphoning was unsuccessful,' one judge remarked, noting Dr Lawrence's evidence that, given their injuries, Jeffrey's parents would have died very quickly after being stabbed and the new carbon monoxide evidence, which held both would have died within minutes, if not seconds, after the fire had started to take hold:

> If the Crown were to continue to rely at any retrial upon the evidence of the cut hose and the smell of petrol on [Jeffrey's]

> breath … it seems to me that the case would need to be reformulated to contend that the attempt at siphoning the petrol was done before the killings and that the mineral turpentine was settled upon as an alternative when the siphoning was unsuccessful.

The other judge pointed out that:

> There is other new evidence which suggests, unequivocally, that [Jeffrey's mother] was sufficiently concerned about her relationship with Christopher to have told her workmates that it was necessary for her to leave work earlier than usual to return home and address the issue. This evidence provides corroboration of [Jeffrey's] expressed concerns about the behaviour of his brother to others in the period leading up to the murder of his parents. It was the Crown case that these concerns were fabricated by [Jeffrey] as part of his plan to divert attention from his involvement with the deaths. Such an allegation would now be difficult, if not impossible, to maintain.

Of course, given what the Court of Criminal Appeal had ruled on the similar stab wound expert evidence, which had also played a key role in Jeffrey's conviction, the similar stab wound evidence would not be available for the third trial. This was another strike against leaving the decision to the DPP.

Even the Crown had no real idea what a strong prosecution case in a third trial would look like. When asked during the appeal hearing, the Crown representative admitted this. 'It is very difficult to see that a satisfactory theory can be now developed,' wrote one of the judges.

After nearly two decades, the question of which brother murdered Jeffrey's parents still could not be answered beyond reasonable doubt. The agreed facts submitted to the sentencing judge in 1995, which remained Jeffrey's account of what happened, could not be disproved, even though it involved Christopher frantically stabbing both of his parents to death and setting fire to the house while not wearing his much-needed glasses or any pants. The appeal judgement set out the account given by Jeffrey:

> [Jeffrey] informed Police that he responded to a frantic intercom call from his mother after he was wakened from his dwelling, being a converted boatshed some 50–70 metres from the main house on the river line at the rear of the property. Upon entering the house [Jeffrey] allegedly saw his brother Christopher standing beside their mother, who was lying on the floor, whom [Jeffrey] presumed was deceased. As [Jeffrey] approached his brother he [Jeffrey] alleged his brother stated, words to the effect, 'I've killed Mum and Dad,' and with that saw a lit match in the brother's hand. As [Jeffrey] drew nearer, his brother placed that match onto their mother's body which ignited immediately. The fire then spread rapidly to the main bedroom where [Jeffrey] saw the presumed deceased of his father [sic] lying on the floor. With that, [Jeffrey] stated that he responded and grabbed a knife, which was allegedly on the floor near to where his brother was standing, picked it up and chased his brother down a spiral staircase to a downstairs room where he fatally stabbed his brother a number of times …

Whether or not to set Jeffrey free was a hard decision. Chief Judge McClellan was clear about his keenness to leave it for the new DPP:

> The gravity of the charges and the relatively short period of time served are powerful reasons for the Court to leave the decision to retry [Jeffrey] to the prosecutorial authorities,

> which are better placed to determine whether a further trial would be in the public interest …

Again, the two other judges completely disagreed. One of them pointed out that before Jeffrey was charged with the murder of his parents, he had been told three times he wouldn't be; first in September 1999 after the first inquest, then in July 2000 after the second inquest and then again the following year after I shut down his uncle Tony's attempt to have Jeffrey prosecuted.

'I regard it as onerous to require [Jeffrey] to wait in anticipation of a further determination by the [new DPP] as to whether he will be prosecuted a third time,' wrote one judge.

Having to make decisions that change people's lives forever without the comfort of knowing that one is 100 per cent correct is something trial judges (and, for that matter, prosecutors) face all the time. The appeal proved there was a real chance that Jeffrey was innocent. He had to be given the benefit of the doubt. Ultimately, in fairness to Jeffrey, the two other judges outvoted Chief Judge McClellan and set Jeffrey free for good that very day.

Outside the court with his wife by his side, Jeffrey made a brief statement to the media.

'This has been a horrendous experience for us,' he said before thanking his supporters. 'I am very happy to be going home a free man, and that's just all I want to do …'

His furious uncle Tony was there and had something to say.

'It's not over yet, Jeffrey.'

Exactly three weeks later, 60-year-old Tony died while staying at a friend's house. Poor Tony. He initially supported his nephew, but ultimately couldn't reconcile himself to Jeffrey's innocence, and essentially drove himself to death over it.

Chapter 13

A VICTORY OVER ANGER: KEN MARSLEW'S TRANSFORMATION

In June 2009, Ken Marslew stood outside a maximum-security jail with a TV crew from *60 Minutes*, one of the country's best-known TV presenters, Ray Martin, and a reporter from the *Daily Telegraph*.

It had been 15 years since the murder of his son Michael. When his son's killers faced court, the anger inside Ken had him calling for the death penalty. He even contemplated paying someone to kill at least one of them. Over the years, the anger remained. It had the power to blind him to almost everything else in his life. At times he didn't give enough attention to his other son, Michael's brother. The anger also took its toll on his health, and he suffered four heart attacks and other problems.

No one would criticise Ken for being angry. But people keep their distance from those consumed by anger. Ken didn't want to live like that, so every day he waged a war with the anger. The battle was never-ending because the anger never went away. It was important to keep busy. Ken's second wife learnt to accept his relentless drive to do as much as possible with Enough is Enough; it was part of his determination to create something positive with his life rather than just let anger take control.

As the years went by, Ken changed his mind about the death

penalty. After all, how could he be the head of an anti-violence organisation if he was calling for the state to be more violent? But no matter how much thought he put into questions of crime and punishment, no matter how many lectures he gave about the need to turn away from violence, the anger remained.

One of the changes Ken lobbied for was the ability for victims of crime and their families to be able to have conferences with the offenders while they were in jail. Ken was one to practise what he preached. Four and a half years after Michael's murder, Ken, Michael's mother, Michael's Pizza Hut co-workers and two of his close friends came face to face with two of Michael's killers: Karl, the ringleader, and Doug, the driver of the getaway car who had been sentenced to a minimum of five years and four months for the manslaughter of Michael. Doug's mother was also present. Vincent, the one who shot Michael dead, and Andrew, the one who sold the shotgun to Vincent and went with him into the Pizza Hut, decided not to face Michael's family, co-workers and close friends.

Michael's mother cried as she told the group how her life had ended with Michael's death. She dropped a bag containing his ashes in the middle of the circle in which everyone sat. Karl looked resentful as she asked him how much money he thought he and the others would get robbing a Pizza Hut. One of Michael's close friends told Karl she hoped he would never be happy again. Doug, clearly full of remorse, sat holding hands with his mother as she told Ken and Michael's mother how truly sorry she was. Both Ken and Michael's mother wholeheartedly told this grief-stricken woman that it wasn't her fault. They couldn't bring themselves to forgive Doug, but they hugged his mother. Once the group meeting had finished, Ken was self-possessed enough to not only walk alongside Karl, but to calmly ask him to hold the bag containing Michael's ashes while talking privately to him about joining his anti-violence crusade once he left prison.

Now that day had come, so Ken was here outside the prison to again ask Karl to join his fight against violence with the cameras rolling. It wasn't because Ken thought Karl had turned into a decent person while he was in jail. In fact, Karl had spent a lot of time in solitary – he had been convicted of assaulting a prison guard, and had also been denied parole, unlike his brother Andrew and the others who were genuinely sorry for what they had done.

Ken was aware of this and his fury towards Karl was as ferocious as ever. That very day, the anger inside him still told Ken to get a gun and blow Karl's head off as soon as he stepped outside the prison gates. It still told Ken that people would call him a hero if he killed the man who caused the murder of his son. The anger that constantly threatened to consume Ken every day would happily tempt Ken into becoming a murderer himself. Today was about Ken saying no to the anger. He would defy it by shaking the hand of a man he despised. Ken knew what the alternative was. He would be condemned to a life not worth living.

The *60 Minutes* team understood the reasons behind Ken's actions and used their expertise to explain it in a way that their huge audience could understand.

'In those minutes before [Karl] came out, what were you thinking?' asked Ray Martin.

'Oh Ray, all sorts of things. Am I doing the right thing, do I really want to be here?' Ken answered. 'Don't get the idea that this bloke is a mate, 'cause that's not what this is about. I haven't forgiven the guy. Let's see what the future brings. At this stage of the process, I have let go of the hate. End of story.'

People do not judge those who are crushed by the murder of a child or loved one, but some did judge Ken for doing things differently, and judged him harshly.

'Those that say that I'm twisted, that I'm doing the wrong thing, you know, comments like, "You've let your son down, you're a coward", "You mustn't have loved your son". How do you reckon that registers in here?' Ken asked. 'I listen to it and I say, "That's your journey, it's not my journey." I'm OK with what I do, Ray.'

No one else was outside the prison to meet Karl, not even his family. After Ken shook Karl's hand and all of them had sat down to watch Karl eat a steak for the first time in 15 years, Ray Martin expressed both admiration and doubt.

'As a father of a boy about the same age of Michael when he died, I don't think I could have done what you have done. I couldn't accept [Karl].'

'Look, how do you know?' replied Ken. 'Had you been where I've been, Ray, you might have a different view of the thing altogether. Maybe you wouldn't, maybe you don't agree with me, that's entirely up to you, you've got an opinion and so do I. I'm just hoping that I can show other dads that there is a better way than curling up in the corner and just literally dying inside. There is a better way to deal with this stuff.'

Ken's new message about his need to defy his anger in order to live wasn't as popular as his earlier messages about just being angry. His criticisms of the legal system struck a chord so long as they gave others permission to use it as a punching bag for their own frustrations. The media spotlight on Ken's work to give victims and their families a voice faded once those changes had been introduced. Politicians were still happy to know Ken, but fewer sought to associate with him publicly. Not because they didn't understand or respect Ken, but because Ken's message was no longer perceived as a vote winner. His message of self-reliance in the face of real adversity was not what people wanted to hear. Hard reality rarely is. It will always be more popular to pretend there are easy answers and to ignore, or even be angry with, those brave enough to say the truth.

Ken's understanding of the criminal justice process, and particularly the limitations created by necessary procedures in the courts, had grown. As it grew, his initial uncontrolled anger dissipated. Ken had modified his own response to his son's killing, and also towards others, including me. Ken and I became fellow members of the NSW Sentencing Council on its formation in 2003. I also became involved in programs explaining criminal justice to schoolchildren through Ken's organisation. He remains involved in matters concerning criminal justice through Enough is Enough and other organisations. Ken has broadened his interest to include programs against bullying amongst young people and supporting young Aborigines and has made himself a campaigner for improvements in personal relationships, particularly amongst younger people. We are still in contact.

Chapter 14

YOURS FAITHFULLY: FACING FORCED RETIREMENT

As Ken continued his inspiring battle with anger, I had another longstanding battle on my hands – fending off efforts by lawmakers to force me out of my position as the DPP and to make future prosecutors' jobs less secure.

When I was appointed the DPP in 1994 it was a job for life, so long as I was not declared insane, became bankrupt or committed a crime (among other things). Back in 2007 the state government had enacted new legislation that would get rid of the complete freedom from political interference that life tenure provided DPPs, prosecutors and other senior legal posts.

When state parliament was debating these changes, it was clear that not all politicians were happy. Faced with debate and opposition, Attorney General Hatzistergos showed that when it came to the government getting its way, pretty words he said from time to time about the importance of the integrity of the criminal justice system were apparently meaningless. He revealed that the state government had resorted to appointing new prosecutors on temporary 12-month contracts that could be terminated at any time for any reason by politicians. This was apparently to avoid appointing prosecutors for life until the law changed. He then revealed this had been going on for the previous two and a half years.

A member of parliament from an opposition party asked if the government intended to hold this gun to the head of the criminal justice system until the Bill limiting the tenure of DPPs, prosecutors, and other senior legal posts was made law.

'That is right,' answered Attorney General Hatzistergos.

The state government got the new law it wanted limiting the tenure of future DPPs, prosecutors and other senior legal positions.

This new legislation, together with earlier enactments, retained the anomaly (probably unintended by the lawmakers) I had identified earlier that applied only to me: if I did not retire as DPP before my sixty-fifth birthday, which was in March 2011, I would lose my entitlement to a pension – completely.

Over the months of May to August 2010, I wrote to the attorney general several times. My sixty-fifth birthday was over six months away. I figured (rather hopefully) that if this problem with my pension was merely an oversight, the attorney general would have time to fix it.

'I am writing to invite you to consider a small amendment to the *Director of Public Prosecutions Act 1986*,' I wrote to him in May 2010. 'I suggest that the [pension] provision that applies to me … is unfairly discriminatory and survives only by omission … I request that it now be amended to align my situation, so far as pension entitlement is concerned, with that of my successors …'

Attorney General Hatzistergos replied that he would seek further advice and respond when he could. A month passed with no further response.

I wrote again, repeating my concern about the legal loophole, adding, 'I also take this opportunity, in the context of various media reports, to note that I have not given notice of resignation / retirement to occur at any particular time.'

Attorney General Hatzistergos left it until about two days before my birthday to give a final answer, signing off 'yours faithfully'. It was clear he had quite deliberately strung the process along. The argument that he eventually put forward, almost at the death knell, was spurious:

> If the Act were to be further amended to retrospectively vary your pension entitlement as you have sought, it could give rise to significant claims from a range of other positions and groups (including statutory appointees, judicial officers and public servants), seeking similar improvements to their tenure, pension or superannuation entitlements.

The logic of that approach was puzzling. I was not seeking an 'improvement' to my entitlements, I was seeking their restoration to the position that applied before 2007 and at my appointment in 1994. Hatzistergos disputed my claim that the loophole applied to me alone. If he was correct, why could he not actually name others who would be able to claim improvements to their tenure/pension/superannuation if my request was granted? If Hatzistergos couldn't name the other legal appointments he vaguely referred to in his letter, then this claim was suspect. His rebuff was unreasonable.

This final letter from Attorney General Hatzistergos added insult to injury. Regardless, I had to accept the operation of the legislation as it stood since amendment had been refused. I had a choice, either to stay there literally for life, which my statutory position still enabled me to do, or to leave before my sixty-fifth birthday and draw a pension.

Attorney General Hatzistergos could have sought to fix the problem by a very small amendment to the legislation. It could have been done at any time, but it didn't come as a surprise that the attorney general was refusing to take that small step. His refusal was consistent with his general attitude towards me and my holding of the office of DPP. In my mind, he wanted to get rid of me and he wasn't going to make it any easier for me to stay.

My view that a powerful politician had deliberately used a technical loophole that he could easily have fixed to force a senior member of the criminal justice system out of their job for no proper reason didn't go unnoticed.

'Attorney-General John Hatzistergos has performed what we can only hope is his final act of bastardry before he is flung out of office,' wrote legal affairs writer Richard Ackland in the *Sydney Morning Herald*. 'As long as Hatzistergos had breath in his body he was going to see the end of the Director of Public Prosecutions, Nicholas Cowdery.'

Chapter 15

SEEING WHAT WE DON'T WANT TO SEE: THE KELI LANE TRIAL

In August 2010, the trial of Keli Lane for the murder of her infant, Tegan, was due to start. On 12 September 1996 Keli had given birth to a baby girl, Tegan, at Sydney's Auburn Hospital. Two days later, Keli furtively left the hospital with her newborn. Tegan was never seen again.

In 2004, given no body had ever been found, the Coroner's Court had to determine if the missing Tegan was dead. For years Keli had told lies to police about the day her infant daughter disappeared. A non-publication order made to protect Keli's privacy had to be lifted in order to appeal to the public for any information as to what happened to Tegan. The coroner found 'that Tegan is in fact deceased', though he noted that 'there is no case against a known person for the homicide of Tegan' and admitted that 'there is a possibility that Tegan … is alive'. With that, the matter had been referred to the Homicide Squad. 'In the meantime,' wrote the coroner, 'I am disturbed at the possibility that Tegan may have met with foul play.'

The day Keli's baby was last seen alive began with both mother and newborn in hospital. Staff had noted that Keli had had no visitors or calls of support during her stay. This was sad, but not unheard of.

Keli had expressed a desire to staff to leave the hospital that day. She had been brought various forms to fill out and health and identification checks for the baby were scheduled prior to her and baby Tegan's departure. However, at 2.00 p.m. hospital staff found Keli's bed and Tegan's bassinet empty. Keli had not said goodbye to any staff and no one saw her leave, and she had left with her baby before the final health and identification checks could be made. Of all the forms she was supposed to complete, only the Medicare form had been filled out and collected by the ward clerk. Keli had named her baby Tegan in that form. The rest of the paperwork, including a form to register Tegan's birth with Births, Deaths and Marriages and a form for a standard blood test, was no longer by Keli's bedside.

Two days later Keli called the hospital and told them to cancel the home visit by a midwife the hospital had planned as she and Tegan were under the care of another midwife. The enormous police investigation into Tegan's disappearance would reveal that was a lie. It was one of Keli's many, many lies about Tegan and her own actions and associations.

People tell lies, big and small, in all kinds of circumstances. Mostly it doesn't do much harm to anybody or give a lot of benefit to the liar. But it is unusual to encounter people who are inveterate and inconsistent liars about important matters affecting their lives and their futures. Through her court process Keli Lane has been shown to have told substantial and changeable lies about very significant matters relating to the death of her infant daughter Tegan and to other activities. Finding that degree of falsehood in one individual is very uncommon.

What was known about the day Tegan disappeared was that at around 3.00 p.m., 21-year-old Keli had walked into her parents' home, alone. Her mother, who had absolutely no idea that her daughter had given birth two days earlier or had even been pregnant, was there. Keli's then boyfriend, who also had absolutely no idea of Tegan's existence, soon joined them. He and Keli were due to go to a friend's wedding that afternoon. Keli changed into a white suit. Her mother drove her and her boyfriend to the wedding. Years later, as police investigated Tegan's disappearance, a video surfaced of Keli and her boyfriend taking their places just before the wedding ceremony began. Keli looked calm. After the wedding, Keli attended the reception, which was full of friends who had known her for many years, some since childhood. Nothing was said about her new daughter. Nobody knew she had been pregnant.

As her mother, her boyfriend and her many friends would tell police years later, Keli was behaving normally, as if nothing had happened. They only found out about Tegan years later when police contacted them out of the blue to ask them about a baby they had never known existed. The only child her family and friends knew about was the child Keli later gave birth to in 2001. She married the father of that child and was universally regarded as a good mother. But she had borne other children.

Tegan was one of three secret children Keli gave birth to during her time as an elite water polo player. Keli was often seen in nothing more than her swimmers during water polo training and matches. Indeed, police had worked out that she had given birth to her first secret child just hours after playing in a water polo final. Her then boyfriend's mother had watched her play. Keli was out celebrating afterwards with friends and teammates when she realised she was about to go into labour. She quietly slipped away from the celebrations, took herself to a nearby hospital and gave birth that evening.

That secret child, and Keli's third secret child, were lawfully put up for adoption. The reason why police and the Coroner's Court had become involved in Keli's private life was that her second secret child, Tegan, had disappeared in highly suspicious circumstances. Despite years of patient and discreet questioning, Keli steadfastly refused to tell the truth about how newborn Tegan vanished.

Bewildered friends and family had given their evidence to the coroner. It was clear that it wasn't physically obvious when Keli was pregnant, even in the later stages of pregnancy (although some teammates had suspicions). Her mother spoke of Keli typically wearing tracksuits and other loose-fitting clothing during those years.

In the years following Tegan's disappearance, Keli had given many different accounts of what had happened the day her secret baby disappeared. Once the police became involved, she told them versions that were different again. Police were quite sure that the story Keli was sticking to at the time of the coronial hearing, that just outside the hospital she had given Tegan to a man she said was the child's father, whom she named as Andrew Norris or Morris, was another lie.

The massive, decade-long police search for the missing secret baby found no trace of Tegan after Keli left the hospital with her. The only records of Tegan that existed were the record of her birth created by Auburn Hospital's administration and the Medicare form the ward clerk insisted Keli fill out. Tegan's Medicare account had never been used.

The enormous police search for the missing child, the scale of which would be described in the trial and outlined by the Court of Criminal Appeal, was continued in earnest during those years. After carefully combing through Keli's life to see if there was any reason to suspect that her startling secretive behaviour and the disappearance of her infant were due to her having suffered abuse or mental illness, the Homicide Squad came to the conclusion that there were no such excuses.

In New South Wales, where Keli's trial was held, the law considers a newborn to be a legal person once the baby has been born whole and taken its first breath. After that first breath, the homicide laws apply. Tegan had taken her first breath two days before the Crown alleged, and the jury ultimately agreed, Keli murdered her.

Broadly speaking, murder is committed when the death of a person is caused with an intent to kill or to cause grievous bodily harm or with reckless indifference to human life. Manslaughter is committed where there is evidence that unlawfully causing the death fell short of murder (for example, there was gross negligence or death was caused by an unlawful and dangerous act, without the state of mind required for murder). A death that results from a genuine accident, without fault, is neither murder nor manslaughter.

The law also provides a third charge of unlawful death that applies especially to mothers and babies. If a person under 12 months of age is intentionally killed by their mother, the offence of infanticide may apply. Infanticide recognises genuine mental health issues, such as post-natal depression, as a reason why some mothers kill their babies, and provides a way for such offences not to be regarded as the murder or manslaughter of a baby.

One of the first tasks facing Keli Lane's trial judge, Supreme Court Justice Whealy, was empanelling the jury. Given the intensely personal evidence about the sex life of a young woman and her choices as a mother that the trial would put in front of the jury, its composition was extremely important. As his Honour would explain to the prospective jurors, not only was Keli's history of secret pregnancies and adoptions going to be part of her trial, so too would the fact that she also had two perfectly legal abortions.

The police investigation had revealed that Keli had two abortions as a teenager, followed by her first secret child, whom Keli put up for legal adoption, followed by her second secret child, Tegan, followed by another pregnancy Keli tried unsuccessfully to have legally aborted (the pregnancy was too advanced so the doctors refused), which ultimately resulted in the birth of her third secret child who Keli also put up for adoption.

Justice Whealy invited those wishing to be excused because they held strong anti-abortion views, or strong views against premarital sex or negative views about mothers who put children up for adoption, to raise their hands. A number of people put their hands up.

This was not an attempt to make people whose religious or moral views differed from the law feel bad, or to put their views on trial. His Honour was making sure that Keli was not considered a murderer by any jury member because she had had extra-marital sex, legal abortions or had put up children for adoption. Knowing this, a number of people moved to where they could wait for their turn to quietly explain to the trial judge their reasons why they could not serve on this jury.

One of the other challenges Justice Whealy had to deal with was the media. On the very first day the jury took their seats in the courtroom, problems with the media began. Keli's trial lawyer reported that photographers and other media had jostled and intimidated Keli and members of her legal team as they entered and left the courthouse. (Such conduct had been the subject of comments the coroner had had to make at the inquest.)

Perhaps surprisingly, the judge did not have as much criminal trial experience as some of his colleagues. Three days into the trial, while dealing with an application from media outlets about what names could be reported, his Honour ended up asking a media outlet's lawyer what could be done about the jostling. The answer was that not very much could be done. Keli and her family had to make their way through the cameras outside the courthouse to the sanctuary within, where the cameras and approaches by journalists were not allowed.

The trial was a long one, running over four months. Keli chose not to give evidence (exercising her right to silence), and had also decided against a clinical psychiatric examination, something the state's chief coroner had suggested. She did not put any suggestion or expert evidence of post-natal depression or any other mental illness before the jury. She maintained what she had told police at different times, namely that she had given her missing child to either 'the Perth couple' or 'Andrew Morris/Norris'.

The police had wanted to know if there was any reason to think incest or any other type of sexual abuse was the explanation for Keli's string of secret pregnancies and children. They had taken blood samples from a large number of men. Through these blood tests the police learnt that the fathers of Keli's first and third secret children were two young men who were simply her boyfriends at the relevant time. Keli's many friends knew about these relationships. In their tight-knit community, private lives were common knowledge. These two young men first learnt about their secret children after the coronial inquest into Tegan's disappearance. Their shock was on full display when they gave evidence at Keli's trial.

It was clear that the police investigation into Keli's private life had revealed a fairly unremarkable history of sexual partners. The normality of her sex life, even after police had gone through it with a fine-tooth comb, made Keli's history of secret babies even more incomprehensible.

What was clear, however, was the extraordinary lengths Keli went to in order to keep her secrets. As the trial would reveal in dizzying detail, Keli was a very accomplished liar. She lied in order to keep her secrets for years on end, often in very serious and stressful situations.

It had taken three years for any questions to be raised about Tegan's whereabouts. These questions were raised as Keli was arranging the adoption of her third secret baby. The adoption worker, who was a kind and non-judgmental person, had been dealing with Keli for several months. The reason the adoption worker had been dealing with her for so long was that Keli was deliberately making herself scarce. She had given the adoption worker lots of false information, including false addresses and phone numbers, was rarely answering messages and sometimes failing to show up to pre-arranged meetings.

One of the lies the adoption worker had uncovered was Keli's claim that this child was the first one she had given birth to. Some routine investigations had revealed that Keli had previously placed a child up for adoption. That was her first secret child. Keli's lying about very serious matters and lack of contrition when found out led to the adoption worker having Keli's mental fitness to consent to adoption verified. Keli was found not to be psychologically impaired and able to make decisions about the adoption of her baby.

During the process of putting Keli's third secret child up for adoption, the infant was in foster care. Difficulties in getting in touch with Keli had meant the infant's stay in foster care was so long that the original foster care agreement was about to expire. By this stage, the adoption worker could not contact Keli to extend it. Child protection officer John Borovnik was assigned as the infant's caseworker and given the task of obtaining a care order.

In the course of his investigations, John, who the chief coroner had described as 'alert', obtained Keli's medical records from the hospital where she had given birth to her third child. This routine investigation led to the discovery of Tegan's existence.

The third child was born in Ryde Hospital, a different hospital from where Tegan was born. However, the hospital where this child was born also had records of Keli being pregnant in 1996. The police investigation would later reveal that in 1996 Keli, heavily pregnant with Tegan, had gone to Ryde Hospital and asked four times to have the birth of her baby induced. The doctors refused her requests. Keli then took her request to Auburn Hospital. By this stage, her pregnancy with Tegan had just become full term. Doctors at Auburn Hospital agreed to do what Keli wanted and induced the birth of Tegan on 12 September 1996.

When Keli returned to Ryde Hospital in 1999 and was asked about the child born in 1996, namely Tegan, Keli lied to hospital staff. She told them that she had breastfeed Tegan for six months and that Tegan was well.

In the course of securing a new care arrangement for Keli's third secret child, child protection officer John contacted her and asked if she had given birth at Auburn Hospital in 1996. Keli said that she had not. When he asked about her first secret child, Keli admitted she had given birth to that child. John again asked Keli if she were sure that she had not given birth in 1996, and she assured him that she was sure. She also denied having attended the relevant hospital in 1996 while pregnant. Instead, she told John that she was not pregnant at that time.

By this stage Keli had also admitted to the adoption worker that she had given birth to two children, but had claimed she had no other children. Keli was denying Tegan's existence to both John and the adoption worker. John told Keli that he would have to contact police.

Details as to why it took so long for a thorough police investigation to begin were also put before the jury. When John contacted police, the matter was quickly sent to Manly police station, that being the station closest to where Keli had lived all her life.

Keli's father was a retired police officer who had spent many years based at the Manly police station. The police John initially contacted in the Blue Mountains had no way of knowing this. Once the case arrived at Manly police station, senior management handled the situation very poorly. Instead of flagging the obvious conflict of interest, Keli's case was dumped into the hands of a talented young detective in the station. Beyond this, as the state's chief coroner had observed, senior management at Manly police station had no input into the case and did not take any meaningful responsibility for ensuring that there was a timely and efficient investigation into it. To make matters worse, the young detective had once served under Keli's father's direct supervision. Realising it was wrong for him to be in charge of the investigation into the disappearance of his old boss's daughter's baby, the young detective repeatedly asked to be taken off the case. His requests fell on deaf ears. In the meantime, the young detective made some inquiries. He located Keli's boyfriend at the time of Tegan's birth, who was living overseas by this time, and arranged for him to be interviewed. He also interviewed Keli in February 2001.

Once police were aware of Tegan's highly suspicious disappearance, Keli proceeded to persistently lie to them for years. The effect, as described by senior crown prosecutor Tedeschi at the trial and by the Court of Criminal Appeal, was to send police on a wild goose chase. Ultimately, the jury agreed that Keli had made police search for a man who did not exist and a baby that she knew was dead.

During the young detective's first interview in February 2001, Keli claimed Tegan was conceived during a brief affair with a man named 'Andrew Norris' who had a partner named 'Mel', both of whom visited Keli twice when she was at Auburn Hospital, and that she handed Tegan to Andrew Norris on the day she left Auburn Hospital and saw Tegan three or four months later. During this interview, Keli revealed that Tegan's name was on her Medicare card. When the young detective asked her why, Keli claimed it was because the Medicare form was amongst the paperwork she was given to fill out and in case Tegan was with her at some time in the future and needed to be taken to a doctor.

In October 2002, having just joined Manly station, which by this time was under new and improved management, Detective Gaut took over the investigation. The search for Tegan began in earnest.

When Detective Gaut spoke to Keli for the first time, he noticed she changed two key details of her story. She was now claiming the man she gave Tegan to was named 'Andrew Morris' and that she had caught a taxi home after handing her baby over in the grounds of Auburn Hospital. A subsequent police search of the records of all taxi services revealed that not a single taxi had picked up any passengers from Auburn Hospital on 14 September 1996.

Another example of the wild goose chase Keli deliberately sent police on was the address she eventually gave for the man she claimed she had given her missing baby to. After being interviewed by Detective Gaut, Keli agreed to accompany detectives to the suburb of Balmain in an attempt to locate the apartment block in which she had said Andrew Morris/Norris lived. After driving around the suburb for some time, Keli identified an apartment block as possibly being where she supposedly had conducted her affair with Tegan's father. They entered the block and, from the outside, Keli identified the apartment she said she believed to have been occupied by this man.

The police investigation revealed this was just another of Keli's lies. The real estate agency that managed the apartment block had no record of any unit being occupied by anyone named Morris or Norris around the time Tegan was conceived. None of the actual occupants realistically could have been the man Keli claimed to have had the affair with.

Two of the actual occupants of the address at the time Keli had claimed to have had the affair were brothers. One brother told police that he had never gone by the name Andrew Morris/Norris, that he didn't know anyone by that name and that he had never received any mail addressed to that name. The other brother, Peter, told police he did know someone named Andrew Norris but he was of Asian appearance, that he had not seen him since 1990 and he had not been to their unit. Keli's description of Andrew Morris/Norris was of a tanned, blond male, so this wasn't the man police were looking for.

Peter turned out to be an unreliable witness. Having originally told police he knew nothing that supported Keli's claims, Peter later started to claim he did remember things that would support them.

When Peter gave evidence at the coronial inquest into Tegan's death he did not give evidence of seeing any mail addressed to Andrew Morris/Norris. However, in August 2008, after a highly publicised police sniffer dog search under Keli's ex-boyfriend's house, Peter started to change his story. He provided the police with a second statement in which he said that some time after his first statement he recalled having seen the name Andrew Norris on an envelope in the letterbox at the relevant address in about 1995 or 1996.

Peter's explanation for changing his story was unconvincing. He said he had not mentioned it at the coronial inquest because he thought he might have been mistaken once he heard the real estate agent give evidence that there was no one by that name living in the block. Peter also said he wanted to avoid placing undue pressure on Keli's family or saying something that would deceive the coroner. Then, just a few months before Keli's trial began, Peter provided a third statement to police in which he said he had seen mail addressed to both Andrew Morris and Andrew Norris at different times.

During the trial the prosecutor wished to cross-examine him, essentially to reveal to the jury that Peter's final statement, which obviously supported Keli's version of events, was unreliable. Against the wishes of Keli's trial lawyer, Justice Whealy allowed the Crown to do that because he was satisfied that Peter had made a prior inconsistent statement. Ultimately, the verdict showed the jury thought Peter was, for whatever reason, making up his claims about seeing mail addressed to Andrew Morris/Norris.

Just about every person Keli had spoken to about Tegan gave evidence that exposed what she had said as a lie. However, there was one person keen to be part of whatever Keli wanted to pretend was true. This person, Natalie, had known Keli all her life and considered her a close friend. Police had interviewed Natalie about what she might know about Tegan. Keli had called Natalie less than an hour after Natalie had finished her interview with police. This conversation was tapped by police. Keli asked Natalie if she had told police she might have once met Andrew Morris/Norris. Natalie told her she had, but that she also told police her recollection was hazy. In fact, Natalie had told police she never met such a person.

In a signed statement to police, Natalie claimed that during or around 2007, Keli had spoken to her about having handed Tegan to her natural father, Andrew Morris, and his girlfriend. Before the jury trial began, Natalie told the court in a voir dire hearing that she recalled Keli talking about a man named Andrew during or around 1995, which was the time Keli was having secret pregnancies. Natalie claimed Keli told her that she had met this Andrew in the suburb of Balmain and indicated she had slept with him.

However, during the voir dire hearing Natalie backpeddled from confirming that Keli had used the name Andrew Morris in the 2007 conversation, despite her signed statement to police. She admitted to reading a book about Keli's case in 2008, the year she had made her statement to police, and many media reports during the coronial inquest that referred to the name Andrew Morris/ Norris, the significance of that name and that police were trying to track him down. She also admitted to telling Keli that police had asked to speak to her about Tegan's disappearance before she was interviewed by them.

The view of Keli's lawyer was that Natalie's evidence was so unreliable it might do Keli more harm than good if Natalie was put in front of the jury and cross-examined. Justice Whealy agreed and Natalie was not asked to appear before the jury.

Natalie and Peter were not hardened criminals. They were misguided people who perhaps thought they could help Keli by telling lies – or they had become convinced by Keli's lies. Identifying and dealing with unreliable witnesses is one of the many challenges trials pose.

As his comments after the trial would show, Justice Whealy was very upset about the prospect of Keli being convicted of murder. If he had let his heart, rather than his head, direct his decisions about these two unreliable witnesses, he may have tried to find a way to allow the wishful thinking of Peter and Natalie to be put in front of the jury without allowing the prosecutor to expose it for the unreliable evidence it was. As a senior lawyer and judge, his Honour knew such an approach would be wrong, no matter what his emotions about this case were. Justice Whealy's intellectual rigour directed his decisions concerning both unreliable witnesses.

The results of the huge, more than decade-long police search for Tegan and the man to whom Keli insisted she had given her baby were placed in front of the jury. The size of the wild goose chase was immense.

The police began their epic search by trying to find whether Tegan was alive and to identify Andrew Morris/Norris. The searches for Andrew Morris/Norris included:

1 electoral rolls for persons of those names living in the Balmain/Rozelle area in 1996;
2 University of Sydney records for persons of those names enrolled in the last 20 years with birth dates between 1960 and 1970 (Keli had told police she thought Andrew Morris/Norris had studied there);
3 records of the New South Wales Water Polo Association, and various water polo clubs;
4 Roads and Traffic Authority (RTA) records;
5 Centrelink records;
6 Australia Post records;
7 Department of Fair Trading records regarding the lodgement of rental bonds;
8 police records concerning reports of missing persons by those names;
9 Registry of Births, Deaths and Marriages records for persons of those names born between 1960 and 1976. (Keli had told police Andrew Morris/Norris was about 36 years old at the time she had conceived Tegan with him.)

None of these searches yielded any person who could have been the Andrew Morris/Norris of whom Keli had spoken.

When the matter was handed back to the Unsolved Homicide Squad by the coroner, some of the searches done by Detective Gaut were duplicated. The police again searched RTA, NSW Births, Deaths and Marriages, telephone records and records of electricity providers in the Balmain/Rozelle area for the man to whom Keli claimed to have given her missing baby.

The police also undertook nationwide searches of electoral rolls and the records of the Australian Taxation Office, the police and the Department of Immigration.

Having searched nationwide, 41 men by the name of Andrew Morris in Australia with birth dates between 1960 and 1976 were identified. Statements were taken from each of those who could be contacted. Those searches produced no Andrew Morris/Norris who could have been the father of Tegan.

One Andrew Morris of a relevant age was found. He had sex once with Keli on Narrabeen Beach. But it was about 18 months before Tegan was conceived. He was not called in the trial.

There were also searches for 'Mel', the woman Keli claimed was the partner of Andrew Morris/Norris. On a direction from the coroner, in July 2005 Detective Gaut had searches undertaken of Births, Deaths and Marriages Registry records throughout Australia for women named 'Mel' or variations thereof – Melanie, Melissa, Melinda – registered as the parent of a female child born in September 1996. This search yielded no 'Mel' as described by Keli or any child who could have been Tegan.

Then there were the searches for Tegan, which meant a search for any child in Australia or who had left Australia who could be Keli's missing baby. This search began with Births, Deaths and Marriages records, covering children born between 31 March 1996 and 30 September 1997. More than 12 000 births were investigated.

No child who could have been Tegan was identified.

Searches were undertaken of New South Wales and interstate Births, Deaths and Marriages registries for a female child whose father's name was given as Andrew Morris. Those searches yielded no results.

Searches were undertaken of foundlings and adoptions, again with no results.

Requests were issued to heads of all authorities responsible for government, Catholic, independent, and home schooling in each state and territory for any female child born on 12 September 1996 with a father named Andrew Morris or Andrew Norris. Nothing was forthcoming.

The Unsolved Homicide Division of the NSW Police Service (who took over the investigation in September 2006) identified more than 1000 children for more detailed investigation as possibly being Tegan under a different name. All were excluded. (A review of Detective Gaut's investigation was undertaken in mid-2007, and many of the inquiries he had made were repeated with similar results.)

In 2008 a more expansive school search was undertaken. No child who could have been Tegan was identified.

Department of Immigration records were searched for passport applications for female children aged under 12 months between 14 September 1996 and 31 December 1996. The search produced no passport application for a child who could have been Tegan.

In all, more than 86000 births in New South Wales between 31 March 1996 and 30 September 1997 were cross-checked against hospital records. No child who could have been Tegan was discovered.

In 2004 and 2005 the police strategy included the use of media to attract attention to the investigation (this was after the coroner lifted the non-publication order). The express purpose was to elicit information from the public. All information provided was followed up. No person who could have been Andrew Morris/Norris was discovered. No child who could have been Tegan was discovered.

The result of this enormous search was to establish that, aside from the few details Keli had recorded on the Medicare form and hospital records of the birth, no record of Tegan existed. The tiny paper trail of her life ended the day Keli left the hospital with her. After that day, there were no health records (the Medicare account had never been used by Keli or anyone else), no belated registration of a birth (other than that registered by order of the coroner during the coronial hearing), no school records – nothing.

In addition to the charge of murder, Keli faced three criminal charges relating to making deliberately false statements in court documents. These court documents were part of the processes of putting her first and third secret children up for adoption. Keli had deliberately included multiple lies in all of them.

The Crown argued these weren't minor offences. The lies had prevented the actual fathers of these children having the opportunity of challenging the adoptions or taking custody of the children themselves or having contact with them. Because of this, the prosecutor submitted these offences were in the worst category of their kind.

Justice Whealy took a different view. At the beginning of the trial, Keli faced three perjury charges. Perjury was punishable by up to ten years in prison. During the trial, these three offences were downgraded from perjury to false swearing. False swearing was punishable by up to five years in prison. His Honour agreed with the Crown that the effect of Keli's deliberate lies was to deny any contact between the children and their natural fathers, but he didn't think that was so serious.

'I would regard these actions by the offender as falling into a relatively low category for offences of this kind,' his Honour would comment when handing down Keli's sentences.

Keli was most certainly a liar, but being proved a liar doesn't in itself prove someone is a murderer. There were, however, three lies told by Keli that were used during her trial to help prove she murdered Tegan. Those three lies were her claim that Tegan was living with a couple in Perth, that she had given Tegan to a man named Andrew Norris, then her subsequent claim that she had given Tegan to a man named Andrew Morris.

Many of the other lies Keli had told about Tegan could reasonably be explained as her wanting to make sure her family and friends never found out about her secret babies. Indeed, it was the Crown's submission that Keli's motive for keeping her pregnancies and babies secret was, at least in part, an overwhelming fear of rejection if her friends and family found out. Another reasonable explanation was that she thought lying would somehow make the process of the adoption of her third baby faster. If such an explanation could reasonably exist, then it could not be said the only reason Keli lied was to hide the fact she had murdered Tegan.

However, the lies about Tegan living with a couple in Perth or having been given to a man named Andrew Morris/Norris were made once the authorities knew about her three secret babies. When she told child protection officer John that Tegan was with a couple in Perth, Keli knew John was intending to report the matter to police. When she claimed to the first detective that she gave Tegan to a man named Andrew Norris, then claimed to Detective Gaut that she gave Tegan to a man named Andrew Morris, the adoption of her third secret child had long been finalised. She persisted in telling the Andrew Morris/Norris lies once all her family and friends knew about the existence of Tegan and her other secret babies, the police having told everyone in Keli's life about them in their search for Tegan.

Near the end of the trial, Keli's lawyer had cause for yet another serious complaint about the behaviour of some press photographers. They were hounding Keli's child born in 2001. Justice Whealy discovered that there was nothing much he could do about that unless an offence was committed.

Years before her trial, Keli had decided to exercise her right to silence in the face of growing police suspicion, then throughout the coronial proceedings and the trial. This had left the police to choose between searching for a baby that had disappeared without a trace or sweeping the disappearance of that child under the carpet as if she had never existed. The police had no choice but to search for Tegan.

Keli's trial lawyer didn't call any witnesses. There was no real argument over the facts. Rather, the argument was over what the jury should make of them.

In his closing address to the jury, prosecutor Tedeschi said:

> The Crown submits to you that there is only one reason why Keli sent police on these wild goose chases for so many years looking for Tegan in a household with a non-existent man called Andrew Morris/Norris and his non-existent partner Mel and that is because she knew that Tegan was dead and would never be found. She knew that because she had murdered Tegan. She had no choice but to pretend that she was assisting the police with their enquiries.

The Crown suggested that part of Keli's motivation for going to such extremes to not have the responsibility of raising children was her ambition to play water polo at the very highest level of competition. Her years of secret pregnancies were the years she tried unsuccessfully to be selected to play for the senior national team.

The defence put forward a very different view of the facts:

> Point number one is that we do not even know that Tegan is dead.

> Point number two is if Tegan is dead, we don't know how she died. There's no scientific evidence at all. There's nothing. Nobody can tell us anything, not one word in this case … if Tegan is dead … we don't know who caused the death … It could have been an accident and people do terrible things to cover things up … we don't know that it was the deliberate act of Keli … that caused Tegan's death …

Most people would shudder at the thought of a police investigation into their sexual history, particularly in their teens and early twenties, and the results being examined in detail in open court.

The reason Keli's private life was examined at trial was to illustrate her tendency to allow herself to become pregnant but to go to extraordinary lengths to avoid the responsibility of child-rearing and to keep her pregnancies and children secret.

There was no suggestion that Keli's two legal terminations were in themselves proof she was a murderer. Rather, they were part of the tendency evidence that she, despite allowing herself to fall pregnant and give birth so many times, had no intention of caring for a baby at that time in her life. The Crown told the jury that Keli's tendency in pregnancies and births prior and subsequent to Tegan was to dispose of them permanently via abortion or adoption.

'So here is a mother that has no plans to take her baby Tegan home, that makes no arrangements to have her baby legally adopted and who is in a desperate hurry to leave the hospital,' the prosecutor told the jury during the Crown's closing address.

> The Crown case is that she had had such a torrid time adopting out [first secret child] the year before and she had come so close to being found out and the whole thing just exploding in her face, she was determined not to put herself through the same traumatic process that she'd undergone with

> [first secret child]. In any event, on 14 September she was in such a rush to get out of the hospital and to get home in time for the wedding that she didn't have any time to even take the initial steps for placing Tegan into care, having foster parent arrangements signed, let alone making arrangements for an adoption and being interviewed by an adoption agency worker. She didn't have time to do those things if she was going to make the … wedding at 4 p.m. on the 14th.

Keli's trial lawyer had a very different view of her tendencies when it came to her secret pregnancies. Overall, the defence told the jury Keli's tendencies were not to murder or engage in other criminal conduct, but to adopt lawful means of ensuring that she was not responsible for her secret children.

> At 19 years of age she found out how children are adopted [with her first secret child] and what is the suggestion? It was such a pain in the neck? Is this really the suggestion? It [was] such a pain in the neck that she murdered [the next] baby? Is that it? … That she murdered Tegan and it was so dreadful, Keli is so stupid that she doesn't know what is involved with a murder of your own child, that she went ahead and did it and to her shock found out it was dreadful, so she reverted back to adoption [for her third secret child].
>
> Keli wasn't driven back to adoption, we submit, by the horror of the act of murder … Sure she goes off the radar every now and then, sure she doesn't ring people back when she's supposed to ring them back and so on … She knew all about the adoption process. She knew that it would be difficult in some ways but we submit the end result of two adoptions [of her first and third secret children] was she never, never tried to pull the plug … on either of [those lawful, permanent solutions].

The Crown and the defence also had very different explanations for Keli's four attempts to have Tegan's birth induced, having been finally induced on her fifth attempt when medical professionals found her pregnancy to be, or at least be on the cusp of, full term at around 38 to 40 weeks. The Crown explained them as Keli wanting to avoid the risk of going into labour at around the time she was due to go to a friend's wedding, submitting to the jury:

> [in relation to the birth of her first secret child] She'd suddenly gone into labour whilst she was at the pub … It could easily have happened when she was in the water, in the [water polo] championship, in the finals of the competition…
>
> So clearly what she knew by the time she had Tegan was that you can't predict when you're going to go into labour. The very last thing that she wanted was to go into labour at an inopportune time: while she's playing water polo, while she's at college or, even worse, while she's at the … wedding [she was due to attend]. So, ladies and gentlemen, here she is having been told on 2 September that she was 39 weeks pregnant … [On Wednesday, 11 September after her fourth attempt to have Tegan's birth induced] she must have gone almost straight to the Auburn Hospital from the [other] hospital. What does she tell them at the Auburn Hospital? She tells them that her estimated due date was back on 30 August, so that she was now two weeks overdue.
>
> Why on earth would a woman, having been to hospital now five times, tell this hospital, the Auburn Hospital, that she's two weeks overdue? She wanted them to induce her. Why? Because it was convenient to have the baby then and there, that she wanted to avoid having an unexpected sudden labour at a time that was inconvenient to her and especially during the wedding, [or] just before the wedding at a time

> when it was going to be much more difficult for her to hide the fact that she was giving birth to a baby in secret. She must have had a very cogent reason to go shopping for hospitals like this.

The defence argued Keli couldn't have tricked any of the doctors to induce Tegan's birth unnecessarily or prematurely even if that was her plan.

The closing addresses complete, the jury retired to consider its verdict. A week later it became clear that, while all the jury members could agree that Keli was guilty of the false swearing charges, only 11 of the 12 could agree as to whether Keli was guilty of murder. To those in the courtroom, it was obvious that 11 members of the jury thought Keli was guilty while one member of the jury had a reasonable doubt that she had murdered Tegan. If the usual requirement for the jury to be unanimous in its verdict remained, Keli may not have been convicted of Tegan's murder. However, his Honour had the option of allowing a majority verdict, meaning 11 out of 12, rather than the usual requirement of a unanimous 12 out of 12.

Justice Whealy allowed a majority verdict. Keli was found guilty of murder and of the other charges.

Despite his limited experience of criminal trials and the epic emotional challenges they pose, despite his personal views of Keli's liability, Justice Whealy's intellectual rigor prevailed and the law was applied. But a few years later, his Honour's lack of experience in controlling his emotional responses would create all sorts of problems.

Chapter 16

SENTENCING A CHILD MURDERER: KELI LANE'S SENTENCING

It requires very strong self-discipline to put aside any emotional engagement with the subject matter of a criminal case, particularly cases where children might be involved, where the deaths or appalling treatment of individuals might be involved. For all criminal lawyers it is a professional task that has to be performed. It is something, I think, that has to be developed and practised – it is an ability to be acquired. Certainly by the time somebody becomes a Supreme Court judge dealing with criminal matters, that discipline should be in place. If they are not able to keep that separation between professional and personal engagement I think they should give serious consideration to removing themselves from any particular case where there is a risk.

Justice Whealy was struggling. Intellectually he knew that Keli Lane had been convicted of murdering her newborn, Tegan, but emotionally he couldn't really accept her guilt.

Seeing this, prosecutor Tedeschi decided to submit some forensic psychiatric reports to help his Honour understand Keli's personality. They had been written by a highly qualified and experienced psychiatrist named Dr Diamond, who had relied on the tapes of Keli's police interviews and other evidence gathered by police.

Dr Diamond's forensic psychiatric reports had not been part of the trial, so they had not been put in front of the jury. They were, however, relevant to sentencing. Justice Whealy wanted to discuss whether he should give copies of Dr Diamond's expert opinions about Keli to the media.

The prosecutor had no strong objections to this, but Keli's lawyer was wary. He could see that Dr Diamond's reports showed his client in two lights. There was her loving side; Keli did love her family and friends and they loved her back. The public support they had shown her for years after they became aware of her history of secret pregnancies and the police investigation confirmed this.

Then there was the side that was very difficult to understand. As Dr Diamond would later say in a brief television interview, it showed that Keli was callous and dishonest to a level that normal people would find hard to comprehend. It was a light that showed signs of a serious personality disorder. In Dr Diamond's opinion, Keli knew right from wrong and she was able to control her behaviour.

Keli's lawyer had to contend with Dr Diamond being put on the stand and being given the opportunity to answer questions about his reports. He also had to contend with a judge who thought that Keli having a personality disorder was something that was in her favour. It would become increasingly clear that his Honour was having difficulty in seeing the difference between mental illness and a personality disorder.

At the request of Keli's lawyer, the sentencing hearing was adjourned for a week to give the defence team time to produce their own psychiatric report to counter those parts of Dr Diamond's reports that supported the notion that Keli was capable of murder. Despite these efforts, Keli still refused to be clinically assessed, so there was no psychiatrist's report to put before the court when the sentencing hearing resumed. However, her lawyer did have Keli's general practitioner.

Keli's GP had spoken to her at her parents' home in November 2004. By this stage, everyone in Keli's life knew about her secret history; police had asked the most important people in her life about her missing baby, the coronial inquest had become a huge media story, she had lawyers and had decided to no longer speak to police. The last time she had done so was 11 months earlier when, during an electronically recorded interview, Detective Gaut asked Keli if she had killed her baby.

Keli had been a patient of this GP for about three years. He wasn't a highly experienced psychiatrist like Dr Diamond, but he was a qualified counsellor. Keli usually saw her GP with her child born in 2001.

'I was called round by the parents because Keli was in a distraught state,' the GP told the court, describing the November 2004 consultation.

> [I]t was all news to me at that stage. I didn't know anything about any court cases ... So I went around to the house just to try and, you know, with no idea what was going on. And Keli was there. She was very distraught and upset and hesitant, kind of looking outside.

The GP recalled that Keli's mother might have been with her at the beginning of her consultation, but she then went out to the back room and left the GP and Keli in private as they sat on the lounge. He said:

> She told me that there were journalists that were hovering around her and giving her a hard time. [S]he told me that a police investigation team had ... given her a hard time and there was this [trial] that might be coming up.
>
> [S]he explained to me ... that she'd been, you know, a young kid that had been good at sport and brought up in a competitive family, in a competitive community. She'd become

> very good at her swimming and this water polo and that everyone was expecting a lot of her and she got caught up in the whole expectation of the whole thing, but deep inside she was not happy and she was wanting something else and she ended up getting pregnant …

'Did she say why she'd got pregnant?' asked the prosecutor. The GP replied:

> No, not that I remember … the whole thing was kind of coming out in a bit of a barrage and I was just sitting there … listening to it … just this story of how it all happened and how Keli had these pregnancies and then felt really bad about a termination and that she said she never wanted to do that again. And so this other occasion she got pregnant, she decided to adopt the baby out. And then obviously there was this second baby that she then told me that she'd given away and the third baby that had been adopted out as well, and that what was happening was that the police didn't believe her, that she'd given this second baby away.

Keli's lawyer wanted to stop further questions from the prosecutor about the pressure Keli felt under during the time of her secret pregnancies and babies. His Honour disallowed this request and agreed with the prosecutor that such an explanation from Keli's own mouth was relevant to determining her chances of rehabilitation, of one day feeling genuine remorse, and other important issues that would determine the sentence the judge would set. The GP recalled:

> It wasn't so much her mum or dad or anyone specifically was pressuring her. It was just that she kind of felt it as a whole big pressure of society or something for her to live up to and that,

> 'what about her' type of thing … she didn't specifically say she deliberately went out to get pregnant.
>
> To me it's like these young kids that they might be top scholars or something and suddenly they commit suicide and people say why and no one really knew. These people should have communicated what they were feeling, but they don't. She didn't do that. But what her behaviours were, with getting pregnant all the time, was another kind of dysfunctional way of managing the situation.

If the courtroom had a jury in it to decide if Keli was guilty of murder, this opinion would not have been allowed in evidence because Keli's GP was not an expert in psychology or psychiatry. However, the jury had done their job. This was a sentencing hearing where the judge had a lot more freedom to inform himself about what sentence the offender should receive. Evidence generally about Keli's state of mind, conduct and communications at various times could be relevant to that task.

Keli's GP also gave the court another opinion, answering a question from the defence about what he observed about her relationship with her child born in 2001: '[Keli was a] very good mother … [S]he struck me as just being a very balanced, excellent mother.'

Keli's lawyer asked the GP what he and Keli said about the investigation while sitting on the lounge in her parents' house:

> I said to her, 'Well, what did the police think has happened then?' or a question like that and she said, 'Well, they think I killed the baby,' … I said, 'Well, did you?' And she said, 'No, no, I would never ever do that,' and she got very emotional about it …

'And in the end what were you able to do with her?' asked Keli's lawyer. 'Did you prescribe any medication, did you counsel her, did you send her off anywhere?'

'No,' answered the GP:

> [M]y advice to her was to tell the truth, that whatever has happened, that, you know, it is important that you tell the truth; that you got yourself into this mess because you've not told the truth, you got pregnant and you've tried to cover it up and not be open with people and that you need to be open and be clear about exactly what happened and bear the consequences of whatever comes from telling the truth.

Keli's lawyer asked, 'Do I follow that nothing untoward was noticed by you about [Keli's child born in 2001] or her?' in the days after this consultation in her parents' house. The GP replied:

> Pretty much went back to business as usual. After that one long consultation with her on the couch in the family home, I then saw her a few days later and I got in my notes here that she was actually feeling better … she seemed more settled and obviously the problems were still there, but maybe she felt calmer in herself.

When Dr Diamond took the stand, he said the evidence of Keli's GP did help illustrate how pressured she felt during the years of her secret pregnancies and babies. He noted that 'within a very short space of time [of speaking to her GP], Keli regathered composure and seemed to feel better.' However, Dr Diamond told the court he was surprised the very serious issue of how Keli felt during those years of secret pregnancies and babies was never really dealt with after that one consultation with her GP.

> When one looks at that and thinks of an issue of that magnitude, that has been an ongoing part of her life in the years since that consultation in November 2004, I was a bit surprised that it was not an issue that had either been raised again or perhaps had even been further addressed by referral to somebody who might have helped her, someone who might have had additional skills or expertise … [T]he matter was simply dropped …

Dr Diamond told the court he thought the evidence showed Keli was not naïve about contraception, having told her partners that she was on the pill. Also, in Dr Diamond's opinion, falling pregnant five times would cure most women of being forgetful about taking the pill. In other words, there must have been another explanation for Keli's very destructive and repetitive behaviour of becoming pregnant.

Keli's lawyer tried to suggest that because Tegan's body could not be examined and no forensic evidence existed of how the child died, Dr Diamond could not contribute a worthwhile view as to why Keli murdered Tegan. Dr Diamond told the court that even with these limitations there was very rich and important information available for his forensic psychiatric analysis:

> [W]e have observed information of Keli's behaviour in very stressful times where she becomes quite emotionally bland, quite detached, dissociated, emotionally unconnected and carries out what she does in an extraordinarily purposeful manner, so that she relies on pragmatic problem solving above all else at those times.

His Honour listened carefully as Keli's lawyer questioned Dr Diamond about what his reports said about her, and observed:

> Well, Dr Diamond agrees that there are limitations on the way in which his material can be used. There is no doubt about that. But even making allowance for that, what do you want to get from that material? … It suggests I suppose in favour of Keli that she was a person who had a particular type of personality disorder.

It would soon become clear that Dr Diamond's answers had not provided what his Honour was searching for. Once the questioning was finished, Keli's lawyer set about trying to identify any means to show that, regardless of the jury's verdict and Keli's disturbing behaviour, she should not be treated like a convicted child murderer. Could the effect the high levels of media attention, the trial itself and the guilty verdict had on Keli's child born in 2001 and her family and friends make a difference?

'Once again, the Court of Criminal Appeal has set a very high bar for this, hasn't it?' noted his Honour, referring to the fact that the obviously acute and very real emotional pain Keli's family was suffering was not a special or exceptional circumstance when it came to sentencing.

'Yes, it doesn't help you …' agreed Keli's lawyer. 'It seems that the authorities regard the potential for a person in her position as a child killer as a risk. They take it seriously.' However, Keli's lawyer urged the judge to see her case as an exception to the court's usual view.

The prosecutor, however, knew the rules and thought they should apply to Keli, just as they would to anybody else.

> Your Honour, we respectfully submit that there is nothing that has been advanced by [Keli's trial lawyer] today that would cause your Honour to come to any conclusion other than that Keli murdered her child Tegan with the intention of killing the

> child and that it was done with some premeditation, certainly by the time she left the hospital on 14 September. The evidence is all one way for the reasons we have already stated.

To which his Honour replied:

> I don't really know what happened, do I? That is where I have a little problem here. I mean for all I know Keli could have simply abandoned the child and the child died. I have no evidence that would suggest that she manually physically took the child's life, on the one hand, or simply abandoned the child and allowed it to die in a neglected state. Not that that helps on culpability [in other words, how much blame Keli deserved or the degree of criminality in her conduct] if that were the case, but I just don't know, do I?

'Your Honour, the evidence we would submit very conclusively proves that there were no abandoned babies.'

'I don't mean that the baby survived.'

'Or any bodies that had been abandoned and found.'

'You could put a baby in a dumpster and leave it there.'

'If a baby was left …'

'No one would ever find it,' interrupted his Honour.

'If the baby was left alive in a dumpster, one would have thought the baby at some stage would be found, if it was still alive,' replied the prosecutor.

'I am giving you that as an example of the difficulty I have as to being satisfied beyond reasonable doubt as to what happened,' said his Honour. 'That must impact on whether I can be satisfied of the precise intention [i.e. the purpose Keli must have had in mind when she did these things, which must be an intent to kill or to cause grievous bodily harm, or reckless indifference to human life] involved.'

But for all his emotional struggles, his Honour's intellectual rigor and adherence to the law always directed his decision-making inside the courtroom.

'I don't know if in a case like this it would make a lot of difference,' he went on to say. 'In terms of culpability, given the age of the victim and the special relationship [the law gives to that between mother and child], it may not matter.'

Prosecutor Tedeschi was not going to give wishful thinking or speculation any place in his submissions as to what his Honour should do:

> [I]f your Honour views all of the evidence as the jury did … when Keli left the hospital she clearly had an intention that the baby was not going to survive. She was not going to take it home. There is no evidence as to how the baby died, that's true, there is no evidence as to where the baby died, but that doesn't detract from the totality of the evidence that obviously the jury were convinced of, [namely] that Keli left that hospital with the intention of killing a baby and did kill a baby. It was always put to the jury on the basis that she killed the baby in those three hours [between leaving the hospital and arriving at her parents' home]. It was never suggested that the baby had been abandoned, [or] may have been abandoned. In fact, the Crown case was that it could disprove abandonment of the baby.

'Abandonment and survival is what the Crown put forward,' retorted his Honour.

'Any abandonment,' replied the prosecutor. 'Not only were there no foundlings who were located, but there were no bodies of discarded babies that were located. We would submit that the jury's verdict must entail a conclusion that she killed the baby with the intention of killing the baby.'

The prosecutor reminded his Honour that the issue of Keli's intention at the time of her crime had been dealt with during the trial. 'Your Honour's directions to the jury were limited to the issue of an intent to kill,' he said. 'We would submit that it was never left to the jury … that she may have done some grievous bodily harm to the baby that caused the baby's death but not intending the death of the baby.'

The prosecutor then listed more facts that had led to the guilty verdict:

> So far as premeditation is concerned, we would submit that it is quite ridiculous to suggest that she left [the] hospital at her own insistence on that particular day, having planned to leave the hospital that day at least on the previous day, having urged the hospital to allow her to leave in time to get home so that she could attend the wedding, … having then left the hospital in time to get home to attend the wedding with [her then boyfriend], spending three hours to get home from Auburn to Manly – we suggest that it is manifestly absurd to suggest that when she left the hospital that she did not have the intention of murdering the baby. Again, that was the case that was quite clearly put to the jury, that when she left that hospital that's what she was intending to do.

The prosecutor also gave his view of the evidence of Keli's GP and Dr Diamond in relation to Keli's repetitive and destructive pattern of getting pregnant, hiding those pregnancies and the different ways in which she sought to find a solution to the five unwanted pregnancies and three unwanted babies:

> [S]he may have a personality disorder that contributed to the way that she dealt with the pressures that she was under from

> the expectation of family and friends and her sporting career …
>
> [T]o use ordinary language, what Keli was saying to [her GP] was: Looking back, I felt at the time that I was on some sort of merry-go-round that I didn't really want to be on, a merry-go-round that wasn't satisfying my inner needs, and I didn't feel that I could get off. And looking back, the fact that I got pregnant all those times was my way of trying to get off that merry-go-round I didn't want to be on.
>
> Dr Diamond's report really says … that was how she got herself into these terrible predicaments which led to her having to have the two terminations, to her having to adopt two children out, to her having to tell all of those lies to everybody, to her having to hide these five pregnancies from everyone, to her having to give birth three times in secret without any support and ultimately to her dealing with the birth of Tegan by murdering her baby.

'How does that assist me, Mr Crown?' asked a distressed Justice Whealy:

> Assuming I accept all of that, where does it actually lead me? Does it lessen culpability, increase culpability? Does it provide some type of explanation that is favourable to Keli or at least has the capacity to tend toward that direction, or towards a more callous and cold-blooded type of murder of a child?

The prosecutor began his answer, 'I think, firstly, what it does is it provides some profound explanation to everyone, including your Honour as to why …'

'There needs to be some explanation, doesn't there, because otherwise the whole story is just too bizarre for words,' interjected his Honour.

'It is a most bizarre story,' said the prosecutor:

> [T]he jury were told in our opening address that this is a bizarre situation that Keli got herself into and this provides some psychological explanation for how she got into such a bizarre, repetitive and personally destructive situation. To a limited degree, I think it is supportive of Keli's position because it shows that back in 2004 she had some degree of insight into how she got into her predicament, but it must be said that since then of course her failure to acknowledge that predicament means that ...

'We move into a complicated area then there, don't we?' interjected his Honour:

> At the moment I suppose you have the situation where Keli is entitled to say 'I maintain my innocence' and that places the sentencing court in a difficult position. There is no remorse in the ordinary sense.

'No, there is no remorse or contrition in the ordinary sense,' agreed the prosecutor.

'On the other hand,' his Honour said:

> ... we know in her life she has now raised a child with whom she has a close and loving relationship and that lends support to the proposition that whatever she precisely did back in this year that she is a person who is rehabilitated and will never offend again. I think I can safely draw those conclusions. I don't know where I go beyond that.

The prosecutor replied:

The evidence overwhelmingly shows that she is a very good mother to the child who was with her until her conviction. The evidence is all one way on that. I suppose the only other relevance of the material that has come out today is that it provides some assistance to understand the motive for the crime. That she had this overwhelming emotional drive or need to get off the merry-go-round that she didn't want to be on that caused her to get pregnant in the first place. Having gotten pregnant she didn't really want to be pregnant, she really didn't want to have a baby, and it provides some additional material to assist the court in what her motive was in committing this offence. It provides a much more profound understanding of the whole offence than your Honour has had up until now.

Most people in the community who don't know the details of the evidence in this case might be inclined to think no mother would kill her newborn child unless she had a mental illness. What the medical evidence that has been provided to your Honour today shows is that this is quite clearly a person who did not have any mental illness. She might have had a personality disorder but that is very different from a mental illness and, for reasons that have been explained by the two doctors, she got caught up in this situation that she felt completely unable to resolve.

It is easy to say she could have just told her parents. That's true, but she felt at the time that she would completely lose them if she told them. Whether that was reasonable or unreasonable is not the point. The point is that is what she felt at the time. The same with her friends. The same with her husband. More than anything else, this medical evidence provides your Honour with a much deeper understanding of the commission of the offence, plus a little bit of evidence

> that Keli back in 2004 understood how she got into the predicament.

As devastating as his Honour's task was, everyone could agree on one thing: thank goodness it was a judge who was going to decide how long Keli's sentence would be.

When we hear of someone being convicted of child murder, many people think they should be locked up and the key thrown away. Politicians know this. In the lead-up to the 2007 state election, Premier Morris Iemma promised to change the law so all convicted child murderers would be sentenced to a minimum of 25 years in prison, with the boast that his political party would 'ensure the judiciary will have no excuse to not come down hard on criminals who choose to break the law'. To many, the promise of a mandatory sentencing law for convicted child murderers would have sounded like a good idea. But in reality, it's not.

There certainly are cases where it is absolutely appropriate that an offender be locked up for at least 25, 30, 40 years, or for life without parole. Those cases are usually obvious. But what about Keli Lane's case? The question of what her sentence should be was difficult.

The mandatory sentencing law proposed in the lead-up to the 2007 state election was all talk and no action. It did not come into force. However, a similar law with some very important differences did.

By the time of Keli's trial, a standard non-parole period for those convicted of child murder had become law. Just like the proposed law being touted by the premier hoping to look tough on crime, this new standard non-parole period was 25 years. However, judges sentencing a convicted child murderer could hand down a non-parole period that was shorter or longer than the standard 25 years, so long as they had convincing reasons why and put those reasons in writing.

Keli's crime had happened back in 1996. The passage of nearly 15 years between her crime and her trial did not save Keli from being convicted. However, prosecutor Tedeschi had found a way to use this passage of time to save Keli from spending a minimum of 25 years behind bars. He submitted an argument that relied on a core legal principle that basically said her crime could not be subject to the new standard non-parole law because it had happened well before the relevant law was passed. Lawyers call this the presumption against retrospectivity. In Keli's case, some might also call it a close shave.

His Honour, fully aware of the important legal principle the prosecutor was using, was grateful. Now the judge didn't have to find convincing reasons why Keli should not be subject to the standard non-parole period of 25 years for convicted child murderers. Given what his Honour would finally decide about her crime, this would have been a tall order.

*

Having chosen to say nothing in a court of law, Keli Lane decided to have her say on tabloid television.

A fortnight before his Honour was due to hand down sentence in April 2011, telephone conversations she had from prison were featured, with Keli's permission, on Channel Seven's tabloid current affairs program *Sunday*, which was broadcast around the nation.

'It makes me angry because they've pulled my life apart for over ten years, and it has still got to this,' Keli was recorded as saying while she cried. 'And here I am being put under the pump for something I didn't do.'

John, the now ex-child protection officer who was the first to notify police about Tegan's disappearance, was also part of the show.

'She is just one cold-blooded killer,' said John.

'There wasn't even anything there to have a bloody charge,'

continued Keli from prison. 'There is not enough evidence. It is just bullshit … This [television show] is going to give us the support to push forward a bit quicker than the average person … The Crown used the media to get me into court to start with.'

'She is either a very convincing liar, or it is the worst miscarriage of justice since Lindy Chamberlain,' commented the journalist.

The Lindy Chamberlain case from around 1980 was a very sore point for the Australian media. Before Lindy had her murder conviction overturned, and subject to the rare distinction of being subsequently proven innocent, the Australian media had crucified her. For those who still thought Keli Lane was innocent, it was a strangely comforting thought. What a relief it would be if Keli's guilty conviction were a horrific blunder.

Keli had a lot more to say on TV.

'I feel I am still being punished for being pregnant, that I am still being punished for adopting children out, and that is difficult to take too because when you are doing it you are supported by people, they want to help you and you think you are doing the right thing. It is hard to understand why I am still being raked over the coals for it … They are saying that Andrew Morris/Norris didn't even exist. I don't know how Tegan came about if he didn't exist. I didn't make her by myself.'

Then came the tabloid TV masterstroke. 'To prove her innocence she needs to find Tegan,' said the journalist. 'We are guaranteeing a $500 000 reward in a bid to uncover the truth [of Tegan's whereabouts or the man Keli claimed to have given her to] … From jail she says the police haven't done enough to find Tegan or the man she says she gave her to.'

'These searches they were doing, they aren't even complete now,' said Keli. 'How do you charge someone on the basis that they can't find Andrew Morris/Norris or Tegan when they haven't even done the searches?'

While standing behind a pile of money representing the reward the TV program was offering, the journalist said; 'Today, we are taking Keli … on her word, or you could say we are calling her bluff.'

'Someone might call in now who hasn't seen the news before or didn't put two and two together … Tegan is now old enough to have her own connections to people … I'm not going to be made to say I did something I didn't do, no matter how bizarre or odd it is,' continued Keli.

The media spotlight on Keli's story was now bigger than ever, and speculation about what might have happened to Tegan was rife.

*

On 15 April 2011, Justice Whealy handed down Keli Lane's sentence. His remarks on the sentence were to be video recorded and broadcast. This did not mean the media or any member of the public was free to bring their cameras into the courtroom. The court had strict rules designed to ensure fair and accurate reporting of the court's judgments.

There was to be only one television camera. There was to be no media organisation's insignia on that camera, and no distracting lights or sounds or any other disruption to proceedings. Recording was to be conducted on a 'pooled' basis: vision and sound were to be shared with other news media organisations as soon as practicable after the conclusion of the judgment remarks. If the vision was to be broadcast live, all news media organisations present were to have equal opportunity to access the live feed at the same time. It was forbidden to record or broadcast footage of any jurors, witnesses, Keli or any of her family. It was only Justice Whealy who was to be recorded. The transcript produced by the official court reporters would always be the authoritative record of proceedings.

His Honour did what he had to do. He acknowledged that Keli was showing no remorse, and that was something the criminal justice system could not ignore. He did not agree with her lawyer's submission that she was at the least culpable end of the range of convicted child murderers. On the other hand, the Crown had submitted, and his Honour agreed, her crime was not in the very worst category either. His Honour found the lack of remorse, plus the nature of the crime she had been convicted of, to be among the factors that made Keli a mid-range offender:

> These are first, the age of the child, a baby of only two days old and secondly, the abuse by a woman of the position of trust as between a mother and her child. These are serious aggravating factors because the life that has been taken is that of a baby, a being who was completely defenceless, and who met her end at the hands of her mother, a person from whom she could ordinarily expect protection, sustenance and care.

Having designated Keli a mid-range offender, to explain why the standard non-parole period of 25 years should not apply to her would have been an extremely difficult task. Thanks to the arguments submitted by the prosecutor, his Honour was spared having to sentence her to prison until she was in her sixties.

Keli's maximum sentence was 18 years. Her non-parole period was 13 years and five months. Having entered prison in her mid-thirties, at the earliest Keli would not get out until she was nearly 50 years old. She would spend some of her best years behind bars and her child born in 2001 would grow up without her. But as severe as her punishment was, 13 years and five months was considerably shorter than the standard non-parole period of 25 years then in force. No one involved in the matter, including the police and prosecutor Tedeschi, thought 25 years was an appropriate minimum sentence for this convicted child murderer.

However, Justice Whealy also expressed his dismay. He could not bring himself to believe that Keli had murdered Tegan so she could make it to a wedding. He referred to the idea of Keli having a personality disorder as though that meant she had suffered from mental illness, or was somehow not solely to blame for her crime. His Honour also hinted at his belief that, while women and girls in very desperate circumstances might kill their babies, no mother could simply murder her child.

His Honour shot the messenger, John, the child protection officer who discovered Tegan's existence:

> [John] was not an impressive witness and presented as a person trying to inflate his own importance in the matter. His role in a recent [TV] program, when he purported to inform the audience of the precise manner in which Tegan met her end, did him little credit, and reinforced the view I had formed.

Such an assessment of John as a witness in the courtroom stood in stark contrast to that made by the chief coroner. In due course, the Court of Criminal Appeal would have nothing negative to say about John.

There were even more serious signs that his Honour was having trouble coping with the facts. The huge amount of evidence collected by the police that ended up proving Tegan had not survived the day Keli left Auburn Hospital with her was simply ignored. His Honour talked about evidence that 'diminished or eliminated' parts of the Crown's case. However, his Honour did not identify what these parts were.

Keli was returned to prison and everyone else left the courtroom. As journalists walked through the ground level foyer of the court building, some of them were approached by an excited man. He was telling anyone who would listen that he was a taxi driver who had had Keli and Tegan in the back of his taxi on the day Keli had left hospital. If what he was saying was true, it would have meant Tegan could have been alive at the time the Crown had argued she had been killed. It was a fantastic claim. Some journalists listened to his story with a sceptical look on their faces.

However, there were those prepared to give public support to what this stranger had to say. Solicitor Chris Murphy, who was not briefed in Keli's case, used social media to announce he thought this man's claims should be taken seriously. He had gone on the tabloid television program aired just before Keli's sentence was handed down to claim there was 'absolutely no evidence' that Tegan was dead or that Keli had killed her.

Keli had been sentenced on a Friday. The following Monday, her solicitor filed a notice to appeal the conviction. The media reported what seemed like a genuine development in the case. However, it was an empty gesture. It would take over a year and a half for the actual grounds of appeal to be filed. Nevertheless, Keli's solicitor did succeed in keeping the media spotlight on the case.

Chris Murphy also kept the media spotlight burning. During an interview on a nationwide media network he repeated the claims that Keli and Tegan had been in the back of a taxi on the day Tegan disappeared. Meanwhile, police spoke to the taxi driver. They advised the media that, after assessing his account, there was no need for police to follow it up. There was no validity to this man's claims for pretty clear reasons that they had been able to establish. Regardless, media reports of the untrue taxi story multiplied and remained online.

There was another media campaign concerning Keli's case, and it was startlingly unusual.

Over a year and a half after Keli's sentence was handed down, Justice Whealy decided to do an interview with the *Sydney Morning*

Herald. Despite it being unheard of for a judge to question a jury's verdict, and inappropriate in my view, he publicly expressed doubt over Keli's conviction. He did this knowing the matter was due to be heard on appeal.

'[I]t did not make sense to me for a mother to do that,' he said.

The emotional toll Keli's trial, and other criminal trials, had taken was too much. Justice Whealy was a highly accomplished civil lawyer and judge, but before becoming a trial judge he had done virtually no criminal work. His Honour had essentially started his criminal trial career by presiding over a few high-profile trials before being faced with Keli's trial.

One of the few criminal trials he had presided over involved high-profile terrorism charges. As the trial judge, he had had to watch videos of hostages being beheaded by extremists. At the conclusion of Keli's trial, his Honour reportedly told the Chief Justice that he wanted to retire from the bench. After spending some time presiding over other types of legal hearings, he did retire a year and a half later.

'[Keli Lane's case had been] such an emotional, harrowing trial, that I really felt at the end I could do no more. I felt worn out from it and I suppose just emotionally affected by it,' he said.

Michael Duffy, a former senior journalist who had written detailed accounts of Keli's trial for the *Sydney Morning Herald*, knew something was wrong. He had left the paper by the time Justice Whealy's interview was published, one of many experienced journalists to leave as waves of redundancies passed through the news industry as it struggled to remain profitable.

'As a former *Herald* reporter who covered … Keli Lane's trial, I feel obliged to write in defence of the jurors whose decision has been questioned by [the] trial judge,' Duffy wrote. 'He says it does not make sense for a mother to kill her child. Unfortunately, there are many cases where this has occurred.' While acknowledging

Justice Whealy's emotional distress, he commented, 'It wouldn't have been much fun for the jurors either, and after [his Honour's] comments I suspect some are feeling even worse.'

His letter was buried in the letters page of the paper.

A senior legal affairs writer, Richard Ackland, also warned about the consequences of the trial judge's decision to publicly doubt the jury's verdict.

'Normally judges, retired or otherwise, don't publicly declare their scepticism about jury verdicts … It could lead to trouble,' wrote Ackland.

When it comes to trials, the only words that matter are those said in court. What is said outside the courtroom is not subject to the rules of evidence or recorded verbatim on the public record. As such, a lot of wishful thinking, speculation and even deliberate attempts to hide the truth are expressed outside the courtroom, and cannot be given the same respect that is accorded to what is said inside the courtroom, even if it is lawyers and judges who are saying it. Outside, it is all just speculation and theatre.

Keli's trial lawyer was no longer part of her legal team. As well as appointing a new barrister, her team made a bold decision. They decided to apply for bail prior to the appeal hearing.

Like any convicted murderer, for Keli to be granted bail the court would have to be convinced that game-changing new evidence or very strong proof of an unfair trial could be shown. Neither existed in Keli's appeal. Her bail application would prove to be a ridiculous overestimation of the strength of her appeal.

'[R]ather than have people possess false hope, I am going to refuse bail,' said the bail judge.

Nearly five months later, the appeal hearing began. Despite its repetition in the media, the idea that there was no evidence that Keli killed Tegan was quickly abandoned inside the courtroom. Instead, the principal ground of appeal openly admitted Keli killed Tegan, but suggested she should have faced the charge of manslaughter rather than murder. The further claim that the lesser charge of infanticide should have been made available during the trial was quickly dropped during a morning tea break. It should be borne in mind that claims and concessions made in court are done on the instructions of the client.

The weakness of the leading appeal point then quickly became apparent. Keli's appeal lawyer had no evidence as to why she should have been tried for manslaughter. Instead, he listed theoretical examples of situations that could be considered the manslaughter of Tegan, for example Keli might have accidently dropped her or hidden her in a bag and then not done anything to make sure Tegan was OK. But for the claim that Keli should have faced a manslaughter charge to succeed, her lawyer needed actual evidence of something like this having happened, and there was none.

Sitting in the courtroom were skilled journalists from a variety of news outlets who were able to understand for themselves what was being said. There were also journalists who relied on others to tell them what was going on. Outside the courtroom there were people spreading misinformation, and among those journalists unable to understand what was happening in court were those reporting misinformation as fact.

Just under five months later, Keli's appeal decision was handed down. It had failed. All three appeal judges wrote unanimously that:

> In all of the circumstances, we are satisfied that the verdict of guilty was amply open to the jury, and we are satisfied that the evidence established beyond reasonable doubt Keli Lane's guilt of the offence …
>
> While courts are not always in a position to make judgments about the quality of police investigations, in this instance, so far as it is possible to gauge, the Crown description

> of the subsequent investigation as 'exemplary' is apt … it can hardly be said that a substandard [police] investigation caused prejudice to Lane.

Instead, the appeal judges described the enormous police search for Tegan as 'a painstaking, meticulous and exhaustive investigation'.

Despite plenty of warning from the judges (other than the trial judge) that this appeal would not succeed, there were TV crews waiting outside the jail where Keli was imprisoned as if they expected her to walk out.

Before Keli's sentence was handed down, Channel Seven's tabloid TV show *Sunday* asked whether there was any doubt over Keli's conviction and whether there was any excuse for Keli's behaviour towards her child. In subsequent years there would be two more national broadcasts, one on Channel Nine's *60 Minutes* in 2016 and the other on the ABC in 2019, that simply encouraged viewers to ignore what had been decided in courtrooms. Both featured Natalie, the unreliable witness. Keli Lane spoke again by telephone from jail. Incredibly, the ABC program *Exposed* featured journalists, academics and Justice Whealy speaking as if the decisions of the Court of Criminal Appeal and the High Court, which by that stage had expressly declined an application to review Keli's conviction, either didn't happen or didn't matter. Such slipshod and misleading reporting, also seemingly designed to turn reporters into amateur investigators in the public eye, risks undermining public confidence in the proper operation of the criminal justice system and that is dangerous.

As an inexperienced trial judge, Justice Whealy had let his emotions overrule his reason again when he had retired from the bench. In expressing his concerns as he did, this very intelligent and accomplished person did enormous harm to his professional reputation.

I think the fact that Keli was a white, middle-class member of the community enabled a large cross-section of people to identify with her. That heightened their interest in her conduct and what happened to her. Public prejudices might be expressed in different ways in the media, depending on the qualities of the individual in the spotlight. In the process they might override findings of courts based on facts found from evidence.

Keli Lane is certainly an unusual individual. Since she has consistently refused to testify in her own case in any court, there has been no opportunity to put challenging questions to her. Television journalists have declined to ask the forensically pertinent ones. If the senior crown prosecutor (for instance) had been able to put to her questions like the following, drawing upon evidence given in the various courts, how would she have answered? Why have journalists not asked such questions when they had the opportunity?

1 When you were first told by the police that they were looking for Tegan and were suspicious about what had happened to her, why didn't you immediately seek out Andrew Morris or Norris, to whom you say you gave Tegan?
2 A boyfriend gave evidence that he was having a full sexual relationship with you for three to four years, including during the time that Tegan was conceived. He even described the 'spooning' position that you insisted on using at the time because (unbeknown to him) you were pregnant with Tegan. How did you know that Tegan was not that man's baby?
3 When Detective Gaut tried to call you after his three months of investigation, why didn't you call him back? If you had really given Tegan to her natural father, for all you knew the detective might have been going to tell you the good news that he had found Tegan.
4 If you had really handed Tegan over to the natural father, you

faced the risk that at some stage (weeks, months or years later) he would turn up with the child and say that it was now your turn to look after her. How would you have explained that to your family and friends?

5 Why did you tell John Borovnik of DOCS that: 'The middle child [Tegan] lives with a family in Perth,' if you had given the child to the natural father?

6 Why did you give eight different versions of what happened to Tegan? Why didn't you just say from the start that the natural father had taken charge of the baby?

7 You told the *Exposed* ABC program that you had handed over Tegan to 'Andrew' in the foyer of Auburn Hospital and that you had been there with him, the baby, his mother and his partner for 15 minutes or so. This was the first time that you had given this version. Your first version to police was that Andrew drove you to Venus Street, Gladesville, where you handed over the baby. Your second version to police was that you handed over the baby in the car park at Auburn Hospital. Why have you now advanced another version? Which version is correct?

8 If you were intending to hand over Tegan to the natural father at Auburn Hospital, why did you fill out a Medicare application form at the hospital putting her membership under your name?

9 When you were adopting out your third child, you used the false identity of Aaron Williams as the father of the child. The real father has since been identified by DNA. There are substantial similarities between your description of Andrew Morris/Norris and your description of Aaron Williams. Is it a mere coincidence that there are those similarities?

10 Why did you lie to Detective Gaut on 16 October 2000 that your friend Lisa had known Andrew Morris/Norris and

had known about the birth of Tegan? Why did you also tell Detective Gaut that you did not know how to get in contact with your friend Lisa?

11 In 2004, your then husband told you that he had looked up all the 'A Norris' entries in the New South Wales online phone book and there were 13 of them, and he offered to ring them all. Why didn't you insist that he do so?

12 Regarding your ambition to represent Australia in water polo at the 2000 Olympics, in March 1995 during the adoption process of your first child, you told the relevant social worker that you were a competitive water polo player and that your ambition was to compete in the Sydney 2000 Olympics and you didn't feel in a position to parent the child. In February 1998, you wrote to a senior person at your sports college, requesting that your five-week teaching practicum for that month be deferred. You wrote:

> As you can see from the enclosed documents I will be in full training for my water polo club team in preparation for the Australian Club Nationals. We also have the Sydney competition finals around this time which will be held in Sydney. From these competitions representative teams will be selected, and with the recent inclusion of Women's Water Polo in the Sydney Olympics, I cannot risk my selection.

13 If competing in the 2000 Olympics was so important in March 1995 that you would adopt out your baby and still important in February 1998, was it also important to you at the time of Tegan's birth in 1996?

Chapter 17

SHIRLEY JUSTINS'S APPEAL

The criminal law is primarily intended to prevent harm to individuals and the community. Just like DPPs, judges are bound by the law and the facts of the cases in front of them, no matter how personally upsetting the outcome may be. But what happens when the law is dangerously inadequate?

One clear example of such a situation during my time as the DPP was the lack of voluntary assisted dying laws. Not long before my tenure ended, this dangerous state of affairs forced three Court of Criminal Appeal judges to resort to confusing and risky arguments in an attempt to bring about a reasonable and just result. However, the cleverest of legal reasoning is not enough to make up for parliament's failure, which puts the police, the prosecutors, the defence lawyers, the judges, the jury, everyone in the process, in a very difficult quandary even today.

In 2010 Shirley Justins decided to appeal her manslaughter conviction for providing the Nembutal that killed her partner Graeme Wylie after he drank it from a glass she left in front of him.

She hadn't helped Graeme die just to rid herself of the burden of caring for someone whose mind had deteriorated so much that he couldn't remember whether he had children. Even though Graeme had changed his will in favour of Shirley only a week before he died, it became clear during her trial that she hadn't helped him die for financial gain. She did it because she honestly believed that was what he wanted.

By 2011 Shirley had finished her prison time. For two years she had spent every weekend in jail. Nonetheless, in 2011 Shirley again found herself facing a trial over the death of the man she loved.

Six months earlier, having considered Shirley's appeal against her manslaughter conviction, the Court of Criminal Appeal had handed down the decision that sent her back into the dock. The three appeal judges appeared concerned about the state of the law that could lead to other loving carers taking desperate measures and then facing serious criminal consequences. Their task was to do justice in an area of somewhat uncertain law that appeared to operate unfairly, which led to this confusing turn of events that saw Shirley back in the dock for a crime for which she had already served her time.

Despite the purity of Shirley's motives in helping Graeme die, the law offered no clear way for her to get rid of her manslaughter conviction. Two of the appeal judges ordered a new trial. One of those expressed doubt that manslaughter should be prosecuted again. The third judge, who would have ordered an acquittal, held that another prosecution for manslaughter would be an abuse of process.

In the present criminal law regime, the offences of murder, manslaughter and (especially) aiding suicide arise for consideration whenever voluntary assisted dying may have occurred or have been contemplated.

For example, a person who administers a drug to another with the intention that it should end that person's life, is (if the drug does indeed kill that person) committing murder – whether by the hand of a doctor, nurse, family member or friend, and regardless of the wishes of the deceased, and regardless of whether the person has other intentions also in mind (such as relieving pain). You cannot consent to be killed by someone else or exonerate that person in advance to release them from criminal liability. The position is therefore brutally simple and there is no way around it as the law presently stands.

This dangerous state of the law was well known by both the senior crown prosecutor and Shirley's defence lawyer at trial, and by the trial judge, all three appeal judges, myself, the retrial lawyers and the retrial judge. We all knew that, despite numerous attempts to change the law, time and time again such attempts in New South Wales and elsewhere failed to gather the necessary number of votes from members of parliament. Parliament's failure meant frail people like Graeme, and Fred's wife Katerina, were instead made to suffer against their will while loving carers like Shirley and Fred were made to watch and also suffer.

In advance of Shirley's 2011 retrial, the Crown decided to accept her plea of guilty to assisting Graeme's suicide. Back in 2005, the Crown had agreed to accept Fred's plea to assisting Katerina's suicide.

Such eventual results might seem appropriate, but it is a huge mistake to think that they mean the current state of the law is no longer dangerous or unjust. Very light penalties for assisting suicide may come after the carer has first faced a murder trial, as Shirley did and Fred very nearly did. The emotional devastation that comes with being charged with murder or facing a murder trial cannot be overestimated. Shirley's guilty plea to assisting suicide came after a particularly convoluted legal path that tested the lawyers and the courts.

One of the appeal judges in Shirley's case thought not only should her appeal against her manslaughter conviction succeed, but there should be no retrial on any charge and she should have no criminal conviction at all. Justice Simpson reasoned that, given the state of the law, if Shirley wasn't found guilty of murder, then a genuine question arose as to whether she was guilty of anything.

Shirley having been found not guilty of murder but guilty of manslaughter, her Honour reasoned the jury must have decided she didn't know whether or not Graeme had the capacity to decide to end his life when she put the poison and a glass in front of him. If the jury thought she knew for sure that Graeme was not able to make such a big decision or, as the trial judge described it, if Graeme told Shirley he understood that if he drank the poison in front of him he would die but it was the understanding of a small child and Shirley knew this, then the jury would have convicted her of murder. Thus, her Honour was able to state that as far as she could see, Shirley's actions and state of mind, as determined by the jury that convicted her of manslaughter, did not include action based on that level of knowledge of Graeme's state of mind.

But this is where it became even more complicated. Her Honour thought that as a matter of law the charge of manslaughter should not have been brought in the first trial.

Overturning Shirley's manslaughter conviction depended on finding fault with the trial judge's directions to the jury. Her Honour thought Shirley's manslaughter conviction was invalid because of an omission from the written directions the trial judge gave the jury; one direction was given only orally. Written directions, she held, were more likely to carry stronger force than oral directions, but they did not spell out a critical ingredient of manslaughter, namely whether it was Shirley's act of putting the glass and the poison in front of Graeme that killed him.

Chief Justice Spigelman took a different approach. His Honour also concluded the manslaughter conviction should be overturned because of errors he said the trial judge had made, but he focused on whether the acts causing death were the acts of Shirley. His Honour seems to have thought that creating different ways for a jury to decide whether it was her actions that killed Graeme was the answer. If they applied, then Graeme pouring the poison put in front of him by Shirley into the glass she provided and drinking it was a legal act of suicide.

The third judge, Justice Johnson, had his own views about what sort of arguments could succeed, but agreed with the Chief Justice's overall approach. Their solution was to put Shirley on trial again and see if the new arguments would result in her again being convicted of manslaughter.

However, the dissenting judge did not share the confidence of her brother judges and described the course of making Shirley stand trial again as an abuse of process. In other words, her Honour thought such a course should not be taken in a court of law.

Ultimately, Shirley, the lawyers and a judge assembled in a courtroom but the retrial didn't happen. Before it began, Shirley asked if she could plead guilty to assisting suicide in return for the manslaughter charge being dropped. She had made a similar request during her original trial and the Crown had said no. This time, the Crown said yes. This wasn't because of any new, helpful development in the law or change of facts. It was essentially because Shirley had already been convicted of a serious criminal charge and had already served her time.

In handing down punishment the retrial judge showed the mood of the court.

'[T]he only order which is appropriate in the present circumstances is that the offender be sentenced to the rising of the Court,' said her Honour. In other words, having to be in the dock at all after already having served her time was punishment enough for Shirley.

*

So how should society deal with the problem of frail or ill but competent people who want to die but are unable or unprepared to do so by their own hand? Some have suggested that DPPs should use their discretion to decide whether or not to prosecute those who help such people die. DPPs do have a degree of discretion, but this is not the best answer to the problem. DPPs' decisions are to be determined by the law, the facts and the Prosecution Guidelines, which require the general public interest to be served. DPPs don't get to make the law, to turn a blind eye to the facts or law, or to pick and choose to whom the law applies. The discretion must be exercised within the limits of the law. This leads to very painful but unavoidable decisions to prosecute, such as in Fred's case. He had walked into a police station and confessed what he had done to help Katerina die – and that, on its face, was a confession to murder.

No police officer or prosecutor or court should be placed in the positions that we were. That is another reason why I think the law should change.

The decision to prosecute Shirley was different. Hers was a case where a weakened person had died in circumstances that pointed to her involvement as someone who, arguably, stood to gain from his death. It was a murder scenario. How can any DPP rightfully choose not to prosecute in such circumstances?

The answer to these dilemmas is for parliament to change the law.

It is important to acknowledge that the criminal law does develop and change over time, in order to accommodate changes in society and in accordance with changes in the will of the people, organisation of society, technological advances and so on. It usually lags a little behind the pace, but that is no bad thing. Conservative development is preferable to sudden and perhaps ill-thought change. Social factors, including changes in social mores, guide and motivate such changes.

There is probably a legitimate social purpose in seeking to discourage people generally from killing themselves and so the law against assisting suicide has a role to play in modern society. But the question is whether it should apply to all cases of suicide, including voluntary assisted dying carried out in carefully controlled circumstances with adequate protections in place.

Those at the front line of the criminal justice system are hardly naïve about the lengths people may go to when money is at stake or to rid themselves of a hopeless burden. I am well aware of the potential problem of frail people being pressured into an early death by those who don't care what the frail person wants, and any change to the law must expressly deal with this reality.

If positive action to hasten death is to be lawful, very great care must be given to the controls put in place, just as they have been in relation to ceasing medical treatment. It must even be recognised that sometimes we humans change our minds about important matters – even matters of life and death.

A few years after Shirley's successful assisted suicide plea, I wrote a paper that considered an interstate civil case concerning a patient's right to refuse medical treatment. It involved a man who clearly stated, prior to becoming unable to care for himself, permanently hospitalised and in an induced state, that he wanted those caring for him to 'turn the bloody machine off' if he was ever reduced to such mere existence. The hospital caring for him knew the withdrawal of medical care would directly cause his death. The court held that not only was it lawful for the hospital to withdraw its medical care, but given the man's undisputed attitude when he was a competent, functioning person, it would be unlawful for the hospital to continue the medical care that was keeping him alive.

It seems to me that a question logically arises in the present state of the law: if it is in the best interests of a person that something not be done and that certain medical attention be ended, knowing that will hasten death, and that is lawful (as determined by a court in the case to which I referred), why can it never be in the best interests of a person (and therefore lawful) that something actively be done, for example that certain medication be administered, knowing that it will hasten death? But the criminal law and possibly present medical ethics appear to be concerned not merely with the best interests of the individual person – other imperatives are at work – and, admittedly, caution is needed.

Amongst the many failed attempts to change the law are legislative models that I am happy to endorse. I can point to legislative models operating successfully in other countries and proposed in Australia and enacted in Victoria that have the right degree of conservative change and safeguards against the unlawful killing of vulnerable people. One such model includes among many safeguards the involvement of at least two doctors in any lawful voluntary assisted death.

It would mean terminally ill people could die at home without their carer being the one left to suffocate them in their sleep with a pillow; or their carer having to enter their home not knowing if the latest suicide attempt has been a success or, if it has failed, if they are going to hear feeble cries for help; or their carer is left looking like a murderer when the will of the person they helped to die entitles them to a large portion of the deceased's estate. It would also mean the terminally ill no longer have to fear being kept alive against their wishes in medical institutions. The moderate changes to the law that would avoid the desperate situations that led to Fred and Shirley facing murder trials are already in black and white, ready to go, in New South Wales and elsewhere. All that is needed is sufficient political will inside parliament.

It's not as if such a change in the law would be a brave jump into the unknown. Lawful voluntary assisted dying under various descriptions and in various forms exists in at least the following jurisdictions: eight of the United States of America (California, Colorado, Hawaii, Maine, New Jersey, Oregon, Vermont and Washington) and in Washington DC; and in Belgium, Canada,

Luxembourg, The Netherlands, Switzerland and Colombia. As far as Australia's own history is concerned, for a brief time it was available in the Northern Territory under the *Rights of the Terminally Ill Act 1995*, and it is now available in Victoria. A parliamentary committee has recommended it in Western Australia. It is being examined in Queensland and South Australia. A Bill is likely to be reintroduced in New South Wales in due course.

The 'slippery slope' or 'floodgate' fears that the introduction of lawful assisted dying will open the way for people who want to live being killed against their will do not appear to have been realised anywhere and stringent legal requirements have been formulated that appear to be achieving the desired ends.

Introducing legal voluntary assisted dying to the state where I once served as DPP has been one of my ongoing campaigns. I particularly favour the model operating in the US state of Oregon, but am waiting to see how the Victorian model, which looks fine, operates in practice.

I think these are the sorts of situations where good men and women should not be left at the mercy of the criminal law for acting humanely and compassionately, in a principled way and with the informed consent of the holder of the right to life. Where is the dignity in that? What purpose does it serve? What harm does it prevent?

Chapter 18

THE DEMOLITION OF THE TRIAL OF GORDON WOOD

In February 2012, the Court of Criminal Appeal decided that Gordon Wood's trial for the murder of Caroline Byrne was a miscarriage of justice. Caroline's family and friends were mute with shock; Gordon's erupted with joy as he walked out of jail, his murder conviction gone.

I didn't anticipate the result of this appeal. I certainly didn't expect the criticism of senior crown prosecutor Mark Tedeschi's conduct to be as strong as it was, even though I accept the validity of that criticism in some respects.

While appeal courts are not there to redo the job of juries, appeal judges do have some discretion to make findings of fact. In his decision, Chief Judge McClellan made a very large number of findings of fact that contradicted those made by the jury. They included:

1 Gordon's remarkably accurate predictions as to the place and position of Caroline's body before police located her as being very important evidence.
2 That Caroline was the weeping woman or that Gordon was one of the men the man who lived in the apartment close to The Gap saw late in the evening Caroline died.
3 That there was a reason why Gordon would want to hide the fact he visited his then boss during lunch the day Caroline died.

4 That despite problems with Associate Professor Cross's lack of objectivity (i.e. his proven desire to be part of the prosecution that convicted Gordon) and other problems with his opinions, the physics Cross outlined as to how Caroline came to be at the bottom of the cliff was supported by another physics expert who gave evidence at the trial, Professor Elliott.
5 That Caroline was likely to have been thrown off the cliff.
6 That the nature of a number of small injuries sustained by Caroline, which the Crown argued proved Caroline probably defended herself from an attack and was probably unconscious when she left the top of the cliff, was important.
7 That the evidence of the two café owners was reliable enough to prove that Gordon was with Caroline the afternoon before she died.

The Court of Criminal Appeal's criticism of the prosecution impacted the evidence to be properly taken into account on the question of guilt: there was simply not enough remaining on which a reasonable jury could be satisfied beyond reasonable doubt that Gordon had murdered Caroline, and that led to a directed acquittal.

Nonetheless, it is important to remember that miscarriages of justice can occur even when judges agree the behaviour of the accused is suspicious.

'His account of falling asleep and then waking, panicking and going about a search instead of ringing [Caroline] or her family to find out where she may have been arouses suspicion,' wrote the Chief Judge, who also stated the suspicion was that Gordon might have had something to do with Caroline's death.

Despite this suspicion, the Court of Criminal Appeal was convinced the prosecutor had pushed far too hard for a conviction. It was also convinced that Associate Professor Cross, the expert witness who claimed there was no way Caroline could have jumped or dived to the place she was thought to have landed, had fought inappropriately for a conviction – and expert witnesses are supposed to be impartial.

That might sound like a strange complaint about the prosecutor. Aren't prosecutors supposed to push for convictions? In his lead judgment, the Chief Judge spelt out in detail the difficult balancing act all prosecutors must perform. But before he gave that homily, the Chief Judge, with the support of two other appeal judges, demolished Gordon's trial.

The Court of Criminal Appeal thought prosecutor Tedeschi had created a motive that helped secure a conviction in a case that didn't have enough hard evidence. In particular, the multiple connections he made between Gordon's boss Rene Rivkin's business woes, fellow Rene employee Tom, and Gordon's relationship with Caroline. The Chief Judge wrote:

> Firstly, [the senior crown prosecutor] was hinting at the fact that [Tom], who he said was a weight lifter, was the second man who the Crown hypothesised was involved in [Caroline's] death. Secondly, he related the involvement of [Rene] in the events of that day with the speculative motive which the prosecutor had created. Any proper foundation for that motive was entirely lacking.

The evidence the prosecutor used to create that motive had been admitted, meaning the trial judge thought it was fair to have it put in front of the jury. The Court of Criminal Appeal thought the trial judge had made a big mistake. The Chief Judge thought none of the evidence about the investigations into Rene, including Rene and Gordon being questioned by authorities the day before Caroline's death, should have been put to the jury. The Chief Judge went so far as to say the inclusion of Rene in the motive for murder was 'a speculative smear'.

Another Court of Criminal Appeal judge, Justice Latham, referred to a High Court judgment, which noted:

> There may be many cases where it is extremely dangerous to rely heavily on the existence of a motive, where an unexplained death or disappearance of a person is not otherwise proved to be attributable to the accused … In my view, this is one of those cases where that danger arose.
>
> It could not have escaped the Crown's attention that, without evidence of motive, its circumstantial case against [Gordon] depended substantially upon the combination of the expert evidence (which was already compromised by the conflict in the evidence surrounding the nomination of the place from which [Caroline's] body was recovered) and the weak 'identification' evidence.

Her Honour added that Gordon's lies were not available to the jury for use towards proof of his guilt, something the trial judge had pointed out to them:

> At the heart of [Gordon's] alleged motive to kill the woman he loved, rather than risk the loss of his employment and all the financial advantages it entailed, was the assertion by the Crown that [Caroline] communicated to [Gordon] that she wanted to finish the relationship. The Crown's submission to the jury recognised the paucity of evidence underpinning this thesis. The submission was: *We would submit to you that she must have intimated to him that she wanted out, and it must have been obvious to him that this time it was going to be forever.* It is difficult to regard this submission as anything other than an invitation to speculate.

'Suspicion and conjecture, even grave suspicion, is not a proper basis for the finding of guilt,' noted the third Court of Criminal Appeal judge, Justice Rothman.

The 50 questions put to the jury by the prosecutor were not seen as a problem during the trial. The Court of Criminal Appeal thought they were a huge problem: they made the jury think Gordon had to satisfactorily answer the questions in order to prove he was innocent, something an accused must never be made to do. By putting these questions, the prosecutor had effectively reversed the onus of proof and caused a miscarriage of justice.

In everyday situations it would be perfectly sensible to demand that someone who had acted suspiciously explain themselves or, in other words, demonstrate their innocence, even if there isn't enough other evidence to prove in a legal way that they have done something wrong. But it is very important that this does not happen in a court of law. It isn't fair for an individual, the accused, to have to prove their innocence and maintain their freedom against the Crown, backed by all the resources of the state. A system that allowed this to happen would see a lot of people go to jail for crimes they did not commit.

The need to prove beyond reasonable doubt first that a crime has occurred and second that it was the accused who did it, is a burden that must be carried by the Crown. This is known as the burden and standard of proof and applies to all criminal cases.

Question 23 of the prosecutor's 50 questions was: 'How would anybody, athletic or not, do a running dive from the top of The Gap in almost total darkness and on uneven ground into either hole A or hole B?'

The Chief Judge found this question reversed the onus of proof by calling for an explanation from Gordon:

> It was for the prosecutor to exclude the possibility that [Caroline] could have dived from the top of The Gap to either

> hole A or hole B (or any other point), not for [Gordon] to show that anybody, athletic or not, could do this.

The Chief Judge found questions such as why Caroline would buy some petrol, a Freddo Frog and withdraw $50 on the afternoon she died, were unfair as they invited the jury to speculate. Other questions 'unfairly invited the jury to be suspicious of [Gordon's] dealings with [Rene] in a manner which was clearly intended to smear his character'.

The other main miscarriage of justice was that the verdict was unreasonable and could not be supported by the evidence.

There was no direct evidence as to how Caroline died. She didn't leave a note and there were no witnesses who saw how she left the top of the cliff. This meant the case against Gordon was a circumstantial one.

Just because a case is circumstantial doesn't mean it is weak. The strength of circumstantial evidence lies in its ability to show that, according to the common course of human affairs, the degree of probability that the proven facts would be accompanied by the occurrence of the crime alleged is so high that no other conclusion can reasonably be supposed. Indeed, circumstantial cases can be very strong, not being dependent on direct human observations or recollections that can be faulty.

As mentioned at the beginning of this chapter, appeal courts do not exist to hold trials or to redo the job of juries. Normally they stick to considering points of law. In this appeal hearing, there were many instances of the Chief Judge making findings of fact that were different from those made by members of the jury that convicted Gordon.

There were many pieces of evidence that suggested Gordon made remarkably accurate predictions as to the location of Caroline's body before police found her. The prosecutor had told the jury that this issue was the 'bottom line of the prosecution case'. It was said to be 'a killer point, an irrefutable point'.

However, Chief Judge McClellan had a very different view. 'It will be plain that I do not accept that this issue had that impact or indeed was of any particular significance at all,' wrote his Honour:

> The evidence of the others present at the time, particularly [Caroline's brother] Peter, was that the night was so dark and the presence of spray and wash on the rock shelf was such that, in combination, it was not possible to see anything at the bottom of the cliff. This must mean that [Gordon] could not have known, even if he was responsible for [Caroline] falling to her death, that she had lodged in the rock shelf with her feet in the air.

The Chief Judge noted it was possible the jury concluded that Caroline was the woman seen by the man who lived in an apartment very close to The Gap, that Gordon was with her, that a second man was near them and walked with them towards The Gap '[a]lthough I would not myself make this finding …'

The Chief Judge was not happy at all with the directions the trial judge made about the evidence of the man who lived in an apartment very close to The Gap, which was important to the Crown's case.

> The jury were earlier told by the trial judge that the Crown would submit 'that if the deceased [Caroline] were there, then the accused [Gordon] her partner, was more likely to be there as well. So you can use the evidence in that way as well.' This reasoning was dangerous and the jury should have been warned against it, particularly in a trial where this was a central and contested issue.

When his Honour considered the evidence of the owner of the restaurant where Gordon's boss Rene had lunch that he had seen Gordon there talking to Rene at about 3.00 p.m. the day Caroline died, and that three times afterwards Gordon demanded the restaurant owner not tell anyone, the Chief Judge wrote:

> There is no apparent reason to doubt [the restaurant owner's] account. However, nor is there any reason why [Gordon] would 'cover his tracks' by seeking to suppress knowledge that he was at the restaurant on that day.
>
> I acknowledge that some of the actions by [Gordon] both before and following [Caroline's] death raise suspicion about his possible involvement. However, many aspects of his conduct before her death which are criticised by the Crown were consistent with him acting out of a genuine concern for her wellbeing. Lying to protect her job with June … and putting about a fake story that her death was an accident rather than suicide are most rationally, and to my mind convincingly, explained by a concern for her welfare and reputation. After discovering her car and probable death his reactions must have been affected by shock and anxiety. The evidence, including that of [Caroline's father Tony] and [brother] Peter, confirm that this was the case. Even if he was responsible for her death he could not have seen where her body had lodged without the aid of the police lighting.

The Chief Judge took very large swings at the evidence used by the Crown to exclude the possibility that Caroline committed suicide by propelling herself off the top of the cliff.

The Crown had heavily relied on the expert evidence of Associate Professor Cross to exclude the possibility that Caroline committed suicide.

The year following Gordon's conviction, Associate Professor Cross published a book titled *Evidence for Murder: How physics convicted a killer* (published by UNSW Press in the NewSouth imprint). In it, he claimed involvement in changing the police's view about where Caroline had landed and influencing the decision to prosecute.

Even though the book didn't exist at the time of the trial, to the Court of Criminal Appeal it revealed a mindset that indicated Associate Professor Cross's expertise was guided by a desire to help convict Gordon. This was a big problem because an expert witness should never take sides. The Chief Judge wrote:

> [Associate Professor Cross] appears oblivious of the serious problems which the book reveals about his own involvement in the police investigations. The energy he applied to assisting the police was no doubt a result of worthy intentions, but then this is almost always the case. Once an expert has been engaged to assist in a case, there is a significant risk that he or she becomes part of 'the team' which has the single objective of solving the problem or problems facing the party who engaged them to 'win' the adversarial contest. It is an almost inevitable result of the adversarial system.

The Court of Criminal Appeal declared Associate Professor Cross's opinion on any controversial matter, such as whether Caroline jumped or was thrown, to have minimal if any weight.

The Crown argued that even if the book did damage Associate Professor Cross's credibility, the physics he outlined as to how Caroline came to be at the bottom of the cliff was supported by another physics expert who gave evidence at the trial, Professor Elliott.

'I do not believe this to be the case,' wrote the Chief Judge:

> Professor Elliott disagreed about critical matters, including the validity of the tests in relation to a struggling conscious woman and the scientific validity of equating bench-press ability with the ability to spear throw.

The Chief Judge was dismissive, even scathing of Associate Professor Cross's experiments. 'They were not sophisticated and I have considerable reservations about the assistance they can provide.' His Honour pointed out that they were all conducted during the day, in conditions where neither the females thrown nor the men who threw them into the water had reason to fear for their safety. 'The circumstances on the night of [Caroline's] death were quite different …' Noting that in one experiment the female volunteer was asked to remain limp, the Chief Judge dismissed this as being similar to an unconscious Caroline.

The Chief Judge dismissed Associate Professor Cross's measurements for both a running dive and a spear throw from the tip of the northern ledge. His Honour did so because such measurements were based on the assumption that Caroline was either thrown or jumped, which, in his view, was 'unlikely to be the case. She died on a dark night and there was nothing to restrain a person from falling off the northern ledge if they approached its tip.'

So how did Caroline's body end up nine metres away from the base of the cliff, head first in a hole in the rock? His Honour suggested:

> … [t]here was always the possibility that… her body may have been carried by the sea to the place from which is was recovered… it may be that the Crown could not have excluded the possibility of suicide, being unable to establish with any confidence the launch point or how far Ms Byrne travelled before being picked up by the ocean and lodged into the rocks.

Attention was also drawn to a lecture posted on Associate Professor Cross's website that he had given where he said that one man was more likely to be able to throw Caroline off the cliff than two men because two men wouldn't be able to throw fast enough. 'This statement is inconsistent with Associate Professor Cross's evidence at trial,' wrote the Chief Judge, quoting the professor telling the court that if two men practised many times, they could achieve sufficient speed to get Caroline to the pyramid-shaped rock.

The Chief Judge damningly remarked that:

> ... this issue ... has far greater significance than the Crown gives it. At the trial the prosecutor sought to take advantage of the suggested presence of a 'second man' at The Gap in the afternoon and evening by raising the spectre of a joint criminal enterprise. It is likely that Associate Professor Cross would have known this when he gave his answer at the trial.

The search for evidence of controversy over the Crown's argument that Gordon was strong enough to throw Caroline or whether two men throwing Caroline was realistically going to work had started during the trial. Gordon's lawyer had requested emails between Associate Professor Cross and police concerning these points, which were provided by the Crown on 4 and 8 September 2008, about a fortnight after the police officer who retrieved Caroline's body gave evidence. Nothing really came of this at the trial, but now, armed with Associate Professor Cross's book and the lecture posted on his website, the Chief Judge dismissed out of hand the possibility that Associate Professor Cross may have made a mistake:

> I do not accept that benign description. Associate Professor Cross must have known the true answer and must have realised it would seriously contradict the Crown's suggestion that two

> men were responsible for [Caroline's] death. The ordinary person would be likely to believe that two men together could throw an object or person further than one man could. Associate Professor Cross should have responded to this possibility as he responded in his lecture.

Regardless of whatever influence Associate Professor Cross thought he exerted on police, the police officer who retrieved Caroline's body always stuck to his original recollection of Caroline's feet pointing towards the corner fence post. Indeed, while giving evidence, Associate Professor Cross said that over the years he had questioned what the police officer who retrieved Caroline's body claimed to have observed about the orientation of her body and 'to this day' he did not know what the officer meant by saying her legs were pointing up towards 'the corner point' [sic].

The Chief Judge made more damning comments. '[Associate Professor Cross] had no reason to dispute the evidence of [the officer who retrieved Caroline's body]. [That officer] had told him of the correct orientation of the body. However, Associate Professor Cross chose to ignore it.' In relation to the professor's claim that he still didn't know what the officer meant, the Chief Judge wrote: 'This was also misleading if he was well aware that he meant the corner fence post, as he states in his book.'

Professor Pandy was an expert in biomechanics called by Gordon's lawyers during the trial. He created a new report especially for the appeal.

In his fresh report, Professor Pandy's opinion was the orientation of Caroline's body meant she left the top of the cliff from the corner fence post, not the northern ledge. Professor Pandy also thought it meant she was more likely to have landed in Hole B, the hole closer to the cliff.

When giving evidence before the Court of Criminal Appeal,

Professor Pandy explained there was a way for Caroline to have left the cliff from the northern ledge, land in Hole A, where Associate Professor Cross and the police thought she had landed, and have her feet pointing towards the corner fence post as the police officer who retrieved her body had observed. It would mean the rotation of her body was different from that calculated by Associate Professor Cross, and 'the only way that that [rotation] could happen is that some force acted to start turning the body'. Professor Pandy told the Court of Criminal Appeal:

> So if the hole is over in this direction and you are leaving in this direction, the only way you could get your legs pointing over there is if some force acted to start twisting the body about another axis other than the axis about which you rotate head to toe.

He added that the prospects of having a forward rotation and an axial rotation at the same time were 'unlikely.' In other words, if Associate Professor Cross was right about where Caroline left the top of the cliff and where she landed, Caroline probably rotated in an unusual way due to some force that couldn't be explained by a normal jump or dive.

'I do not believe it possible or necessary to conclusively resolve this issue,' said the Chief Judge. It didn't really matter because, in his opinion, there was no reliable evidence that placed Gordon at the top of the cliff when Caroline left it. What's more, even if it could be proved that Gordon was there, there was still the problem of proof that he had anything to do with her leaving it.

As mentioned above, underlying this critical attitude towards the expert evidence the Crown had relied on to rule out the possibility of suicide were problems with the identification evidence.

When it came to the discussion of a joint criminal enterprise during the trial, in other words the idea that Gordon and another, unidentified man may have thrown Caroline off the cliff, the Chief Judge heavily criticised both the prosecutor and the trial judge:

> At the trial the Crown Prosecutor was no doubt concerned that the Crown case would be diminished if the presence of 'the second man' was not explained and for that reason embraced the theory of a possible 'joint throw'. Furthermore, he no doubt assumed that the jury would reason that a joint effort would enhance the probability of reaching the identified landing point.
>
> [T]he trial judge's direction [to the jury] contained no discussion of any facts which may have supported a joint criminal enterprise. Beyond the evidence that [the man who lived very close to The Gap] saw two men and a woman, there quite simply were not any.

The problems with the evidence of the café owners and the man who lived in an apartment very close to The Gap were well known from the start. Honest witnesses may end up recalling what has been suggested to them, rather than what they actually saw. This is known as the 'displacement effect'. The trial judge had spoken to the jury about these problems.

Aside from one criticism, the Chief Judge was happy enough with the directions the trial judge made in relation to the evidence of the café owners. The Chief Judge noted that, without wanting to criticise June Dally-Watkins, Caroline's well-meaning employer who had shown photos of Gordon and Caroline to them, the evidence of the café owners:

> ... was so compromised and their recollection so unsure that little or no weight could be given to it. To my mind it could

> not have justified a conclusion that [Gordon] was lying when he said that he had not gone to The Gap that afternoon.

In relation to the alleged sightings of a green Bentley, the Chief Judge took another swing at the prosecutor. 'The evidence about the sighting of the car raised a false issue and served only to reinforce, as the prosecution no doubt intended, the relationship between [Gordon] and [Rene].'

The Chief Judge then turned to the expert evidence of the medical doctors. They had noted the nature of Caroline's number of small injuries, which was used in the trial to support the conclusion she probably defended herself from an attack and was probably unconscious when she left the top of the cliff. 'Given the controversy as to whether [Caroline] could have jumped to hole A, [the expert evidence of the medical doctors] does not assist in resolving whether [Caroline] was thrown off the cliff top,' wrote his Honour.

There were many other alternative findings of facts made by the appeal judges, but even these were not the full extent of the demolition of Gordon's trial.

Associate Professor Cross told the Court of Criminal Appeal that he learnt before the trial in 2008 that the photo of the northern ledge marked '1996', which featured a bush, was actually taken in 2003 and that he didn't tell prosecutor Tedeschi. Fresh evidence, namely different photos and signage at The Gap, were accepted by the Court of Criminal Appeal as also proving the photo marked '1996' couldn't have been taken prior to 2003.

This fresh evidence wasn't new. These photos had been gathered by Gordon before his trial. However, the Chief Judge blasted the Crown for not submitting these photos during the trial.

'The photographic material discovered by [Gordon] was not disclosed by the prosecution at the trial. It should have been,' wrote the Chief Judge. '[T]here is no reason why the defence in a criminal trial should be obliged to fossick for information of this kind and to which it was entitled.'

Aside from evidence proving the photo relied on in court was dated incorrectly, there was also evidence from the NSW National Parks and Wildlife Service that there was no vegetation on the northern ledge in 1988, seven years before Caroline's death. However, there was vegetation cleared from there in 2004.

Nonetheless, the Chief Judge dismissed the possibility that there was a bush restricting the run-up on the northern ledge on the night Caroline died, noting 'it does not follow that the vegetation removed in 2004 was present in 1995, some nine years earlier'.

Aryan was one of Caroline's friends at the gym who gave evidence that just before she died Caroline was unhappy in her relationship with Gordon, that she wanted to leave and was sometimes fearful of Gordon. He also gave evidence that supported the motive involving Caroline knowing something about the investigation into Rene's business concerns. Not long after Gordon's trial, Aryan pleaded guilty to an offence that was unrelated to Gordon or Caroline. This was made known to the Court of Criminal Appeal.

The Crown argued that even if the jury knew about Aryan's illegal conduct, it would not have been likely to have caused the jury to consider Gordon innocent of Caroline's murder.

The Chief Judge did not agree. He thought the unrelated offence cast serious doubt on Aryan's honesty, that his evidence was more important than the Crown said it was, and that with knowledge of his true character the trial judge may have rejected his evidence. If it wasn't for the Chief Judge's view that Gordon should be acquitted, he thought the effect of Aryan's unrelated offence on his credibility would justify a new trial.

While the Chief Judge dismissed out of hand the part of Professor Pandy's fresh expert evidence concerning how Caroline must have moved through the air if she landed in Hole A, there was another part of Professor Pandy's new expert evidence his Honour wholeheartedly embraced. It involved further calculations upon the assumption of no vegetation restricting the run-up distance on the northern ledge.

Professor Pandy's fresh report concluded that, with this greater run-up, the majority of the women involved in Associate Professor Cross's experiments could have dived into Hole A. The Chief Judge found this new expert opinion, with the obvious implication that a suicidal Caroline could have propelled herself into Hole A after all, would itself merit a new trial.

A prosecutor's principal role is to assist the court to arrive at the truth. It is never about winning at all costs. For example, even if the Crown has evidence that the defence doesn't know about that would ruin the chances of a conviction, a prosecutor has to disclose it to the defence and it may be put in front of the court. Prosecutors are supposed to press for a conviction, at times vigorously, and when necessary, attack. Their duty to be fair means they must never resort to prejudice or emotion in order to persuade a jury. It is a difficult balancing act that no set of guidelines has ever made easy. Tactics that may need to be employed in one trial may be out of place in another.

On top of that difficult balancing act, a prosecutor must carry a heavy load. The Crown alone must carry the burden of proof. If the criminal justice system is serious about keeping innocent people out of jail, it has to be this way.

In this decision, the Court of Criminal Appeal found prosecutor Mark Tedeschi had created fiction, and that one of his core submissions was 'a speculative smear'. Flaws in Gordon's defence, including his legal team's decision to accuse Caroline's ex, Andrew, of being the killer with next to nothing to back such a serious accusation, barely rated a passing mention.

I agree that it could be argued that the prosecutor had encouraged the jury to think Gordon had to explain himself, or as lawyers put it, to reverse the onus of proof by putting the 50 questions, even if that had not been his specific intention. I also agree with the court's criticisms of Associate Professor Cross and his evidence. It follows that the conviction was unsound. However, I think the Court of Criminal Appeal's overall criticisms of Mark Tedeschi were excessively harsh.

A question of malice

The professional standards for prosecutors are extremely high. No one is a harsher judge of whether the prosecutor and the criminal justice process has reached those high standards than the criminal justice system itself.

Practitioners become accustomed to being held to these standards and to the stinging criticisms they occasionally receive from senior members of the profession (including judges) if those standards are not met. After all, what is at stake is the liberty of the accused. It doesn't matter if those in the dock have huge clouds of suspicion hanging over their heads, are loved or hated, pitied or feared, have people in their lives who care about them or have no one. If the rule of law is to be maintained, the extremely high standards needed to ensure everyone gets the fair trial they are entitled to must always be maintained.

I think it is clear enough that every court that has dealt with Gordon Wood has acknowledged, one way or another, the strong suspicion of his involvement in the death of Caroline. The issues that have been addressed, however, are the issues of proper criminal process and evidence. Suspicion has never been enough for a conviction, but the question of whether or not Gordon was responsible for Caroline's death remains open. His successful appeal meant that his presumption of innocence had been restored – not that he was found innocent.

When Gordon's conviction for the murder of Caroline was overturned in 2012, the Chief Judge at Common Law made damning criticisms of Mark Tedeschi, the senior crown prosecutor, including branding him as having created fiction and relying on speculative smear. His Honour's words rang not only in the ears of the media and the public, but also in the ears of Gordon's lawyers. In February 2017, a few years after he left jail, Gordon sued the state in the Supreme Court for malicious prosecution. Chief Judge McClellan's criticisms were quoted throughout the claim and in the judgment.

Gordon named a detective who was key to the police investigation, prosecutor Mark Tedeschi and expert witness Associate Professor Cross as people who were out to get him before and during his trial. Gordon even named and sued me before his lawyer almost casually conceded in open court that there was absolutely no evidence to support any allegation against me and publicly apologised. The allegation against me was quietly dropped two weeks after the malicious prosecution hearing began, with her Honour remarking:

> [I]t is a grave allegation to make, if only in a pleading filed. Mr Cowdery … is a person who gave high public service to this State over many years, in his position as the Director of Public Prosecutions, and it was entirely, as I now see it, unwarranted that he be named in this prosecution at all.

The State of New South Wales, the subject of the malicious prosecution claim, argued that only Mark Tedeschi should be considered in this action, as the prosecutor, and that the others shouldn't be in the firing line. In her judgment, Justice Fullerton agreed.

Her Honour's task was different from that of the three judges who heard the appeal against Gordon's conviction. However, one thing both courts had to do was make an extensive examination of the evidence and arguments that led to Gordon's murder conviction.

Justice Fullerton carefully outlined the undisputed evidence of Gordon's suspicious behaviour, including his claims of how the 'spirit world' led him to The Gap in the middle of the night and his remarkably accurate claims as to where Caroline's body had landed and its unusual head first, feet up position, before police were notified and discovered what he had said to be true:

> [S]ome of [Gordon's] conduct might still be regarded as inconsistent with having had no knowledge of [Caroline's] whereabouts both during the afternoon and at the base of the cliffs at midnight … it bears repeating that [Gordon] is entitled to the full benefit of the quashing of his conviction for her murder and the verdict of acquittal that was entered [by the Court of Criminal Appeal].

In deciding whether Gordon had been maliciously prosecuted, her Honour had to consider two tests. The first was whether Tedeschi had prosecuted Gordon maliciously; that is, predominantly in pursuit of some improper, illegitimate or oblique motive extraneous to the proper invocation of the criminal law. The second test was whether he had acted without reasonable and probable cause.

Her Honour thought police had gathered evidence capable of excluding suicide as an explanation for Caroline's death. It was universally agreed that Caroline's body landed nine metres out from the base of the cliff. Her Honour dismissed Gordon's argument that waves might have taken Caroline's body out that far and placed her head first into a hole in the rock shelf at the bottom, a possibility that Chief Justice McClellan had suggested. She found the post-mortem evidence concerning Caroline's injuries supported the view she had landed where she was found and that there was simply no evidence the waves could have put her there. Her Honour had no argument with the part of Associate Professor Cross's evidence that concluded Caroline must have been travelling at a minimum of 4.3 metres per second to land nine metres out.

Unlike the Chief Judge in the appeal, her Honour did not think the jury were wrong to use the evidence placing Gordon at the top of the cliff when Caroline plunged to her death.

However, just like the Chief Judge in the appeal, her Honour was scathing of those parts of Associate Professor Cross's evidence concerning how Caroline was allegedly thrown off the cliff to her death, and made multiple criticisms of Associate Professor Cross's experiments and findings:

> [I]t must have been obvious that significant and important aspects of his evidence concerned biomechanics – a specialist field of learning in which he neither had, nor claimed to have, any formal expertise, qualifications or training ... [about] the capacity of a female of [Caroline's] age, height, weight and athleticism to launch herself from the cliff top at The Gap and to arrive head first into Hole A, and the capacity of a male of [Gordon's] weight and assessed athleticism to 'spear throw' [Caroline] to arrive at the same location.
>
> ... Were it the Crown case simply that she was thrown off the cliff, Associate Professor Cross's evidence that the 'spear throw' by a single strong man was the only technique that could replicate her landing in Hole A by experimentation would have been otiose ['otiose' being an uncommonly used word that means serving no practical purpose].

Nonetheless, her Honour found the problems in Associate Professor Cross's experiments and calculations were so great that they undermined the capacity of all the other evidence to exclude beyond reasonable doubt suicide by jumping as an explanation for Caroline's death. She found that prosecutor Tedeschi should have known that prior to advising me as DPP that the matter was ready to go to trial. Her Honour found Tedeschi objectively had no reasonable and probable cause to hold the view that Gordon should have been tried for Caroline's suspected murder, but that subjectively he believed he did.

That still didn't answer the question of whether he had been malicious. Her Honour had to decide if the other test, namely if the prosecution went ahead because of an illegitimate motive, had been satisfied.

Despite suing for malicious prosecution, Wood's lawyers had not questioned Mark Tedeschi about any desire to harm Gordon, or any tendency to be unfair, self-aggrandising or to have an unreasonable obsession to be the one to put Gordon behind bars for a hitherto unsolved homicide.

Prosecutor Tedeschi had argued that Associate Professor Cross's evidence was very significant but not crucial to his case during the trial. Justice Fullerton rejected that argument, describing it as 'somewhat disingenuous'. She looked for any signs that the former prosecutor had manipulated the evidence during the trial to cover up the deficiencies in Associate Professor Cross's evidence.

The prosecutor remained convinced Associate Professor Cross's 'core findings', namely that Caroline could not have landed where she was found unless she was thrown, which meant he was justified in submitting Associate Professor Cross's problematic expert evidence to the jury without drawing attention to his view that it would be more difficult and dangerous to throw Caroline over the cliff if she was conscious and struggling. He also openly admitted to changing the Crown case during the trial from 'it wasn't important whether Caroline was conscious or unconscious when she was thrown to her death' to 'she was likely to have been unconscious or incapacitated when she was thrown to her death'.

Prosecutors cannot make radical changes to their cases during trials, in other words changes that are not supported by the evidence and the opening the prosecution began with, without serious consequences. Her Honour found the changes made to the Crown's case by the prosecutor during the trial were within acceptable limits. The second test of whether there had been a malicious prosecution had failed. But the reasons why Gordon was not going to win did not stop there. Her Honour decided the ultimate reason why this wasn't a malicious prosecution was Tedeschi's personality. It was her Honour's view that he was too egotistical and defiant to recognise the fundamental problems in parts of Associate Professor Cross's evidence, so he honestly held the wrong view that going ahead with the prosecution of Gordon was the right thing to do. Her Honour also blamed his personality for his refusal to agree with the Court of Criminal Appeal's criticisms of other issues, such as the motive for Gordon to kill Caroline.

It was hard to get past her Honour's stinging, even personal, criticisms of Mark Tedeschi and Associate Professor Cross. Having made her findings, Justice Fullerton even invited speculation about whether the former senior crown prosecutor was fit to be a barrister.

The judge found Gordon had been subjected to a trial that contained 'gross unfairness'. As no finding of malice had been made, Gordon was not going to get any of the multimillion-dollar compensation he sought for spending three years in prison as a convicted murderer. However, her Honour's judgment had yet another sting in its tail. She also decided to order Gordon to pay all parties' legal costs. This was guaranteed to place him under a debt of hundreds of thousands of dollars. Her Honour had chosen, in the exercise of her discretion, to burden the man she found had been imprisoned after an unfair trial with a debt from which he would probably never emerge.

Gordon appealed against the malicious prosecution judgment and the appeal remains on foot at the time of writing.

Whatever the result of the appeal, it is interesting to note that the two judges who criticised prosecutor Tedeschi the loudest couldn't agree on key facts, such as whether Gordon was at the top of the cliff when Caroline died. The reason we know this is because judges are held to extremely high standards of transparency, integrity and accountability. Judges literally must give their reasons for their decisions in public and in writing. This book, which has relied on judgments for all the descriptions of cases and trials you have read, is a testament to that. Also, having given their reasons, judges can't go back and change them should they realise they have made a mistake or if they change their opinion of a case.

The fact that two highly competent judges couldn't agree on key facts of this case also suggests that, despite being unquestionably very intelligent and skilful, judges are not necessarily superior to juries when it comes to being finders of fact. In my opinion, juries that have been properly instructed in well-run trials are very good at making fair decisions about whether the accused is guilty or not guilty. Also, the general public does tend to accept verdicts that have been made by 12 objective, ordinary people, even if those verdicts are unpopular or distressing. This is immensely important to the maintenance of public confidence in the criminal justice system.

Chapter 19

LIFE AFTER BEING THE DPP

I retired as DPP the day before my sixty-fifth birthday, pension preserved. Eleven days earlier the ABC screened an *Australian Story* on my time as DPP. It ended with Ken Marslew solemnly presenting me with the jar containing the two olives he had kept in his garage for years – my symbolic testicles. To say all was forgiven might be putting it a little high – but much had been.

Despite the frustrations that attended my departure from office, I must honestly say that it was unlikely that, given a choice, I would have stayed much longer, anyway – maybe a couple of years. (Of course, without a pension I would probably still be there!) Just short of 16 and a half years is a long time as DPP – an Australian record for a single jurisdiction, and likely to remain so.

I had served as an acting judge before appointment as DPP, so I had tasted judicial life and I am grateful for that. I thought that I could contribute more as DPP than from the bench.

I didn't have time to miss the job. A week after retirement I was working in London on a Commonwealth Secretariat project. I was quickly offered and accepted teaching roles at Sydney University and the University of NSW which have continued to the time of writing. I remained engaged in criminal justice projects, in Australia and internationally (especially with the International Association of Prosecutors of which I was President), and speaking engagements have continued to be offered.

I am all too aware of the limitations of the criminal justice (or criminal legal) system. It has a task a bit like that of an undertaker. Something bad happens and somebody must deal with it in socially acceptable ways. The criminal justice system does that with crimes and criminals. But it cannot do much more than tidy up after the event in the best socially acceptable way possible and look forward to the next one, despite all the efforts made at crime prevention.

I did not retire after my tenure as DPP ended. Retirement? I wonder now how I had time for a proper job. There are too many urgently needed reforms to the criminal justice system to work towards, and other interesting pursuits to follow before I truly retire, and time will probably beat me.

Voluntary assisted dying laws still do not exist in New South Wales at the time of writing. Drug law reform is urgently needed and the wheel is turning in that direction – but very, very slowly. The over-incarceration of Indigenous Australians is scandalous and governments seem most reluctant to seriously address it or even to seriously address the Australian Law Reform Commission's excellent recommendations published on 28 March 2018. And the country needs a national Bill of Rights – and an effective national Anti-Corruption Commission.

The law surrounding legal abortions remains unclear and unfair in New South Wales. There's a prohibition against unlawful abortion. That word 'unlawful' is in sections 82 to 84 of the New South Wales *Crimes Act*. A lay person reading that would read the 'abortion' word and think all abortions are therefore unlawful, prohibited and criminal (which was probably the original intention of the lawmakers in 1900).

In fact, the courts have determined there are conditions that would make an abortion no longer 'unlawful'. Those conditions are if the physical or psychological health of the mother is likely to be adversely impacted by carrying the pregnancy through to the end or there is the risk of harm to the foetus by the continuation of the pregnancy.

Obviously the law is not clear to people who might be affected by it. Obtaining proper advice is a lottery. If someone goes to their GP to seek advice about abortion, the personal views of the medical practitioner may guide the advice the practitioner gives. In the absence of clear guidance from the law, the stage until which a lawful abortion can be performed comes down to the policy of a particular clinic. Ironically, you can have quite late term abortions in New South Wales under the current law, so long as you are in the know.

When you consider that there are something like 85 000 cases of legal abortion in the country every year, there must be women and girls in New South Wales who have not gone down that path because they haven't had proper advice and haven't known where to get it or it is simply unavailable – especially in country areas.

I am told that it is the policy for police in New South Wales not to charge abortion offences. But in 2017 there was a case of a young woman, who had obtained abortion inducing drugs via the internet and administered them to herself, being prosecuted in the Blacktown Local Court by an ODPP prosecutor and convicted. It was rather surprising. No doubt the DPP was brought in because of the general public importance of the issues.

And I should declare that it has been an honour to be a member of the NSW Pro-Choice Alliance that came from initial work of the Women's Electoral Lobby Abortion Decriminalisation Roundtable (of which I was the only male member). At the time of writing there are signs that decriminalisation may be achieved.

The problem of politicians passing unnecessary and faulty legislation after bikie gangs committed acts of violence that upset mainstream society surfaced during my tenure as DPP and the problem persists.

There is no escaping the reality that some motorcycle clubs conduct themselves in a way that is a menace to society. They are involved in drug manufacture and distribution, violence, offences of dishonesty and sexual offences, and it seems to be part of the culture of some clubs to act that way.

However, most anti-bikie legislation passed after a public act of bikie violence has generally been a waste of time and effort on the part of all those involved. For a very long time now we have had provisions in our *Crimes Act* directed against criminal gangs. Those laws have been enforced against bikie gangs very effectively. We've even had people plead guilty to offences of those kinds.

I know why additional anti-bikie legislation comes into being. It's so politicians can make some kind of political point to the electorate, that they are being 'tough on crime'. But if politicians properly explained existing laws and the way in which they are enforced they wouldn't need to take these steps. Instead, they could be 'smart on crime'.

In my view new anti-bikie legislation usually opens up a whole new set of issues about its impact on the rights of the people against whom it is directed and others. This leads to more legal arguments and appeals against its application all the way through to the High Court as has happened in several states around the country, thus creating a lot more work for the criminal justice system without demonstrable benefit to the community.

Juries are under threat. I believe that the jury serves an important purpose in the trials of serious offences. Its role has changed over the centuries and there are probably improvements that can be made even now, but its erosion from the landscape needs to be halted.

Politicians should learn the lesson that mandatory punishment for anything but minor regulatory offences (e.g. fixed fines for traffic and public health offences) is antithetical to the doing of justice –

and I do not know any judicial officer who is content to be an agent of injustice.

Back during the 1995 and 1999 New South Wales elections, strong action needed to be taken by the legal profession and by me as DPP to moderate the calls by politicians for harsher and harsher penalties and harsher and harsher criminal law enforcement.

In later elections there hasn't been the same level of 'law and order' auction discussion but that is not to say it won't come back. I think even if the politicians of the day aren't pushing that particular barrow too strongly, the profession and others concerned with the rule of law and achieving justice in the criminal justice system need to remain alert and ready to resist the pressure.

Diversionary programs for offenders and rehabilitation programs in prisons need to be given prominence and funded appropriately. While some people simply do need to be kept away from us, most offenders are capable of returning to stable and law-abiding lives in the community, given the right support.

The way criminal laws are made in our system does not generally inspire faith that they will be designed to – or even be likely to – provide justice in our best common interests. The *Bail Act* is a prime example, having been inspired in its present form by a report from former Attorney General Hatzistergos before he was appointed to the bench. Too often criminal laws are the product of fleeting moral panic, real or imagined, on the part of persons with influence or the tabloid media. That law is supplemented and sometimes moderated by the common law, judge-made law. Often judges wrestle with the parliament-made law to try to make it achieve justice and we should be thankful for that.

Justice is a fragile quality that depends for its assertion on ideas such as the rule of law and the protection of human rights, and all that imports into the application of the criminal law. And it depends on the courage of those in positions of power, including judges who choose to accept the responsibility to implement those ideas.

One problem we continually face – in the legal environment generally and especially the criminal law – is that once rules are created, controls are put in place. Some people resist controls and humans generally have a history of selectively disobeying rules, so the criminal law provides sanctions for breaches of those laws. And when there are controls in place, that inevitably means that some persons have power. And when there is power, there is abuse of it – by conduct or omission. So we need to control the abuses, too.

The foundation stone for making the decisions a DPP must make and managing the crises a DPP must manage is, and always has been, independence – with appropriate accountability. Particularly (but not only) in New South Wales, that independence of prosecutorial decision-making and administrative independence were hard-won and must constantly be defended. Just as the independence of the judiciary is the foundation of a fair trial, so the prosecutor's independence underpins the best prosecutorial practice and it is reflected in the Prosecution Guidelines. Yet there are always those in government, lacking in essential understanding, who would like to get their claws into the DPP's operations, even in administrative roles, and they must continue to be resisted.

So much flows merely from the fact that we are human. We are very strange animals at times – but always interesting and often challenging. Rolling with the punches is one way of dealing with people – but so, too, is taking a stand on principle when it is needed.

Appendix

REFORMS ACHIEVED AND REFORMS STILL NEEDED

As noted in the Introduction, I saw working for improvements in the criminal law and its processes as part of the role of the DPP. Many seemingly dry procedural and evidential reforms can have a big, practical impact within courtrooms. I am proud of the reforms that were achieved during my tenure through the hard work of many in the system, but more remains to be done.

Reforms achieved during my tenure as DPP

- The ability of the defence to make an opening address after the Crown's opening in a trial was introduced in 2000 (section 159 *Criminal Procedure Act 1986*, commenced 1 January 2000). I had encouraged that informally for some time before it was legislated, so I take some credit for that one.
- Unsworn statements from the dock were abolished in 1994 (by the *Crimes Legislation (Unsworn Evidence) Amendment Act 1994*, commenced 10 June 1994). This had been a hangover from times when the general level of education in the community was dismally low and, indeed, when an accused person was not able to give sworn evidence in his or her defence. Although this provision commenced before my appointment, its ramifications were still being addressed when I began.

- Victim impact statements were introduced in 1997 (by the Charter of Victims' Rights which was provided by section 6 of the *Victims Rights Act 1996*, commenced 2 April 1997). They may be made in writing or orally – but there is still some argument about how they are to be regarded. In principle they are not to affect a sentence (with very limited exceptions) – but in reality…?
- Majority verdicts of 11 to 1 were introduced in 2006 (by the *Jury Amendment (Verdicts) Act 2006*, commenced 26 May 2006). I strongly advocated for this development, enabling the one rogue juror to be neutralised – and such people tend to turn up in the longest, most expensive and most demanding trials. There are checks and balances in place and I do not see any dilution of the quality of justice in the cases in which they have been returned.
- Retrials from jury acquittals are available in limited circumstances (and none have occurred at the time of writing). (Part 8, Division 2 of the *Crimes (Appeal and Review) Act 2001*, commenced 15 December 2006.) In limited circumstances there may be appeals from judge alone acquittals.
- Appeals may be brought on points of law from acquittals by direction – (Part 8, Division 3 of the *Crimes (Appeal and Review) Act 2001*, commenced 15 December 2006).
- Disclosure by the police to the prosecution is now required by legislation (section 15A of the *Director of Public Prosecutions Act 1986* inserted by the *Criminal Procedure Amendment (Pre-trial Disclosure Act) 2001*, commenced 19 November 2001).
- Charge negotiation and agreement and the settling of agreed facts have been put on a proper footing and expanded after the Samuels Report of 2002 and pursuant to (essentially unnecessary) legislation in February 2011 (G Samuels, *Review*

of the NSW Director of Public Prosecutions' Policy and Guidelines for charge bargaining and tendering of Agreed Facts, 2002, at <www.ipc.nsw.gov.au/report/lpd_reports.nsf/pages/report_gsamuels>.

- The legislated trial, in Sydney, of Criminal Case Conferencing made significant advances into bringing forward in the prosecution process the time at which pleas of guilty are determined and the issues between the parties identified (the *Criminal Case Conferencing Trial Act 2008*, commenced 16 April 2008). That initiative was discontinued but later revived in a different form with extra features and is now working well.
- There have been some moves towards greater defence disclosure in some circumstances (notably in relation to claims of mental impairment).
- There is now the possibility of greater judicial case management in some matters (the *Criminal Procedure Amendment (Case Management) Act 2009* commenced 1 February 2011, following recommendations made by the Trial Efficiency Working Group); but there is judicial reluctance to take that course.
- There have been exchanges of personnel between the Crown Prosecutors and Public Defenders chambers.

Reforms I think still need to be achieved

There have also been some important matters (at least in my view) that we have not been able to change, so far:

- The conduct of all prosecutions should be with the ODPP and Police Prosecutions should come to an end. A trial of a takeover at Campbelltown and Dubbo Local Courts in 1998 almost led to it in 2000 and the ODPP has ready a detailed plan.

- The ODPP should approve all serious charges before they are laid and pre-charge bail should be able to be given by police (as in England and Wales).
- The *Bail Act 1978*, mucked about by successive ad hoc legislative knee-jerk interventions, should be reformed in a way commensurate with the original and with the NSW Law Reform Commission review.
- Immunities should not be the province of an elected politician and the DPP should have the function of providing indemnities and undertakings (as in some other Australian jurisdictions and elsewhere).
- Trials for multiple sexual assault victims of the same accused should be joint trials, normally (some progress in that direction has been made).
- Appropriate comment should be able to be made on the failure of an accused to testify at trial (as in England and Wales).
- Sentencing law should be revamped and simplified and standard non-parole periods abolished (without any extension of existing mandatory sentences). The NSW Law Reform Commission reported on its review of sentencing law in 2013. Delayed and only partial implementation of its recommendations in 2017 has been disappointing, but better than nothing.
- The review of the *Crimes (Forensic Procedures) Act 2000* which began in April 2010 and was still underway when I retired, generated the proceedings of the Working Group directed towards rationalising and simplifying this cumbersome legislation. Those outcomes should not be lost.
- A better approach – one that does not bring us into conflict with our international human rights obligations – should be

taken to the problem of serious sex and violence offenders who refuse to participate in rehabilitation programs in prison.

- Such programs in prison and post-release support programs should be greatly expanded.
- The verdict of 'not guilty by reason of mental illness' should be recast so as to accurately and acceptably describe what has actually occurred and better measures should be put in place for dealing with the mentally ill within and alongside the criminal justice system.
- Drug laws should be reformed, with personal possession and use and small-scale trafficking not being criminal, leaving the criminal law to address growth, manufacture and trafficking for profit. Portugal provides a case study of how the first phase could work and I would favour legalisation, regulation, control and taxation of all presently illicit drugs. The rest of the world is moving on these issues and Australia needs to catch up.
- There should be a federal anti-corruption body with a broad remit.
- There should be a statutory Charter or Bill of Rights at the federal level with comprehensive coverage of rights, judicial enforceability and compensation available for breaches.
- And it really is time we got rid of the wigs!